THE
PRINCESS
MATILDA
COMES HOME

Also by Shane Spall:

The Voyages of The Princess Matilda

THE
PRINCESS
MATILDA
COMES HOME

The adventure of a lifetime
around Britain on a barge

SHANE SPALL

EBURY
PRESS

3 5 7 9 10 8 6 4 2

Published in 2014 by Ebury Press, an imprint of Ebury Publishing
A Random House Group company

Copyright © Shane Spall 2014

The Random House Group Limited Reg. No. 954009

Addresses for companies within the Random House Group can be found at
www.randomhouse.co.uk

A CIP catalogue record for this book is available from the British Library

The Random House Group Limited supports the Forest Stewardship
Council® (FSC®), the leading international forest-certification organisation.
Our books carrying the FSC label are printed on FSC®-certified paper.
FSC is the only forest-certification scheme supported by the leading
environmental organisations, including Greenpeace. Our paper procurement
policy can be found at www.randomhouse.co.uk/environment

Printed and bound in Great Britain by Clays Ltd, St Ives PLC

ISBN 9780091941826

To buy books by your favourite authors and register for offers visit
www.randomhouse.co.uk

*For my young friends Alec, Susan and Krissy
who didn't make old bones, and for my dearest
husband and best friend Timothy Spall who
beat the odds and is hopefully only halfway
there. And Jenny Baker, Miriam Jones and
Frances Barber – my rocks in a stormy sea.*

*And to the next generation: my grandchildren
Matilda, Lena, Rex and Bertie and our
blended family Kyou and Honoka.*

CONTENTS

Chapter One
DANGEROUS DICK

Cardiff to Swansea: 42 nautical miles

I am married to a loose cannon. His name is Timothy, most of the time he is rational, but very occasionally he becomes a crazy man. I suppose this is what makes him a genius and an extraordinary actor. The Tim Spall madness doesn't happen overnight, it is a slow build. Every now and again my doolally detector picks up something. I just stare at him.

'What, what?' he will ask me accusingly.

'You have wild eyes, Tim!'

My husband says that I am a saint, but I always answer, 'No, my love, I am your wife, but sometimes I wonder if you should be on medication.'

Usually Tim's madness begins with a stressful job, or long-haul travel, or a family celebration, or a trip out to sea on *The Princess Matilda*. We had a perfect cocktail for Spall madness during the early months of 2010. The job was a film called *Upside Down* starring Kirsten Dunst and Jim Sturgess. It was being made in Montreal. Tim was doing an American accent; it worried him a great deal. There is nothing worse than an English actor doing a bad Yank twang. Also, our youngest daughter, Sadie, was getting married. But on our return from Canada the wedding arrangements were all in hand, so we had a month to spare before the big day.

Tim and I caught the train from London to Cardiff, where our 35-ton, 54-foot-long Dutch barge, *The Princess Matilda*, had spent the winter. Tim had his sea charts spread out on the train's table and I looked out of the windows. Canada is a beautiful country, but nothing beats the splendour of an English landscape. It was late March and bright golden daffodils and clusters of pale-yellow primroses smudged the banks of the spring green railway cuttings.

I pulled out my AA road atlas to look at how far we had already travelled, getting to Wales from Chatham on the river Medway, moving my finger around the coast of the south-east tip of the map at the front. It seemed such a long way while we were actually doing it aboard *The Princess Matilda*. The train takes a couple of hours to get to Cardiff – on our boat it took four years, and we had only done the bottom end of the UK. But what a journey it had been.

We had travelled by sea from Kent to Cornwall around the infamous Lizard Point and Land's End and finally up the Bristol Channel to Cardiff.

'At this rate I'll be drawing my pension before we get all the way around the British Isles. Do you think we'll ever get back to Chatham?' I asked Tim.

'Eventually,' he replied. 'If we can get to Cumbria this summer, we could be home next year.'

Chatham is where Tim had cut his navigational teeth. It had been our home port for two years; after two abortive attempts we had finally left in the spring of 2007. Tim and I always manage to do things the hard way; we had more than a few hairy moments getting to Wales.

'But Cumbria is miles away,' I said wistfully. 'The road atlas stops at Barrow-in-Furness!'

I turned the page to look at the rest of the country. My eye scanned the Solway Firth before resting on Kirkcudbright. The name rang a bell. I pronounced it how it was written, but Tim interrupted me: 'Kirk-cew-brie, we might go in there next summer.'

'Five years from now you mean. I'll qualify for a winter fuel allowance before we get there,' I said. 'But I'd settle for Aberystwyth this year...'

Tim nodded his head in agreement, adding, 'First we have to get to Swansea and that means going back down the Bristol Channel. When's Paul Crompton joining us?' Paul was responsible for us filming our trip from Fowey to Wales the summer of 2009. He had managed to edit it down to three half-hour episodes and it was going to be broadcast in May this year.

'Paul just sent me a text,' I replied. 'He's travelling down tomorrow, but he says he's still not got a commission from BBC4 to shoot a second series yet.'

Tim cut in, 'Oh, bugger the BBC, we'll film it anyway, if only for ourselves and the grandkids!'

I was distracted again by the glint in his eye. I was not sure if it was the dappling sunlight coming through the train window or a hint of Tim Spall madness. I was tempted to text Paul and put him off, tell him not to come down to Penarth Marina. To the uninitiated, it can be slightly unnerving to encounter Tim this way.

When I married Tim, we had been strangers; we had only known each other four months. I had been in a dark unhappy place when we met; my mother used to say he was my knight in shining armour, and he was, but it was a motorbike that he rode and not a white charger. The first hint of his madness came early on in our relationship, because he bought the motorbike so he could ride it from the Aldwych Theatre, where he was performing in rep three nights a week, to Euston Station. The bike was put in the guard's van and retrieved as the train pulled into Wolverhampton, where I lived. He would ride the bike to my council flat, arriving after midnight, and leave at five the next morning. His day job was 70-odd miles away in the

Cotswolds, where he was filming a *Play for Today* for the BBC. Then at five in the afternoon, three times a week, he put the bike on the train at Cirencester to go back to London where he would perform on stage, and this went on for several weeks. Needless to say, he didn't get much sleep and, come to think of it, neither did I.

One night, he returned from London wearing his usual ankle-length ex-army raincoat, with his open-fronted 1950s helmet and goggles in his gloved hands, but I noticed he was missing his white silk scarf. He used to wear it like a World War One fighter pilot, for whom the scarf would act as protection from the splattering oil thrown up from the prop. Tim used his to keep flies out of his mouth. He explained that he had thrown the scarf away.

'Why?' I asked him.

'I almost drowned,' he said. 'It was pouring with rain, I had the scarf around my nose and mouth, I was doing about 90-miles-an-hour down the M5, when I realized I couldn't breathe.' As he was telling me his story, with his wild-looking Heathcliff eyes, he was going through the motions of trying to tear off the rain-sodden scarf with one gloved hand, while the other steered the bike. 'I managed to pull onto the hard shoulder, but I still couldn't get it off. It was like it was glued to my face by the G-force and every time I tried to gasp some air I swallowed water. I almost died!'

'You almost died for love,' I replied, laughing. 'You really are quite mad.'

'You really are quite mad at the moment, aren't you, Tim?' I had said on the morning we waved our goodbyes to our new friends at Penarth Marina, off Cardiff Bay. Stupidly, I had not put Paul off. Tim the loose cannon crashed *The Princess Matilda* against the holding pontoon as we went through the lock, despite having six feet either side to spare – this did not bode well. Not only did we have Paul filming, but we also had Matt David aboard too. Matt had filmed us from the land a couple of times in 2009, but he had never filmed on the boat, until now.

Matt and his camera were all over the place; he is twenty years younger than Paul and our Geordie cameraman Phil Shotton. Matt was an enthusiastic gazelle jumping onto the roof and running down the gunwale. It was rather nice having someone so young onboard.

'It will only take us about twenty minutes to cross over the bay to Cardiff today,' I explained, before going inside to the galley. I returned up top with a couple of bottles of beer for the guys. Paul seemed to be happy to let Matt run around and stood next to Tim in the wheelhouse.

By the time we were moored in front of the iconic Welsh Assembly, I realized Tim was entering the next phase of his manic madness. This was exacerbated by several glasses of Chablis over the course of the evening and mainly took the form of general ranting – encompassing the film industry, the television industry, long-haul travel, jet lag, the weather, English football and that he was a crap skipper and hadn't a clue what he was doing. I suggested to Paul and Matt that they should leave us to it, but I saw the look of panic on their faces. They both wanted to make a good TV programme, even though they still hadn't received the green light from the commissioning editor of BBC4. This didn't help Tim's stress levels.

'What time shall we come in the morning?' Paul asked, as they stepped off the boat onto the pontoon.

'Bollocks to that!' Tim shouted through the window. 'We ain't going nowhere!'

'We'll see you about 7.30,' I whispered softly. 'The weather's looking reasonable, so we hope to get through

Cardiff Bay Barrage at 8.45 tomorrow morning, but bear in mind it's been months since we've done a sea passage and he's feeling really anxious.'

Paul nodded and whispered, 'We don't have to film anything. There's no pressure, Shane.'

'He'll be fine,' I replied, crossing the fingers on my left hand as I waved them goodbye with my right.

Tim was fast asleep when I joined him in the saloon. I filled the hot-water bottle and put him to bed.

The Princess Matilda is our home from home with all mod cons, including two bathrooms, but during the winter months we remain cocooned in a safe sheltered mooring and it is hard then to remember she is actually a sea-going barge. There have been occasions when we have both said – usually after a nasty sea passage – 'Why are we doing this?' We both know why: it is a compulsion, our way of cocking our fingers up at fate. Because, once, Tim had been so weak that he had been unable to get out of his hospital bed.

Tim tossed and turned all night and was up at first light; I wasn't far behind him. He was already at his charts. I put the kettle on and checked the weather forecast.

'A slight sea and a nor'east wind. That's good, isn't it, Tim?' But he was no longer at the table. I looked for him in our cabin. He was on his knees, and looked like he was praying. I thought back to the last time I got on my knees to pray but quickly swept the memory away.

'What are you doing?'

'I can't do this, Shane! It's been over six months. I've forgotten how the autopilot works, never mind the satnav. I've lost my bottle and my sea legs. Tell Paul we're staying where we are. It's too much, too much pressure, I can't do it!'

At times like these, I can do three things: ignore him, cuddle him or shout. I left the cabin and went up into the wheelhouse to get shipshape. Tim joined me half an hour later, muttering under his breath and swearing as he put his course in the autopilot and set the radar. We had had this fitted over the winter because the trip out of Padstow to Ilfracombe the previous summer had made us both aware how poorly equipped we were. The visibility had been frightful; tankers could have rammed us or, even worse, perhaps we could have rammed a smaller craft.

Roy Jones, an overactive teetotal Welsh Baptist with an interesting love life, had fitted the radar. Roy, who is whip thin and unable to sit still, regaled us with stories about his diving exploits.

'They call me Dangerous Dick,' he announced on New Year's Eve.

Tim and I always try to see in the New Year on our boat, but this year we had been sitting in the dark for a couple of hours, with a few spluttering candles and a smoking fire. None of our electrics was working, the shore power had gone off and the batteries were flat. We tried the generator, which farted and died. Fortunately, the wine was well chilled or we would have been seriously cheesed off.

I phoned Roy, apologizing for bothering him at 6.30pm on a wet and windy New Year, and explained the situation.

'Oh, I'm in the Valleys, on my way to my fiancée's; it will take me at least an hour to get to Penarth,' he said in his singsong lilt. 'But I can't let you see in the New Year in the dark. I'm sure Diane, my fiancée, will understand.' He didn't sound too convinced.

Tim and I hardly had time to drain the wine bottle before we heard a knock on the window. The rain-lashed Welshman waved and shouted he would join us inside as soon as he

fixed the problem. It didn't take Roy too long to get to the
source of our lack of electrics, but nevertheless he was out
on the pontoon in horizontal sleet for about twenty minutes
before the lights came on. Tim and I cheered when he came
inside. He didn't seem to be in a rush to leave us; he had
left his dripping-wet coat in the wheelhouse and made himself
comfortable by the fire.

'Wanna cuppa, Roy?' I asked him.

'Don't put the kettle on special for me,' he replied. He
then proudly presented me with a video. 'Don't lose it, it's the
only one I have, but it might be of interest, might explain why
I'm called Dangerous Dick.'

'Put us out of our misery, Roy!' Tim exclaimed.

'Oh, you've twisted my arm up my back,' Roy laughed
more to himself than us. Then he looked around just in case
anyone had snuck in the saloon.

'I use the explosives, see, when we dive the wrecks.'

'Why would you need explosives, Roy? I thought you
divers just liked to swim around a bit?' I asked, as I put a
steaming mug of tea in front of him.

'No, there's a lot of money in salvage, but sometimes you
can't get to it, so a bit of dynamite comes in handy.' Once
again he chuckled. 'That's why I'm known as Dangerous Dick,
Dangerous Dick Dynamite.'

Dangerous Dick was always popping by *The Princess Matilda*
during that damp Welsh winter; he put a web cam on our
bow, which was connected to the TV. Tim had visions of us
having a leisurely lunch, while on autopilot and being able to
see on the TV where we were going. Roy worked on several
boats in Penarth Marina, and would come aboard if he saw
our lights on. 'I don't want to be a nuisance,' he would say.
He must have spotted our boat moored on the Cardiff visitor

mooring pontoons the day of our planned departure. I heard him before I saw him. Roy doesn't walk anywhere, it's more of a skip and trot. I waved. 'Hi, Roy!'

'Is Timothy still in the arms of Morpheus?' he asked me as he stepped into the wheelhouse.

'No, Roy, he's been up for hours fretting. Go inside.'

I left them to it for a few minutes while I finished tidying up the back deck.

When I joined them, Tim and Roy were discussing our intended route to Cardigan Bay, so I put the kettle on. I noticed Tim had calmed down; he still had the mad glint but I could tell he was holding it in check. Tim had admitted how nervous he was because we had not been to sea for six months, and Roy was offering him lots of advice.

'It's enjoyment, it's not a test,' Roy sagely remarked, 'but you wouldn't be human if you weren't nervous.'

'We were a couple of idiots when we came out of the Thames, Roy, but the more we do the less confidence I have. You see no one has taught me. I just wish I knew if I was doing it right—'

'You must be doing something right, Timothy,' Roy said interrupting the skipper's diatribe, 'you came around Land's End, didn't you, boyo?'

Roy was at the lock later that morning as we came through the barrage, he lowered me down a paper bag full of Welsh cakes. 'That'll keep you going till Swansea. It's a bit fresh out there!'

This was an understatement, for as we came out of the lock I saw the grey, frothing, unforgiving channel galloping by the sea wall. I quickly joined Tim in the wheelhouse.

'Look at it!' Tim shouted.

'It's doing a fair old pace out there, but it will be fine once we turn into the stream!' I shouted back. 'We just need to get back our sea legs; we'll be fine.'

'We won't be fine, look at the way that buoy's moving.'

I had to agree with him that it did look scary, but we were out in the lumpy, swirling, choppy channel in seconds. *Matilda* took it in her stride but Tim looked pale.

'My heart's beating, my guts are churning and I feel like I'm going to die, but I'll be all right in a minute!'

Ahead of us were the two islands of Flat Holm and Steep Holm and suddenly the sun came out. I looked at Tim and saw that he too was looking at the sunrays illuminating the passage between the islands. This was an omen, the future was beckoning us, and I could sense the Spall madness ebbing away with the tide.

Chapter Two
THE HAVEN

Swansea to Milford Haven: 55 nautical miles

Our trip to Swansea went without incident, and Tim and I settled into our old routine of drinking tea and eating cheese sandwiches. We left Swansea Barrage on free flow at nine the following morning. Free flow is when the tide is the same either side of a lock, so we didn't need to 'lock through'.

'Look at that,' Tim said, pointing towards the azure-blue horizon. 'The sea is dead calm.'

'Not a ripple,' I agreed. 'What time will we get to Milford Haven?'

'Well, according to my calculations the tide will be running behind us, and we should get there about half five.'

I looked at my road atlas. 'So we'll be crossing Carmarthen Bay?'

'And too far out for you to see much, but look to our starboard side – that means right, Shane – that's The Mumbles. It's a shame we didn't have time to explore, but we have to make the most of the weather; there's not a breath of wind. We don't get many days like this.'

'I'm glad we went for it when we came out of Cardiff Barrage, that sea looked horrendous. It's amazing how it calmed down once we passed the islands. I wish it could be like this every time we venture out, hey, Tim?'

'You give me the confidence to do this, darlin'. I was a bit of a wreck before we left, wasn't I?'

'Just a bit,' was my reply.

Tim was right about the lack of scenery; for three hours, it was just the monotonous sea, thankfully dead flat.

'I wanted to get a good look at Tenby,' I complained.

'You'd better get a train next time,' Tim laughed. 'Go and put your feet up inside, or find a good book to read. I'll give you a shout if I see anything interesting.'

I am ashamed to say that I fell asleep. Tim woke me as we came into the estuary that forms the natural harbour of Milford Haven.

'Come on, love, you're missing it all. I've been dodging ferries and tankers.'

Milford Haven is Wales' largest port and the third biggest in the whole of the United Kingdom. It is also home to oil refineries.

'Our favourite kind of landscape,' Tim commented. 'You got a text from Matt, while you were asleep.' Tim handed me the mobile that I had left in the wheelhouse. 'He says he's going to film us as we go into the marina, but we have to go onto a holding pontoon first before we can lock through.'

'I better put the kettle on then. I bet he'll be freezing cold, Matt never wears the right sort of clothes.'

Both Tim and I had taken a liking to Matt, who was the same age as our son.

We actually had an hour-and-a-half to drink tea in the saloon before we were allowed to go through the lock at free flow.

It had become chilly and, except for Matt, we were all wrapped up against the damp of the Welsh twilight. There were a couple of marina workers waiting for us and we were grateful when they helped us moor. I was OK because I had had a nap, but Tim had been on his feet for over eight hours. Accidents happen when you are tired.

On our first night in Milford Haven, Tim slept solidly for ten hours. I woke him with a cup of tea, telling him he needed a day to relax.

'What's the weather forecast?' he asked, as he sat up in bed.

'Perfect,' I replied, 'but we need to chill.'

'We also need to do a bit of spring cleaning—'

'And then we can have some lunch,' I interrupted. 'I'm determined to get a Sunday dinner.'

We zigzagged our way up a steep incline towards the town that overlooks the harbour and estuary. We still had Matt with us, and when he wasn't filming we chatted.

Matt had spent the winter in Dover, working on a documentary about the lifeboat.

'We moored in Dover a couple of years ago; it looked pretty depressing and rundown,' I said.

'I think it's the transitory nature of the town. People arrive on the ferry and head for the M20,' Matt replied. 'I was staying in digs, and missing my girlfriend, so it was pretty grim, just waiting for the pager to go off, then I'd have to tear down to the lifeboat station. If I wasn't quick enough they'd leave me behind, which didn't please the producer! "Seconds costs lives!" the coxswain used to say.'

'Did you have any rough trips out with the lifeboat, Matt?' I asked him.

'Not half,' he replied, 'but I'm looking forward to coming with you to Fishguard if you leave tomorrow. The weather forecast is looking good, isn't it, Tim?'

Tim was walking just ahead of us and stopped and waited for us to catch up. 'Yes, yes it is, but I've been told so many conflicting things about the best time to leave. I think I'll spend the afternoon crosschecking the *Reeds* and the pilot books.'

We had reached the top of the path and all stood to catch our breath. Before us was industrial Milford Haven, with a backdrop of the glorious Pembrokeshire coastline and the Preseli Mountains.

'The oil refineries and natural gas terminals will be lit up like a Disney magic kingdom tonight,' I observed. 'It was just as well it was the afternoon when we arrived, as all of those lights would have thoroughly confused us in the dark.'

Tim and I loved the juxtaposition of the beauty of the river and the hills beyond and the industry for which Milford Haven is now famous. However, the port still has the largest fishing fleet in Wales, with 3,000 tonnes of fish landed a year. We saw a trawler offloading that morning; it made us quite nostalgic for Newlyn. We'd had such a great time watching those Cornish fishing boats coming in the previous summer, a couple of the smaller craft even rafted against us to pass the time of day. Our little freezer had overflowed with red mullet and mackerel.

We had lunch in the Lord Nelson Hotel, which has panoramic views over the harbour, although there was no fresh Welsh fish on the menu. Matt was with us and I force fed him champagne.

'So how far is it to Fishguard, skipper?' he asked Tim, while covering his glass to stop me refilling it.

'You are such a lightweight, Matt!' I laughed.

'Approximately 55 nautical miles and one of the fishermen said it would be blowing from the north, maybe a force 4, so we might be back here for lunch again tomorrow. If we do go, we'll leave about eleven.'

'Great, that'll give me an hour to go to that dress shop on the harbour. I have to find a frock for our youngest daughter's wedding,' I explained to Matt.

Image by Vanessa opened at ten; I left Tim in the marina office paying our mooring fee.

'I'll see you in the chandlery in half an hour,' I told him.

Vanessa was very accommodating and kept pushing clothes through the changing-room curtain. I bought several outfits and made my escape before I ended up with a hat to match.

'How much did that lot cost?' Tim enquired when I joined him.

'Not much,' I replied innocently. 'Did you get some more rope for the fenders?'

He picked up the three large dress bags and gave me a small brown paper bag in exchange. Inside were half a dozen white corded strands of short rope for the fenders. I shoved them in my handbag. At the time, I wasn't aware of how vital these ropes would prove to be.

Back onboard *The Princess Matilda*, I changed into one of the outfits, which in the shop I'd thought looked rather fetching – a pair of white trousers and a blue smocked blouse. Tim was too busy putting his course into the chart plotter to take any notice. He was also complaining to Matt: 'It seems like we'll be leaving two hours too late to use the full benefit of the tide to take us around St David's Head, but a slight sea is forecast, so we should get to Fishguard around nine tonight.'

Then he turned and saw me. 'What the fuck are you wearing, Shane?'

I twirled, 'I've been imaged by Vanessa. What do you think?'

'Vanessa should be flayed. Now let's get a move on, we have to go through the lock.'

When we arrived, we had waited an hour-and-a-half to go through the lock on free flow, to get into the dock. This time they needed to empty it for us to go in, then fill it for us to leave. To make a passage through an 'average' lock takes about fifteen minutes; this lock was the size of a football pitch. I tied up the bow and sunbathed, thinking what a perfect day it was.

The marina had shimmered and the water was like a millpond. I had time to think.

I was brought up in Staffordshire on the edge of the ancient royal hunting forests of Cannock Chase. There were no mill-ponds in my neighbourhood. Instead, there were mines dug deep under the forest, and where I lived there were aban-doned flooded open-cast coal pits. From an early age, I had been warned to keep away from these hazardous lakes. When the sun was burning down the local children jumped in, but not me. In the winter, the deep manmade ponds froze over and were peppered with rocks and branches as the local kids tried to break the icy crust. These kids had mottled-blue bare legs and slimy-green candlesticks of snot running down their faces, and if they were lucky their mothers gave them a pair of old socks to wear as gloves. Two brothers from my primary school tried to retrieve their branches from the ice. At the next school assembly, the headmistress told us what had happened to them. The thin skin of ice cracked and they drowned. So I have always been aware of the fragility of life. One moment everything is marvellous and the next you have to fight for survival, thrash and try not to panic. Even still calm waters are deceptive.

During the summer of 1996, after Tim was diagnosed with leukaemia, we had learned how to tread water. After his second course of chemotherapy, Tim contracted a virulent fungal infection in his lung that further threatened his life. He still had three more courses of chemo to get through before he could be given the all clear.

It was sticky and humid in London that year, and I used to have nightmares that I was sliding down the shifting shale of a coal-black slag heap. The slag heaps were my playgrounds, but I never slid down the heaps that went into the ponds, except in my nightmares. In my sweat-drenched dreams, my only escape was to throw myself into the cool, flooded, bottomless coal pit of my childhood. The 'midnight notes' I wrote when Tim was diagnosed with cancer stopped me from drowning. I felt I could remove myself from what was happening; it was a way of making sense out of the medical roller-coaster, or, as Tim liked to put it, the bungee jump into hell.

29th July 1996
Midnight
Results of the latest bone marrow (how could I have made such a fuss that first time?): 2 per cent cells, complete remission. We can't believe this yet, but we know you will not get the 'all clear' until you have had at least two if not three more courses of chemo. We must not think too far ahead, you keep saying, 'One day this will be something that happened to us and not something we are living through.' But the fact of the matter is your platelets are still low, so this means you could haemorrhage. You are very, very tired. We left the hospital today, and very slowly walked to a pub across Tottenham Court Road. You felt stronger because of the transfusion you'd had the night before. It was weird being out. You ordered a Yorkshire pudding and it came with a huge sausage in the middle of it; it looked horrible. You couldn't eat it – you looked like an old man, reminded me of my dad.

30th July 1996
Midnight
More platelets tonight. You may be home tomorrow after seven long weeks. It should have been four – that last lot of chemo and the fungal infection almost killed you. I've seen visitors come and go on that ward, weeping as they came out

of rooms, and I never ask the nurses what has happened to patients when the name on the door is changed. The lucky ones are the patients like you, who finally emerge, like a bald chrysalis, weak, unsure on their feet, shuffling up the corridor to the nurses' station. You did it.

It's no way to carry on, is it? So home for a few days and then back in to begin the third course...

31st July 1996
Midnight
You're very fed up, I can't get a smile out of you, you won't talk to me, you won't eat because you get atrocious heart burn, your guts aren't used to food, and you think something might happen in the middle of the night if you come home. I leave you sitting at the table looking out of the window and come back with an Indian takeaway. You said you didn't want any, but you eat a few mouthfuls and enjoy it.

2nd August 1996
Midnight
You came home yesterday, but I took you back to the ward tonight. I'm wearing your pyjama top but I can't smell you on it. Too much snot, I'm like one of those bad actresses who let it slime down their face. You were skinny and bony in bed last night, I thought you'd stopped breathing, I'm almost relieved that you are not here. We're both paranoid now, aren't we?

10th August 1996
Midnight
You came back home on the 3rd and everything has been OK. You have been back to the hospital a couple of times for platelet transfusions and you had a CT scan on Thursday.

Dr Panos said the shadow of the fungal infection on your lung looks larger, so you have to go on the ward for a few days for some more antibiotics. I wish I was stronger, I wish it were over, but they can't begin the third chemo until the fungal infection is sorted out. One way or another I wish I had faith in God. I can't pray, except every now and again something slips out. I wish I could believe it works.

Five hours after passing through the lock at Milford Haven, I was sitting on the floor of our cabin, with my back against the bottom of the bed and my feet on the bulkhead wall. This was to stop myself being thrown around the bedroom. 'Oh, God,' I kept saying to myself as we were hit by another merciless wave. I was surrounded by chaos, our cabin looked like Homeland Security had searched it looking for the smoking gun.

Since leaving the haven of Milford Haven, *The Princess Matilda* had been tossed around by the raw power of the sea. Our boat weighs 35 tons but she felt like a child's balsawood model ship. A few hours earlier I had been writing in the logbook, 'We have a short chop as we pass around the outside of Skokholm and Skomer islands, we shall then cross St Brides Bay, to St David's Head. Through the binoculars we shall see the beaches of the Pembrokeshire Coast National Park...' Then Tim had yelled, 'SHANE! SHANE! SIT DOWN!'

I threw myself on the step of the wheelhouse and hung on to the grab bar as a wave the size of the Thames Barrier bashed against the whole 54 feet of our vessel. *Matilda* rolled with the force of the water and Tim hung on to the steering wheel at a 45-degree angle; everything that had not been tied down moved. I could hear objects being smashed inside the boat. It was as if time had stood still, *Matilda* seemed to be frozen, just hanging at the top of a wave. Then she slammed down as the wave dumped us like a sack of coal, the whole boat shuddering and rolling so far to one side I thought she would never come back upright.

'WHERE'S MATT?' I screamed. My blood turned to ice as I realized our new young cameraman wasn't in the wheelhouse and I knew he wasn't inside the boat. Unexpectedly, the boat stopped rolling and I was able to stand and look around. The closed doors to the rear deck flew open and Matt appeared. He was soaking wet from the spray. Tim and I were both trembling, but Matt had a look of sheer joy on his face. 'That was amazing—' he started, but Tim interrupted him, 'Matt, mate, I'd rather you didn't go outside again, not until we're in calmer waters. Hang on, everybody, there's another roller...'

Again *Matilda* revolved.

Once she righted herself, Tim opened the door a little bit and told me one of the bowlines had been swept into the sea.

'Can you get hold of it?' he asked me.

'Not on your nelly. I'm not going out there, Tim!'

'You don't have to; pull it in through the porthole from the bedroom. Do it now while we have a lull. If it gets fouled around the propeller, we'll be completely buggered!'

Matt came to help me as I made a dash down the steps to our cabin. Everything was on the floor, books, my printer and the big ring binder that I kept on top of the wardrobe. The whole lot decorated my carpet, along with six hats and all Tim's sea charts. This, however, was the least of our problems, as I frantically opened the porthole so I could get hold of the rope.

'Hold it open for me, Matt!' I yelled, pushing my arm through the gap. I think it was pure luck that I managed to get hold of it on my first attempt. I tugged with all of my might. 'Slam the porthole as soon as I have it all out of the water!' I shouted.

We both had trouble standing up and were being thrown like a couple of ragdolls against each other. I now had yards and yards of heavy wet rope on my bedroom floor, and I knew I had to secure it somehow. Then I remembered I still had the fender rope in my handbag, which fortuitously was on the bed. I rolled up the bowline and secured it in a tidy bundle. Matt opened the window wide enough for me to chuck the rope back outside, and we both swiftly turned the sea catches. During all of this, Matt was filming me. God knows how he did it with one hand.

We both sat on the wet floor.

'That was one of the most amazing things I've ever seen, Shane! Can we go again please?' Matt said breathlessly.

'Fuck off!' was my reply.

He left me on the floor and staggered through the saloon and up the steps to see what was going on with Tim in the wheelhouse. I knew exactly what was going on, the same as had been happening since we came around St David's Head. We had got the tides wrong when we left Milford Haven; 'haven' was the clue, and now we were being punished by rough, turbulent, unforgiving waves.

I joined them. Tim was still struggling with the steering wheel, trying to go over the waves instead of having them catch us on the side. They were eight or nine feet high.

'It's what I was saying about the elements,' Tim shouted to me, 'this is when they tell you who's boss.'

From where I was hanging on, I thought the sea might win this battle.

'How much longer?' I yelled.

'At least another four hours,' he replied. My heart sank.

'We've spent two hours going nowhere. We're still doing eight knots, but the tide's against us,' Tim continued, as if by saying it, it all might stop.

'Talk about being lulled into a false sense of security!' I shouted over the roar of the waves. 'We've had two perfect passages, the sun was shining, the sea like a millpond, and now it's teaching us a lesson and I feel sick. I'm going below to tidy up, hopefully without breaking my hip.'

20th August 1996
Midnight
We just got back from the Norfolk Broads. We had hired a boat after staying in a hotel in the New Forest overnight. It was pouring with rain on Friday, and Rafe and Sadie were behaving like little pigs, but the sun came out when we picked up a type of boat known as a 'Gin Palace', so that suited me down to the ground. Last night we moored in quite a secluded spot, and there were gale-force winds predicted. It was quite scary, because the night before I was woken up by banging; the mooring line had come undone and the boat was bouncing against the one next door. I managed to get us tied up again without waking you up. Not to be caught out twice, I phoned Jenny in Scotland, the boat expert, the woman who crosses Loch Lomond in the dark on the little ferry boat and jumps off with five-foot waves to tie up. I asked her advice how to tie up properly. The wind was really blowing and I discovered there wasn't anywhere I could walk to civilization for help (in case of an emergency). Thank goodness we had a signal on the mobile, but one can't help but think of all the 'what if' scenarios...what if you haemorrhage, what if you need an ambulance, what if the boat sinks...what if...
YOU STILL NEED MORE CHEMO...

'I've never felt more grateful to see a lighthouse,' Tim said wearily, as we came into Fishguard Harbour. The sky was a slab of smudged purple, and in any other circumstances we would be waxing lyrical about the beauty and stillness of the night sky; but we just squabbled about where we had been told we could moor. I used a torch so I could look at the pilot book.

'The bloke on the phone said to go by the lifeboat station.'

'No, we can't go there, it's a foul area. It dries,' Tim kept saying irritably.

It took us an age to moor up; characteristically, Tim was trying to be in two places at the same time.

'I can manage, Tim,' I snapped at him as he came to the bow, where I was hanging onto a dangling chain from the high harbour wall. I gave it to him and went to the stern, where he yelled at me to manoeuvre *The Princess Matilda* forwards and backwards: 'Turn to starboard! No, not that way, STAR-BOARD, STARBOARD!'

Fortunately, Matt was able to get onto the ladder and he took a line from Tim. I left them to it. I had had enough of yelling to last me a lifetime. I hate people shouting at me, and hate it even more when the person who is doing it is supposed to be my best friend.

I took off my lifejacket, went inside to the galley and poured myself a large gin. Fishguard might be a major port, but, unlike Milford Haven, the actual town is far away from the docks. I looked through the window towards the flashing lighthouse and thought, 'We are in the middle of nowhere, miles from civilization, welcome to paradise.' And there was a ladder, I hate ladders.

Chapter Three
VISITORS

Next to our mooring in Fishguard was a corn-yellow crane and a grim rusted-ginger ladder that became longer by the day. Even when the tide was in, the ladder continued to grow. It reminded me of a pantomime seaweed-encrusted beanstalk. Tim is not afraid of heights, but I became giddy craning my neck to look up. It may have been a trick of the still low-lying spring sun, but the top of the ladder and crane appeared to disappear into the ether. The grungy grey, granite blocks of the harbour wall contrasted with the clear, cloudless sky. I could imagine a pointy curl-toed boot suddenly stepping out of the blue sky curtain. Although it was not Jack or a fakir that descended our ladder, but a couple of angels. On closer inspection, I recognized them as RNLI lifeboat crew.

'Permission to come aboard?' asked the first. Tim had already made their acquaintance that morning, asking their advice about getting fuel for *The Princess Matilda*. The last time we had filled up was in Swansea, so we knew we were getting low. We have two 100-gallon tanks, one for the engine and the other for the generator and central heating.

'This is Paul Butler,' Tim said, as I shook his hand.

'I'm the coxswain,' he explained gravely, his eyes taking everything in. 'And this is Hosey, our mechanic. He's come to look at your fuel tanks to see if he can swap them over.'

I shook hands with Hosey who immediately spotted the empty beer bottles in the wheelhouse recycling bin. 'Had a party, have we?' he said, winking.

Then Paul reached into the waste bin and pulled out a set of broken dividers, which Tim uses to measure distances on his sea charts. 'Every picture tells a story. The skipper tells me you had a rough passage last night?'

Up to this point, Tim and I sensed they were holding back. We felt like a couple of foreigners; they were both exceedingly Welsh. But Hosey with his cheeky grin broke the ice. 'Haha,' he said, 'you deserved a good drink after a lumpy crossing!'

'Fancy a beer, Hosey?' Tim asked him, as he led the way down the steps into the saloon. I suspected he would have answered yes if he had been on his own, but he shook his head. I put the kettle on, while Tim showed them around.

'So, Hosey's an unusual name,' I heard Tim say, as they all went into the forward bathroom.

'I used to be in the fire brigade,' he replied, as they all came out. 'Nice boat. I'd like one of these, Paul!'

Paul was a little shorter and slighter than Hosey. Tim and I worried how the jovial, beefy mechanic would get into the restricted space beneath our wheelhouse deck. The skipper lifted the hatch and turned on the light. In a flash, Hosey took off his jacket and descended the ladder, squeezing and contorting himself around the confines of the engine room. Paul and Tim kneeled and hung their heads down the hole, the coxswain occasionally asking Tim questions about our trip.

'We're going all the way around the British Isles. We've been filming some of it. The series is coming out next month and my wife writes a blog; she'll probably write about you when you've gone.'

Paul looked up at me as I relaxed on my fold-up director's chair. Unsurprisingly, I was tapping away on my laptop.

'What's it called, the blog?' he asked.

'Spalls at Sea,' Tim replied.

'Fools at Sea?' Paul looked at us both with astonishment. 'Fools at Sea, haha, that's very funny!'

Hosey climbed out of the wheelhouse and explained what

he had done with the fuel tanks, but Paul insisted he draw a diagram, 'Just so you know for the future!'

Hosey wiped his hands down his trousers and chuckled, 'That's why we came down today, saved ourselves a trip out on the lifeboat to bring you back. We get a lot of shouts for boats running out of fuel.'

'You should get a fuel gauge fitted on here,' Paul added, 'but that other tank should keep you going until you get to Aberystwyth, they've got a fuel barge there. But I can't see you going anywhere for a few days as the weather's changing. You can use our emergency buoy if it gets too rough for you against this wall.'

'We might take you up on that; we've been banging about a bit. But we have a journalist coming tomorrow, doing an interview with us about our new series—'

'Fools at Sea?' Hosey interrupted.

'Yes, that's the one,' Tim laughed. 'So we'll stay by the ladder until he's been.'

After Paul and Hosey left us, I sent Tim to the shop to get in some more supplies. With a guest due the next day, we needed to stock up on crisps and Chablis. While Tim was away, I sat on the roof and watched a fishing boat offloading bags of shellfish. *Annie* had come in shortly after us the night before, and they had been unloading ever since. Fishguard has a busy commercial harbour and we were also moored by the Fishguard-to-Rosslare ferry terminal. The Stena Line ferry had been lit up like a dazzling block of flats as it arrived from Ireland just after midnight. We heard it before we saw it, a deep pulsating rumble. Tim had only just come inside after checking our mooring ropes for the twentieth time. Both he and I rushed to look out of the window.

'It's heading straight at us!' Tim cried. 'Turn on all our lights!'

'Of course they can see us! They're not going to crash into us and the harbour wall,' I yelped. But I did what I was told just in case.

The sound of the growling engines suddenly changed as the ferry was put into reverse gear, and turned and backed onto the terminal dock.

By the time Tim came back from his shopping expedition, it was low tide. Like a boy scout, Tim had returned to me prepared. I heard him yodelling above our rocky harbour crag. 'I'm going to lower the shopping down on a rope!'

We had come a long way since we had first done this; lowering down provisions when we first picked up *The Princess Matilda*. That was in Brentford, in the summer of 2005. At the time we thought that *that* was a long ladder. In retrospect, in comparison to this one, it was a couple of rungs. Back then, we had been like a couple of clowns participating in some game show, as Tim swung down our worldly goods for me to catch, ready to get *Matilda* shipshape for our maiden voyage.

After stowing away our shopping, Tim and I cleaned the boat from top to bottom in preparation for the morning. We wanted to make a good impression on our newspaperman. I was anxious because I had never been interviewed before; this was all new to me. Tim, the expert, advised me to be myself.

The journalist was bringing a photographer with him, so I dressed in my 'Image by Vanessa' specials the following day.

'Get 'em off!' Tim said, and he wasn't propositioning me. 'You look like you're off to a Conservative ladies' garden party.' I looked in the mirror and thought I looked rather smart, so refused. He pushed me onto the bed, tickling me while trying to remove my clothes. 'Come on, Vanessa, get 'em off.'

Tim was outside sorting out some fenders when we heard someone shout. It was Bill, the journalist. I secretly watched him climb down the ladder as I continued putting on some makeup, although I had relented and the Image by Vanessa was back in the wardrobe.

I joined our visitors in the saloon. Having lived with an actor for three decades, most of them with him being 'famous', I can gauge how an encounter with a stranger will go. Nine times out of ten they only have eyes for my husband. This is understandable, I don't take it personally. And so, when Tim introduced me to Bill, I wasn't surprised when he looked at me for a split second and carried on his conversation with Tim. I persevered and stuck out my hand and said, 'Hi, I'm Shane Spall. Welcome aboard *The Princess Matilda*!'

Bill didn't introduce me to the photographer, I did this myself too.

'Can I get you a glass of wine?' I asked them both.

'I'd better not, I have to get the pictures and I'm driving,' the photographer replied.

'Bill?'

'Yes please,' he said, barely drawing breath as he chatted to Tim.

I poured the Chablis and interrupted: 'Would you like a tour?'

It didn't take long and we all returned to the saloon. I sat in my usual chair, the photographer took the other. Tim and Bill sat at the table.

'Would it be better if Shane sits at the table too?' Tim asked.

'No no, she's fine there,' Bill replied, as he pulled out two tape machines.

I stood up, expecting to be handed one, but he gave me his empty glass instead. Retreating to the fridge, I began to half fill his glass and glanced briefly out of the window at the long ladder. I filled our guest's glass to the brim.

Bill ignored me as I put down his wine.

'Right, one two, one two...' He pressed the buttons and played back. 'We're ready to begin! Now, tell me why you like to spend so much of your time on the barge.'

'Well it's our home—' I began, but before I could finish the sentence Bill's hand came up. He didn't look at me. I noticed Tim grimace a bit and he began to explain that the boat was our home from home. I took the wine bottle out of the fridge and refilled the glasses. I mimed, 'Do you want a cuppa?' to the photographer who was leafing through yesterday's *Daily Telegraph*. He shook his head and went back to the paper. He was obviously used to not being part of the conversation.

I poured myself a glass of champagne and decided to have another go at joining in. Tim was talking about all the wildlife we see on our journeys. I added, 'We saw the first swallows three days ago...' The disapproving silencing hand came up so I half-heartedly mumbled, 'Or maybe they weren't the first ones.' Tim knows I love birds and I could tell he was encouraging me to say more when he said, 'And the guillemots...' But I had had enough of the hand by now. It is the one my mother used to use when she was on the phone.

I excused myself and went to the bathroom. The window was open so I craned my neck, checking out the length of the ladder. Low tide was in two hours. I applied a splash of red lipstick and returned to the saloon. I did another refill. This, I thought, is his fourth, and I wondered if I'd get done for manslaughter if he were to fall overboard. Suddenly, I realized all eyes were on me. I noticed Bill's hand was now beckoning me to speak.

'Darlin', what did I say we'd get when I was so ill in hospital?' Tim asked me again. Bill's hand was really becoming animated.

I spoke as commanded and replied to Tim's question. 'That when you got better we'd get a Rolls and a boat.'

Then the silencing hand came up again.

'What a rude man!' I said to Tim after our guests left us. 'I liked the photographer, but that Bill was plain insulting.'

'I'm sure he didn't mean to be,' said Tim. 'But he did look like a big daft girl climbing that ladder.'

Chapter Four
UNDER MILK WOOD

Paul, the coxswain, had been quite right about the change in the weather and we decided we would take up his kind offer and use the RNLI buoy. *The Princess Matilda* and crew had had enough of being banged against the side of the harbour wall, which was now known by us as the Welsh Grand Canyon.

'If you want a laugh,' Tim had told the coxswain, 'have a look through your binoculars. We usually have a screaming match getting a swing mooring, and we're both a bit rusty; it's been a while.'

I felt there were several sets of binoculars observing us from the window of the lifeboat station as the barge approached what looked like a giganic tin of Lucozade. Tim had no choice but to remain in the wheelhouse on the helm as I stood on the bow with my boat hook. Rivulets of sweat trickled down my back, even though there was a keen wind blowing. I am sure I saw the sun reflect off yet another set of binoculars. Kneeling down on the deck I made a grab for the float but missed it, and stood to signal to Tim to reverse so I could attempt it again.

'You can do it, you can do it,' I muttered to myself, as once more we approached the float and once again I threw myself on the deck. I missed it, but quickly tried again before the tide pushed us away. 'I've got it!' I squealed, as I tried to lug the float aboard, but it was attached to the thickest chain I have ever seen. Tim was at my side in an instant and I fell backwards, still holding the slimy float to my chest. I scrambled to my feet, while Tim groaned and yanked the sopping clanking chain out of the water. Swearing through his teeth, he managed to get both of our bowlines attached to the chain. We both then collapsed on top of the gas locker and hugged each other.

'Well done, darlin',' Tim said, as he gave the thumbs up to the RNLI station window that was about a quarter-of-a-mile away.

I went below to have a wash and change my wet grungy clothes, but I could hear Tim on the roof. He dangled his head down through the open skylight in the bathroom and whistled. I swatted him with a towel and put on my dressing gown.

'No one can see you,' he said, laughing at my attempt at modesty. 'I'm going to blow the dinghy up.'

'And I'm going to wear Image by Vanessa,' I replied, as I shut the bathroom door behind me to go into our cabin.

Tim sometimes surprises me and this was one of those occasions. Not only did he inflate and launch the dinghy that had been sitting on the roof since we had used it in Newlyn nine months before, but he got the outboard started first time too.

'Come on, darlin',' he shouted impatiently, as I put on my lifejacket. 'I'm taking you to the pub! Don't bother locking up, there's no pirates around here and we have the Welsh Mafia keeping an eye on the old girl.' He waved towards the RNLI station.

I slid into *New Si*, our dinghy, and we cast off from the mother ship and set sail.

'Where are we going?' I asked Tim, as I made myself comfortable on my usual spot at the bow of the tender. I held on to the painter, the thin mooring line, for balance, as we bobbed over small waves.

'Lower Town Fishguard. Paul says there's a pub called The Ship.'

'I hope they serve food, I'm starving,' I replied.

Tim laughed. 'Forget about your belly, look at the scenery, it's glorious. How many people get a chance to do this?'

It took us about ten minutes to cross Fishguard Harbour. We were the only craft on what appeared to be an oversized boating lake. Naturally, I had the camera out, clicking away. The gently pulsating water was a cold emerald green; I was pleased I was wearing thermals under my Image by Vanessa.

'The Lower Town is up the River Gwaun,' Tim said, pointing towards a narrowing between two grey craggy outcrops. The steeper and bleaker one to our left was haloed with angry-looking gorse. At the base was an ugly concrete slipway.

'It looks like an obscene tongue telling us to turn around,' I said.

But this made us more curious to see what was around the corner.

Tim and I felt *New Si* push against the rippling undercurrent at the mouth of the fairway. We felt rather than saw what at low tide would become a tumbling stream; at the moment the river gorge was swollen with salt-tinged sea. Around the next bend was a handsome fishing village and on the other bank were bare deciduous trees. But Tim and I didn't have time to admire the view, as the little port was dotted with small boats. They appeared to be attached to long lines coming from the harbour wall. The water was crystal clear, allowing us to dodge these seaweed-smothered strands of rope. Tim slowed down the outboard and we played dodgems in and out of the small moored craft. Many had not been moved for months, their owners awaiting the return of long summer days. It was early April and there was no one around. Tim cut off the engine, took out the oars and began to row.

'It's like a ghost town,' he said, nodding his head towards the town quay.

'Or a film set,' I replied, as I pushed bobbing seagull-shit-encrusted craft out of the way.

'Paul said we should moor on the cobbled slipway,' Tim said, pointing ahead.

This was easier said than done. I could sense Tim becoming irritable, but I ignored him until our dinghy nudged the wall of the quay. 'Slipway is a perfect name,' I thought, as it occurred to me that Tim now expected me to leap off *New Si* onto the oily cobbles.

'I can't get off here, Tim!' I complained. 'I would kill myself.'

'Do you think you'd be able to get off on that ladder,' he said, keeping exasperation out of his voice.

I looked towards where he was pointing; it was a low wall.

'Even you could manage that tiny ladder!'

He paddled towards it, so I didn't have a choice. I made a grab for a greasy metal rung, and Tim moved his weight to one side as a counterbalance as I stood gingerly.

'Go on, love,' he said gently. 'You can do it.'

It was surprisingly easy and I climbed the little ladder, then quickly scrambled onto my hands and knees and stood up in case anyone was watching my ungainly disembarkation. But there was only Tim and me. He had rowed back to the slipway and I watched as he tied up our little boat.

'I'm leaving a slot of slack,' he said, 'we don't want to get hung up on the wall when the tide goes out.'

I threw my lifejacket in the dinghy, and we strolled hand in hand along the empty quay.

'Let's find The Ship,' Tim said, picking up speed so I had to jog to keep up.

The pub wasn't hard to find, standing pebble-dash pink in a narrow street, flanked by double yellow lines.

'At last, civilization,' Tim said, squeezing by a brewery delivery lorry that filled up the whole road.

We went inside the wood-panelled pub where three men were sitting on high stools at the bar. They stopped talking when we entered. Tim ordered a Guinness and a glass of wine, and was told by a friendly barmaid that they didn't serve food. 'I'm Val, the landlady; as you can tell, I'm not local.'

'She's Canadian,' one of the blokes at the bar explained.

'From Vancouver Island,' she laughed.

The local Welsh ice was broken.

Tim was still wearing his lifejacket, and the conversation changed from local politics to boats and the sea. We explained that we were moored in Fishguard on the lifeboat buoy. As we chatted, the draymen were in and out delivering barrels of beer. Val gave them a drink when they were done.

'Thirsty work,' one of them said, downing it in one. Then he peered at Tim; we were sitting in a dark unlit corner. 'You're off the telly!' he said.

'Not at the minute, mate,' Tim replied.

'You're not the first actor we've had in this pub,' Val remarked, pointing to some old framed photographs above our heads. I stood and inspected them.

'It's Richard Burton,' I exclaimed to Tim.

'That's right,' one of the draymen said proudly. 'They filmed *Under Milk Wood* around here, 1971 it was, starring Richard and Elizabeth Taylor, Peter O'Toole and that girl out of *Bouquet of Barbed Wire*...'

'Susan Penhaligon?' I said.

'That's the one,' Val said, 'but it was way before my time.'

I would have liked to have added it was before my time too, but in the early seventies I used to live in West Wales. We didn't have time for me to reminisce though, because one of the blokes at the bar said we had better get a move on if we wanted to get back to the RNLI buoy.

'The crew all drink in here,' he said proudly, pointing to all the commendations on the wall. 'But, if the tide goes out too much, you'll have to walk home and it looks like the weather's about to change. Lower Fishguard is sheltered but...' He didn't finish his sentence as a gust of wind blew the door of the pub open – it was our cue to take our leave.

'Bloody hell,' Tim said breathlessly a few minutes later. 'This is your fault!'

The mooring line to our dinghy was taut, holding the bow out of the water. My lifejacket had slid down the slope of our almost upended tender.

'Take your shoes off,' he added. He already had his tied by the shoe laces around his neck. While I took off mine, he pulled a knife out of his pocket and cut the end of the painter. The weight of the boat had made it too tight to untie, and time was of the essence. *New Si* slipped into the deeper water. Tim followed closely behind with his trousers rolled up to his knees; he splashed through the shallows and launched himself in to the dinghy.

'Get in, get in,' he instructed urgently.

'It's fucking freezing!' I complained, as I joined him flopping into *New Si*.

Tim managed to shove us away from the slipway using the oar on the bottom and I dragged us around the moored boats until we hit the flow of the outgoing tide. I was pleased I was wearing thermals under my Vanessa specials and pulled down my bobble hat to cover my ears.

'Let's hope the outboard works...' Tim mumbled under his breath. This is always a nail-biting moment, but I was more concerned with getting my lifejacket on. The weak sun had disappeared behind the hill and there was a chill wind blowing. The engine fired up first time, which was just as well, as we were now in the mouth of the river. The river water and tide was running quickly and we shot out. I fell backwards against Tim's knees before righting myself and grabbing onto what was left of our painter.

We both instinctively looked across the bay of Fishguard Harbour towards our mooring, but *The Princess Matilda* had disappeared from view. Now the warning from the customer in the pub made sense, Lower Town Fishguard was a safe haven, protected by the high hills of the gorge from the wind and the tide. The 'boating lake' we had experienced just two hours earlier had become a maelstrom. A grey froth-topped wave hit us both in the face.

'Wind across tide!' Tim yelled. 'Hold on, Shane...'

The nose of the dinghy ploughed into the next icy cold roller. Fear engulfed me, because a few months previously we had found ourselves in a similar situation on the Helford River. Tim and I had thought we might drown; there'd been no one around to come to our aid because it was the end of the holiday season. We'd been the only ones stupid enough to be out in gale-force conditions in a rubber dinghy.

Once again, I found myself having to hang on in case I was thrown overboard. 'People pay money at funfairs to do this,' I thought, as I struggled to stay upright and retrieve my phone from my pocket. In a panic I pressed redial. I hadn't a clue who I was calling. The bow of the dinghy began to climb up a hill, then the wave disappeared and we hung in mid-air before falling with a thump. Cascades of seawater almost blinded us.

'Good afternoon, Fishguard Lifeboat Station...hello, hello...'

My feet were turning blue in the sloshing water that was trapped in the dinghy.

'Is that Paul, the coxswain?' I yelled, as Tim kept us head on to the breaking waves. I left him no time to answer before continuing. 'Can you see us? We're crossing the bay from Lower Town, and if our outboard cuts out we're buggered!'

'I've got my binoculars on you. Just tell Tim to keep her bow on to the waves,' Paul calmly replied. 'You'll be OK, you've got your lifejackets on and we'll come and get you if you go over.'

'That was Paul, the coxswain,' I shouted to Tim as I hung up. 'He's keeping his eye on us; he says take them head on!'

The outward journey had taken us ten minutes, but the return trip took us thirty. It felt like hours. Tim was sitting behind me, but I knew he would be as grim-faced as me.

'Why are we doing this?' I yelled.

'Because we're fuckin' alive!' Tim screamed back.

Tim managed to steer New Si 'inside' of The Princess Matilda, so she acted as a windbreak. I didn't waste any time getting our short painter tied around the bollard, and I was up and out like a seal in a circus. Tim followed close behind. We both stood bare-footed and dripping water on the gunwale and waved towards the lifeboat station. I pressed redial as we entered the wheelhouse.

'Thanks for keeping an eye on us, Paul,' I said through chattering teeth.

'Best get inside and have a hot shower,' he said, laughing. 'Watching you get that buoy then cross the harbour was the best laugh me and the boys have had for ages, but we were ready to pluck you out the water if you'd sunk!' I could hear guffawing in the background. 'We might buzz you in the lifeboat later on as we're going out on an exercise. You're welcome to join us.'

'I think we'll give that a miss, thanks Paul, and tell Hosey we've heard all the gossip in The Ship,' I replied.

I could hear Hosey in the background: 'If it's about the police and a pushbike, it's all lies...'

We couldn't turn on the central heating because we were conserving fuel, so I tried to light a fire. Tim calls me 'the fire starter'. I boast that I can light a blaze with two sheets of newspaper, but all we got that blowy day was smoke belched back down the chimney. I turned the gas rings on and made us something to eat. A green-eyed baked potato for me and an expired tin of Fray Bentos steak and kidney pie for Tim was all I could find in the cupboards.

We went up into the wheelhouse before we went to bed and looked towards Lower Town. It was a dark evening and the quarter moon had not risen. I shivered, and Tim put his arm around me and cleared his throat. I pulled away from him and opened the door so he could gob outside, but he pulled me back and whispered in my ear, 'The sloeblack, slow, black, crowblack, fishingboatbobbing sea. That's all ours.'

'Did you just make that up?' I asked him.

'No, Dylan Thomas. I did *Under Milk Wood* at RADA. Come on, let's go to kip.'

Our wakeup call the following day was the rolling wake of a bobbing fishing boat leaving the harbour. I jumped out of bed to open the curtains. The sea was satin smooth and the sunrays danced on the surface. I made a pot of tea and climbed back under the covers. 'I'm glad the lifeboat didn't have a shout last night,' I said, as Tim blew on his steaming mug.

The crew had warned us, when they 'buzzed' *The Princess Matilda* the night before, that if they had to bring in a rescued boat they would need to use the emergency buoy.

The boat might be too damaged to put alongside the harbour wall, so it would mean we'd have had to do so instead. We had watched the lifeboat cross from the station towards us at thirty knots. Paul was high up on the fly bridge and the crew were on the bow, all dressed in their orange waterproofs and lifejackets. When the lifeboat slowed and came alongside us, Hosey appeared from below, the only one of them not in waterproofs. I was about to ask him about the pushbike, but noticed the boat was named *Blue Peter VII* and remembered all the milk bottle tops I had sent to Blue Peter over the years. Tim was talking to Paul: 'We plan to leave two hours before high water...'

'That'll do it,' Paul replied. 'You'll push a one-knot tide but then you'll have it behind you all the way to Aberystwyth.'

Chapter Five
GOING BACK

Fishguard to Aberystwyth: 41 nautical miles

'I used to live over there,' I said to Tim, twelve hours later. We had crossed this first segment of Cardigan Bay on a tranquil flat calm sea, but we were too far away from the land to pick out any landmarks. I looked down at my AA road map. 'Can we not go into Aberaeron?' I asked him.

'No, darlin'. I've set our course to Aberystwyth and Aberaeron dries out and we don't want to be stuck there if the weather changes.'

'That's a shame...' I replied, but Tim didn't let me finish.

'Keep your eyes peeled, I need a slash!' He disappeared below.

The Princess Matilda was on autopilot but I scanned the horizon for any shipping. Something else caught my eye.

'Tim!' I yelled. 'Quick, quick!'

He dashed up the steps to the wheelhouse, bumping his head. His flies were still undone and he was about to tell me off for scaring him when he saw what I was pointing at. The one fin I had spotted turned into five bottlenose dolphins, and we watched enchanted as they swam alongside us.

'Oh my God, oh my God,' I whispered.

Our camera was in my pocket so I began to click away as the creatures leapt and dived, changing places in a spectacle of choreographed acrobatics. Then they all disappeared under the hull and we rushed to the other door to see them reappear.

'Fuck me!' Tim said.

I looked behind us and three more dolphins appeared and

joined the pod. Sunbeams danced on their sleek, silver-blue, glistening skin as they arched, twisted and soared out of the ocean.

They swam alongside us for twenty minutes, Tim and I now silent as if we were in a holy place, then, as if by a pre-arranged signal, they disappeared.

'Can you believe it?' Tim eventually asked me.

'It's one of the most amazing things I've ever seen,' I replied, as I looked at the photos I had captured. We had seen two dolphins when we were in Cornwall and regretted not having taken any pictures of them.

'It's just as well you didn't take a video 'cos the sound track of you oooohing and ahhhhhing would've sounded like a porn movie,' Tim said, laughing, as he peered over my shoulder.

I punched him on the arm and said, 'To think of all the time I lived in West Wales, I never even knew that dolphins lived in Cardigan Bay.'

'Is it going to be weird going back to Aberystwyth?' Tim asked me thoughtfully, as he took the camera out of my hands.

'I want to take you to the Castle. It was my favourite pub, I had some good times in there necking Southern Comfort and—'

'Pissing away your dole money?' he said, interrupting me.

'No! I was one of the only hippies to have a job,' I said defensively.

'I know, I've seen the photos,' Tim replied, laughing.

There used to be a photographer in Aberystwyth called 'Mr Mo'. None of his 'models' knew his real name, but he paid them £3 an hour for 'arty' shots. I still have a few of them that Tim has had framed. It took our kids a few years to realize that in a couple of them I was naked under my crochet shawl. I bought a great deal of Southern Comfort with those three pound notes.

'Is Paul meeting us in Aberystwyth?' Tim asked, dragging me out of my reverie.

'Yes,' I replied.

'And has he got the commission for the second series or are we still bankrolling this ourselves?'

'If we're skint, I can always see if Mr Mo's still taking dirty pictures!' I said, laughing.

Paul was standing on the edge of the breakwater as we came into Aberystwyth. I waved to him from the bow, as Tim found the pontoon we had been allocated by the harbour master. 'Hi, Paul,' Tim called out to him, as we walked up the gantry to the locked gate of the marina. We all chatted as we walked into the town, or rather the two of them talked. I felt like I had a lump in my heart.

Instinctively, I led the way to my old local pub. I almost expected to see faces that I had once known, but I knew this wasn't likely to happen. The pub was smaller than I remembered and looked tatty and unloved from the outside. There was a time when this old boozer was the centre of my universe, standing a stone's throw from the beach and the medieval castle ruins. I once loved a boy and we made the crumbling battlements our own personal jousting ground. The sun went in, and I wrapped my scarf around my face to hide my tears.

'So are we going to go in for a drink?' Tim quizzed me.

I shook my head and walked back the way we had come.

'Let's find an Indian?' I suggested, once I had regained my composure.

Over our curry we discussed our plans for the near future.

'The weather's on our side,' Tim told Paul, 'and we just want to get a little further north and find somewhere to leave *The Princess Matilda*—'

'Sadie's getting married next week,' I said, interrupting him, as I leaned across the table to replenish my tarka dal.

'Then we're flying back to Montreal so I can finish that film,' Tim added.

I left Tim onboard the following morning. Paul joined me, as he wanted to see where I used to live. Tim wasn't interested. I couldn't blame him, what man wants to know about his predecessor? Besides, he already knows all about my past, well most of it...

'Is this where you lived then?' Paul enquired, as we stood in front of a nondescript terraced house half an hour later. I could sense his disappointment. We had left the characterful streets and alleys of the tourist town behind us.

'Yes, up there in that room on the first floor, that's where I lived with my first husband and a ginger tomcat and a load of hippies.'

'How old were you?' he asked me.

'Nineteen.'

'A child bride?'

'I was a rather wild child bride, but then the whole town was wild. The university is just up the hill there,' I said, pointing ahead. 'Aber was like the hippy mecca and the police and the local councillors didn't like us very much. I had a boyfriend called Dai—'

'Hang on,' Paul interrupted me, as cars whizzed by us breaking the speed limit, 'I thought you said you were married.'

'My husband was always too stoned to be jealous. Come to think of it, so was Dai, but he could play the guitar,' I said, laughing.

'What happened to Dai?' Paul prompted me.

'Dai was one of the few black guys in West Wales. Well, actually his dad was white but his mom was Ethiopian. The police hated him because he was a chippy sod and they ended up beating the crap out of him. Come to think of it, they bashed everyone in the house. It was a bit of a riot, but it was Dai they wanted. He ended up doing six months in Swansea Prison; my husband Alec got three months, 'cos he was under twenty – but they were both charged with attacking police officers. Alec was out of his brain on downers at the time; he couldn't stand up, never mind be aggressive. It was me that jumped on the back of the copper to stop him bashing in Alec's head as he lay stoned in bed.'

I turned and walked back the way we had come. Suddenly, I wanted to be alone. The 19-year-old girl I used to be was a stranger to me now.

'I'll see you back at the boat, Paul,' I said. 'I'm going to find a supermarket, get some shopping in.'

Paul looked relieved.

The supermarket was behind the train station.

I have always been ashamed of something I did at this station. It was the day I met Alec, my vulnerable boy-husband, off a train when he got out of prison. I watched as he slowly walked towards me. He had become fat because all he had eaten for three months was potatoes and chocolate. For two of those months I had been a good wife, writing him letters and visiting him every fortnight, but then one night in the Castle pub I met someone. His name was Robin and he was the drummer in a band that Alec and I had heard play at the university in the spring. By then it was mid-December and Bing Crosby was singing 'White Christmas' on the Castle jukebox. The drummer bought me a large Southern Comfort. I spent that Christmas with Robin and the rest of the band at a remote hillside farmhouse. The house always had a blazing fire and homemade bread baking in the oven. I was sick of shivering and going hungry where I had been living.

The first thing I said to Alec on the platform of Aberystwyth Station a month later was 'I don't love you anymore...' Poor Alec looked like he had been punched in the guts, but I was a teenager and had fallen head over heels in love with the drummer. I thought it was best to be cruel to be kind. We had separated a few times during our brief marriage, but this time Alec knew it would be for good. He was a troubled soul, and this wasn't helped by the cocktail of drugs he used to take.

'They will kill you one day, Alec, and I'm not going to hang around to watch it happen.'

Chapter Six
A WEDDING

We needed to refuel *The Princess Matilda* before leaving Aberystwyth and pushing on to Pwllheli but the fuel barge already had a boat against it, so Tim and I patiently waited and waited. Tim left the engine to tick over while I sorted out knots in some of our ropes.

'I think they are moored there,' I said to Tim after some time. All the knots had been undone.

'Looks like they are just painting the deck,' Tim said thoughtfully. 'This is going to be tricky. Go up the front and ask if we can come alongside.'

I scooted along the gunwale, dropping the fenders. The moored boat had seen better days and I didn't want our paintwork damaged. A woman looked up, and sullenly nodded her head when I asked if it was OK to moor against them while we took on fuel. She put down her paintbrush on some newspaper and reached over to take a line from me. 'Sorry to bother you. Isn't it a lovely day? That paint will be dry in no time!' I laughed, trying to be friendly. She shrugged her shoulders and assumed her painting position once more. I heard Tim ask a man at the back of the boat for permission to come across them. I noticed there was someone holding a fuel hose. I recognized him from the marina office.

'Hi, Dai!' I shouted. Everyone is called Dai in West Wales.

He waved to me as he chatted to Tim. Meanwhile, the crew of the boat carried on painting, and I noticed several open pots of different-coloured paint on the deck.

The fuel hose was a heavy monstrous thing and Tim had to wrestle with it to bring it across the inside boat to get to ours. It wasn't an easy exercise with all of the clutter on their deck. Suddenly, all hell broke loose as the snaking hose knocked over one of the woman's pots. 'If looks could kill,' I thought, 'Tim would be dead.'

'Sorry, sorry!' he exclaimed. 'Quick, Shane, go get some kitchen roll.'

'It will take more than kitchen roll to clear up this mess,' she seethed. 'And it's all we had of this colour.'

A man joined her, and handed her a pamphlet out of his pocket. 'This has happened before,' I thought. Hardly surprising if they moor by a fuel barge. They both scooped up the paint using the pamphlet as a ladle and poured it back in the tin. Tim pulled out a £20 note.

'Sorry, sorry, mate, will this cover the damage?'

The woman stopped scooping and glared at him but took the cash and put it in her pocket. We quickly undid our mooring lines, both of us apologizing, but they ignored us.

'She took the twenty quid!' I said crossly, when I joined Tim in the wheelhouse a few minutes later. 'I bet that's a scam. They moor that old rust bucket on the fuel barge 'cos they know their paint will get knocked over.'

'It is a rust bucket!' Tim replied. 'And I cut myself on their stanchion.'

I noticed he had kitchen paper wrapped around his hand, with blood seeping through.

'Go and run it under the tap now!' I ordered him.

'I already did. Have we got any antiseptic?'

I dashed below and found some out-of-date Germolene in the first aid kit, but I also grabbed the gin bottle out of the fridge. Tim swore when I poured the Gordon's over the fleshy wound on the inside of his hand and bound it in a bandage.

I looked behind us as *The Princess Matilda* left the harbour, the sea shimmering like an uncut emerald and as flat as a village bowling green. My eyes were drawn above the town, to the main road that leads to the university. I didn't need the AA road map to tell me it was the A44, because it was a thoroughfare I had travelled on many times. Mostly I hitchhiked. I still maintain that Fred West once picked me up.

I spent a lot of time in Hereford and Gloucester, as this is where Alec was from. My guardian angel must have been watching me the day the weird man picked me up. The first thing I noticed was his hands, huge and hairy, as they patted the passenger seat for me to join him. He didn't speak to me, but just stared ahead, and I became quite afraid as he turned off the main road and onto a country lane that became a track surrounded by forest. He stopped the car and climbed out. My heart was beating so hard I thought it would burst. I watched as he walked away, and then I opened the passenger door to run but hadn't a clue where I was. I saw a rock on the track and picked it up and hid it on the seat, and waited for him to come back. Maybe he was taking a leak, but if he was it was taking a long time. Then I saw him approaching the car. He bent over and his eyes were full of hate and malice. 'You fucking bitch,' he growled. My hand tightened around the rock as he climbed into the driver's seat. I noticed a damp patch on his trousers and realized he had just masturbated. He started the car and dropped me back on the main road. I recognized his face immediately when he was on the news all those years later. I realized then I had been lucky that day.

The A44 cuts through the Cambrian Mountains, and Tim and I could see them clearly as *The Princess Matilda* cut through the calm pea-green sea.

'I'm so used to seeing those mountains from the land, it all looks so different from here, doesn't it, Tim?' I remarked. 'How's your hand?'

'I'll live,' he replied. It wasn't so long ago that a cut hand would have resulted in him being in hospital on a course of antibiotics.

'Do you remember what happened to you in New York?' I asked him.

'I'll never forget that,' he replied, knowing immediately what I was referring to.

28th September 1996
Midnight
Secrets and Lies *opened the New York Film Festival last night! The thought of getting here has helped you so much, you've been in and out of UCLH all summer, having tests, scans, transfusions. We spent Wednesday at the hospital, not sure until virtually the last moment whether you would be able to go, but the consensus was that you would be OK to fly if you had a couple of bags of platelets. Very hectic, phones ringing: 'Are you well enough?' Mike Leigh's PA Debs came round from Thin Man Films with the tickets. I've spoken to her so many times it was great to see her face, but she looked a mite bewildered with all the comings and goings on the ward. Dear Cath, the nurse, had a huge bag of equipment for me to give the nurses in New York, and instructions about flushing your line, medi wipes, distilled water, plasters. And you just sat there very calmly, watching the platelets drip into your line. You look so lovely, your hair has grown back and you have a little beard. I couldn't believe it when the car arrived and took us to the airport. Free, we felt like kids playing the wag from school, and savouring the fact that no one now could nab us and go, 'OI, YOU TWO, GET BACK HERE!'*

We arrived in JFK about 8pm that Wednesday night, or early Thursday morning in London, and were picked up in a stretch limo, and crossing over Brooklyn Bridge was magical, the skyscrapers of Manhattan. You said, 'The thing about America, it looks just like it does in the movies.' It's true. Neither of us could believe we were here. We were booked into the Radisson Empire, just across the road from where the film's going to be shown, and Simon Channing Williams, the producer, was in the bar when we arrived so I left you downstairs while I unpacked. The room was rather small but Simon says all the hotels are full because of the festival.

You had far more energy than me. I left you all downstairs after dinner and said I was going to bed. It was like old times. I tried to shut the blinds but the whole lot fell on the floor, so I had to call reception to get someone sent up to fix them. This took an hour, and then as I was getting into bed I thought I'd try and move the mini-bar up a bit, as it was right next to the side where you sleep, but I couldn't get a proper hold of it so I opened the door to get my hand inside and the fucking thing fell off. So now, really pissed off, I called reception and spoke to the duty manager and said we need to change rooms. There weren't any! 'But there must be something, for goodness sake. My husband's just got out of hospital, and it's bad enough that the blinds fell down, but now he has to sleep with the fridge door open.'

The manager replied, 'What is it you would like me to do, madam?'

'Well, let me tell you what I will do if my husband gets an infection from this room. He's been on antibiotics for months!' Then I slammed the phone down and phoned Carin from October Films, who's distributing the film, and told her what was happening. She phoned the hotel and there were no empty rooms, so someone came up to try to jam the door on the

fridge shut. The handyman arrived just as you did. Of course, you thought it hugely amusing and told me to chill out. You took me to the window, but the handyman said, 'I wouldn't touch that blind if I was you, sir!' So we peeped through.

'Look we're in New York,' you said joyfully. 'I'm alive!'

The next day we walked for miles down Broadway, everyone we passed shouting and yelling, yellow cabs hooting their horns. Even in the lift going up the Empire State Building, the tourists were barking at each other. It was a relief to enter a quiet restaurant where we had arranged to meet up with Mike Leigh, Brenda and her husband Michael, and Michael Gambon (who is doing a Broadway show here). We love Gambon, who surreptitiously puffed on a sneaky fag during lunch. He said it gives him a great deal of satisfaction to smoke in New York restaurants; sometimes he gets away with it. The new 'junior suite' we had been given is much bigger than the room that fell to pieces on our first night.

We tried to have a sleep later but were too excited and even though the venue for the screening of Secrets and Lies *was only a five-minute walk away we went in a convoy of limousines, first of all to a dinner, a very strange affair, meeting up with Bingham Ray, the head of October Films (he liked my red gloves, the ones I'd planned to wear at Cannes!), and then another limo ride, fifty yards this time, and everything went mad with cameras flashing. I went to move out of the way but you held on to my hand. We were both shaking because it was so very emotional. We'd seen on TV Bren, Mike and Marianne arriving at Cannes for the premiere, the day that you had begun your first day of chemotherapy, and now here we were in New York. I was so proud of you as we moved up the line of photographers, you stopping off to give sound bites like you'd never been 'away'. We were taken into the green room while the audience were sat down, and you were so lovely, chatting to Mike, Bren, Marianne, cracking jokes. I was taken around to slip into a seat at the back of the auditorium (it was huge) while you went with the others. Mike introduced you all and I felt my heart would break with pride to see you back on stage. It was all so exciting, the party afterwards, the Inn on the Green, fairy lights twinkling on the trees, everyone coming up to congratulate you on your performance. Hundreds of people milling around, table-hopping, schmoozing, but we didn't stay too long, as we were both completely knackered. A night at the circus, you said, as we flopped into bed.*

29th September 1996
Midnight
All you needed was a platelet transfusion, so you could fly home to London without you haemorrhaging. It was all arranged, faxes sent from UCLH to the doctors in New York…Everything stops when you become ill, we'd forgotten, hadn't we? I sit alone opposite the hotel, the one where the blind fell down and the fridge door fell off. Above my head is a heater. I watch as crowds turn out of the Lincoln Centre, Secrets and Lies *opened there just a couple of days ago. Conversations drift by me, people talking about the orchestra and food, the weather. It is so cold, even with the heater, that the muscles around my face feel like they might shatter and break. I want to be one of these people with just the thought of the performance on my mind – not staphylococcus or entero-coccus faecalis. The waiter called me sir when I sat down. I'm wearing your jacket and hat. I think I look rather nice but inside I feel like I did years ago when I first came to London; I used to sit on a bench down Ladbroke Grove watching busy people coming and going – much as I'm doing now except today I'm wearing pearls. How I long for someone*

to sit down and talk to me – I'd make a horrible widow, I would! I'm no good on my own, and recently you and I have become you and I again, despite the almost daily transfusions and blood tests. We'd become a pair again – out and about – but now you are in The Sloan-Kettering Cancer Center and I am here, waiting to offload my despair onto strangers ANYBODY but no one looks my way, no one sits down next to me. When they flushed your line to give you the transfusion, you rigored and all hell broke loose. People rushing in: 'He's got a temperature of 104!' I wanted someone behind me to hold me up, and I cried and you cried, but I couldn't get near you, it was like time had stopped. And, my Timmy, you never complain. You are braver than me: being poked and messed about with – you poor bugger. I cough like Camille; do I have consumption? Did I contaminate you? You still have the fungus in your lung and, as long as you have a strong immune system, it won't grow anymore. But now you have some horrible lurgy that had been festering in your line and entered your bloodstream. The American doctors hope it's not one that is resistant to antibiotics. I don't want you to be ill; I want you to be in charge, I'm not strong enough.

The sun was dancing on the slinky silk sea. I had my road atlas open on my lap, but I was looking through the binoculars. I passed them to Tim, accidently catching the cut on his hand. He winced, but Tim being Tim he didn't make a fuss.

'Sorry, darling,' I said, before pointing towards the coast. 'See those sand dunes? That's Borth. I used to live there for a while, after Alec was sent down. God, it was a freezing winter with no central heating. All I had was a paraffin heater.'

Tim laughed. 'You certainly got around.'

'Just wait until we get further north, then I can bore you about where we went for our holidays when I was a kid.'

'Let's get to Pwllheli first. We're going to cut right across the bay,' Tim said, pointing to my map. 'God, you've got me at it now!' he said with annoyance. 'Look at the charts. We're going to take a 327 degree bearing for 17.6 miles...'

I yawned.

'You really aren't interested, are you, Shane?'

'As long as you know where we're going, that's all that counts,' I replied. 'I'm going to make some sandwiches.'

I had just got the bread knife out when Tim shouted, 'Shane, quick, quick!' I dashed back up the steps to the wheelhouse. The pod of dolphins was back. Tim already had the camera in his hand. 'I'm going up to the bow to film them,' he said.

'Don't fall in!' I said anxiously, as I watched him walking along the gunwale, filming.

There were six dolphins swimming next to where I was standing by the steering wheel; I could almost bend down and touch them, but then they would tease me and disappear, only to reappear on the other side. So I kept running backwards and forwards from one door to the other. Every now and again I could hear Tim yell, 'There's eight of them...nine...ten!'

Again, they disappeared, but this time they left us for good, and my heart sank with disappointment. I scanned the sea, willing them to return.

Tim came back to the wheelhouse.

'They were amazing, I counted a dozen at one point!'

'That's not counting the ones I had at the back. Did you get them on film, Tim?'

'I think so, we'll look later, but for the moment we have to keep an eye out for that,' he said, pointing towards the horizon. For a moment I had hoped it was a dolphin that he had spotted, but it was a sail.

'That's the first yacht we've seen this year,' I commented.

'Yes and we're on a collision course,' Tim said, looking through the binoculars. 'I can't believe it, we're six miles out but if we keep on the autopilot we'll cut straight through them. I'll have to change course, the International Regulations for the Prevention of Collision at Sea are legally binding. The IRPCS rules require all vessels to maintain a lookout at all times,' Tim continued. 'Out of this vast expanse of sea, our paths are on a collision course and motorboats always give way to sail. We're off the auto so in about ten minutes I'll turn around, give them time to move safely out of our way.'

I love when we do this on a smooth sea. *The Princess Matilda* left a perfect circle of plate glass behind us as we spun 360 degrees. I waved to the yacht, but they did not acknowledge us.

'Bad manners is what I say!'

'That was fun,' Tim said, laughing, 'and if you look very carefully over there you can see Snowdon.' He was looking through the binoculars, but I could just about make out Wales' highest mountain. 'The sea is a millpond, no wind, no waves and the sun shining. We don't get many days like this, hey, Tim?'

'Don't speak too soon,' he replied, 'we have St Patrick's Causeway benignly hidden under the sea to starboard, and there's a few wrecks down there.'

'You always look on the bright side, don't you, darling?'

'This time last week, we were preparing to lock out of Milford Haven, and look what happened to us, eight hours of hell, so I have to know where all the bogeymen are now.'

Fortunately, all the bogeymen were on a sabbatical that day, and a single dolphin led us into Pwllheli Marina. The mountains of Snowdonia, rising up like a trio of uneven breasts, dominated the skyline. That evening we walked the couple of miles into the small seaside market town looking for dinner. It began to rain when the starter arrived, so we booked a cab to drive us back to the boat at the end of the meal. We still got drenched as *The Princess Matilda* was moored at the end of several long pontoons, but at least now we had shore power and the use of electric fan heaters to warm us during the April showers.

'I'll get the bike out and get the Sunday papers for you tomorrow,' Tim said, as I drew the curtains against the lashing Welsh rain.

'You'd better wear waterproofs then,' I replied.

Tim has a fold-up motorcycle that lives in a bag on the back deck. Mostly it just gets in the way. If you take a look at the website, it will tell you the 'folding motor scooter gives you immediate mobility in just three seconds'. This, in Tim's case, should be altered to three hours because he can never remember how to do it. He thinks brute force is the answer. It was a Sunday morning, so the marina was busy with people enjoying their boats and doing odd jobs. A few joined us on our pontoon. They watched with interest as Tim used physical violence, and with a couple of kicks the miniature bike was unfolded. He was very pleased with himself, but I knew the best was yet to come.

'All I have to do now,' he said to Paul, the man from the boat next door, 'is start it.'

His foot began to pound up and down on the starter pedal to kick start it, but the chap from next door tapped him on the shoulder and said, 'I think you need to turn the fuel on, mate.'

Tim laughed and replied, 'Yeah, petrol helps.'

He then resumed ramming his foot down like some frenzied Rumpelstiltskin, and everyone cheered when the bike's engine fired up. The cheering turned into coughing, gagging, grumbling and wheezing as clouds of blue smoke belched out of the exhaust. Then with one enormous, lengthy, shrill wheeze it died. Tim scratched his head and looked at me and said, 'I don't know what's wrong with it.'

'When did you fill it up last?' I asked.

'I can't remember. Pass me one of the outboard cans, darlin',' he responded hopefully.

I handed him one of the green plastic fuel containers and he filled the petrol tank, only spilling half a pint. I gave him some kitchen roll, which he used to wipe up the residue.

Tim was just about to begin kick starting again, when our neighbour Paul suggested it might be a good idea to add some two-stroke oil to the tank.

'Oh, yeah, I forgot about that,' Tim said, as he pushed by me. I was standing at the door of the wheelhouse.

'Why does he need oil?' I asked Paul, who caught me as I fell onto the pontoon.

'Lubrication,' he replied, but I missed the rest of his explanation as I was distracted. I could hear Tim in the back cabin, emptying drawers and swearing.

He returned with a plastic bottle.

Our audience had grown and people clustered around to watch him add the oil to the petrol.

'I wouldn't put that in if I was you, mate,' Paul said anxiously.

Tim put on his glasses and looked at the label. He was just about to add hydraulic steering fluid.

'I've got some oil you can have,' Paul continued. 'Hang on...'

He disappeared into his boat and returned with some two-stroke. 'May I?' he asked. Tim nodded, looking sheepish.

The bike fired up first time and we all watched as Tim climbed aboard his bike.

*

The Princess Matilda would remain in Pwllheli for several weeks, while Tim finished work on *Upside Down* in Montreal. But first he was father of the bride at our youngest daughter Sadie's May Day wedding.

Our eldest daughter Pascale had made her sister's nipped in at the waist, 1940s, Hollywood glamour wedding dress, and it was all going well until after I'd left the house for the church. The back of the corseted bodice was fastened with thirty tiny hand-stitched, raw-silk-covered buttons that Pascale needed to fasten one by one. Everyone was relaxed and chatting when I arrived at the church, but forty-five minutes later the groom's head had sunk to his chest as he stood with his best man at the altar. According to my daughters, back at the house, Tim kept hollering up the stairs, 'DON'T KEEP THE HOUSE WAITING!' – a theatrical term for getting onstage on time. The shouting did not help with the fastening of the tiny buttons as Pascale's hands began to sweat and Sadie began to tremble. Later at the reception, I asked Sadie what was the most memorable part of the day so far.

'Besides Dad hollering?' she replied with a laugh. 'The morris dancers and the champagne bar you set up outside the church while the pictures were being taken.'

Chapter Seven
HOME AND BACK

London to Pwllheli via A5: 205 miles

Tim and I drove our car back to Pwllheli at the beginning of June. For once I didn't need to look at the road map, because I knew the route to North Wales. I am a Midlander. This is where my family used to go on holiday. My father was a gambling man and one of our holidays was spent in a farmhouse which he had won in a bet. That's the holiday not the house.

There were no motorways in the late fifties; come to think of it, there was no family car either. My dad had a 'wagon' that he used to transfer wastepaper from factories to paper mills. His paper yard was next to the bookmakers and a scummy canal in Walsall. I used to sit watching him, and when he wasn't placing a bet he was always checking his rat traps, with a cigarette in his hand. Rat catching and a flutter on the horses were his greatest pleasures in life. My mother was not so enamoured by either of these hobbies, although she was pleased when he proudly threw £50 in five-pound notes on the table after a day at Chester Races. The rats never made her smile and she would insist he check the wagon every night, just in case there were any ratty stowaways.

Dad used to be extra vigilant when we were going on holiday, because my brother and sisters, my grandma and various animals travelled in the back. My mom with my baby brother on her lap sat in the cab with my dad. There was a tarpaulin over the rest of us in case it rained, and my granny, wrapped in blankets, sat on a sofa with her cat in her arms. Jacqueline, known by the whole family as Jack, my Ava Gardner look-a-like elder sister, sat next to Grandma, holding her pet goat by the collar to stop it eating the cat. I thought this was how everyone travelled.

The A5 is now mostly dual carriageway, but in the fifties a line of traffic would build up behind our wagon, waiting for a gap to overtake. I would leave off stroking the dog to wave.

'Have I ever told you about going on holiday with the goat?' I asked Tim, as we traversed another traffic island.

'The one where your nan got stuck in quicksand? No, you've never told me that one,' he answered, laughing. 'But I bet you are going to show me where it happened. We've a few miles to go yet, do you want to stop and have something to eat?'

'Let's wait until we get to Porthmadog,' I said, as I turned on the radio. There was a report about shootings in White-haven in Cumbria.

'I thought we might winter the boat in Whitehaven,' Tim said thoughtfully.

Over the next hour, we listened with horror as the tragedy unfolded; a lone gunman called Derrick Bird killed twelve people and left another eleven injured. We were both feeling rather shell-shocked by the time we crossed the border into Wales. From past experience, Tim and I know just how quickly your life can change; there is no epiphany or warning.

We didn't go to the beach where my grandmother got stuck in the sand, the sparkle had gone out of our day. Also, they say you should never go back. I had made this mistake in Aberystwyth, but the drive from Bala through Snowdonia was full of memories for me anyway. I could still hear the echo of my mother's voice as she pointed out the purple, smoky-topped mountains.

We didn't always travel in the back of a lorry – my dad eventually bought a second-hand Ford Consul, but we still managed

to fit the whole family in it, including my granny. Just down
the coast from Porthmadog is a beach that stretches for miles.
At low tide, you can walk there from this bustling tourist town.
This is where my Granny Nance got stuck up to her knees in the
soft mud of the outgoing tide. I can see her now, holding up
the hem of her skirt so her pink bloomers were showing, and
howling that the quicksand was dragging her down. Her six
grandchildren all laughed, and those nearest to our mother got
a clip around the ear and the others told to use their spades to
dig her out. The Baker family were handy with their spades. The
beach is called Black Rock Sands and is one of the few beaches
where you can park your car. Sensible drivers leave their vehicle
on firm sand but we were always on hand to dig out the daft
ones for a tanner – that's two-and-a-half pence in new money.

We had arranged to meet Paul Crompton in a local restaurant in Pwllheli the evening we were reunited with *The Princess
Matilda*, because he was going to join us to commence filming
the following day. Our series *Timothy Spall: Somewhere at Sea*
had been shown on BBC4 while we were away in Montreal.
Tim and I had thought long and hard when Paul first suggested
we film our trips. We eventually agreed because it was something we could show to our grandchildren when we were in
our dotage. Now our barge had become a 'reality TV star'. We
discovered many messages and gifts from her fans on her back
deck, including a bouquet of flowers, a bottle of whisky and
a holdall full of new ropes. The series was so successful that a
new one had now been commissioned, so we no longer had to
pay for it all ourselves.

Paul predictably was excited about coming onboard with
us again. We explained to him that someone had arranged us
a mooring on an RNLI buoy in an unpronounceable place:
Porthdinllaen.

'It's going to be an early start, Paul,' Tim said, as he passed him the poppadoms. 'I've been worrying about this passage for six weeks. We have to leave three hours before low water to get through Bardsey Sound.'

He reached in his pocket and pulled out some crumpled 'cruising notes' from the marina office. He pushed them over to Paul who read them silently, but every now and again out loud.

'Tidal streams run strongly through the sound...can be evil...fifty foot standing waves have been reported...Only tackle it in fair weather and at slack water...The shoals lying offshore of Bardsey Island...cause severe overfalls which can constitute a danger to small vessels.'

'Oh, it will be fine,' I said. 'Anyone want another Kingfisher?'

Chapter Eight
PARADISE

Pwllheli to Porthdinllaen: 38 nautical miles

Tim and I were both up at 4.15am but Paul Crompton had an even earlier start than us. He hadn't been able to get a cab to bring him to the marina at that time of the morning; however, he assured us that he enjoyed his four-mile walk from the hotel, carrying his rucksack, sound equipment and camera.

'Red sky at night, shepherd's delight,' he said, rubbing his back. 'What do they say about red sky in the morning?' He groaned as we helped him stow away his gear.

'The weather forecast is perfect. Do you fancy a bacon sandwich, Paul? I'll make some once we get going,' I replied.

We managed to leave our mooring ten minutes ahead of schedule.

As Tim had predicted over last night's curry, the sea as we left the safe haven of Hafan Pwllheli was a little bit choppy. 'But that's because of the overfalls,' he reiterated, as I brought the bacon butties up into the wheelhouse. I almost dropped the lot as I fell up the steps from the saloon.

Paul had his legs splayed with his knees bent. I wasn't sure if this was to stay on his feet or to rest his back. 'So what's an overfall, skipper?' Paul asked Tim, as he focused his camera.

'We're pushing against the tide,' Tim replied, 'and going over a shallow patch on the seabed, so as you can see and feel it's causing what's known as a confused sea. We're going to be altering course soon—'

'Do you want a bacon sandwich, Tim?' I interrupted.

'Nah, you know I can't eat when I'm anxious!'

Paul ate for two.

While he ate, I read the cruising notes and took a look at my road atlas. Tim had been talking about Bardsey Sound for weeks.

'*Swnt Enlli*,' I shouted to Tim over the noise of the engine.

'I told you I didn't *swant* any breakfast,' he laughed.

'No, that's Welsh for Bardsey Sound. Well, that's what it says on the road map. And the island is called *Ynys Enlli*...'

'If you say so,' he said thoughtfully, looking down at his various charts.

'Oh...I just found out what *Ynys Enlli* means!' I wished I had taken better notice of the cruising notes before we had left.

'I know what it means, Shane,' Tim said tersely. 'Why do you think I've been worrying so much? It means the island of eddies. See those two small islands to port? That's to your left, Shane. Those are the St Tudwal's and up ahead is Bardsey, but thankfully the sea's much calmer now.'

We both watched as Paul walked along the gunwale, following Tim's instructions to keep a hand on the grab rail at all times.

'The tide is slowing, that's good. I just have to make sure we get this timing right to get over Devil's Ridge.' Tim looked at his watch. 'At this speed, we should be there about eight o'clock, but I'm going to slow down.'

For the next forty minutes, we were able to enjoy the sunshine dancing on a dead calm sea. Meanwhile, the scrub-encrusted cliffs of Bardsey Island rose out of the sea like a verdant-green humpback whale.

'We have three nautical miles to go,' Tim said quietly, once more looking at his watch. 'Slack water is at 08.37, that's when we want to go through the sound...'

I also began to look nervously at my watch. It was 8.20. There had been a sea change; it is amazing how these nautical terms make sense when you are actually experiencing them. Our flat calm sea now resembled the surface of a Jaffa Cake. We felt *The Princess Matilda* corkscrew slightly as if she had been knocked off course, and then she shuddered a little as the bow cut through low, short, choppy wavelets.

I pointed to our Welsh courtesy ensign, the small flag we flew in their waters. 'There's not a breath of wind though, the flag's not moving...'

Tim interrupted me. 'I don't believe this!' He was tapping various screens on the control panel. 'According to the autopilot, we're still pushing a two-knot tide!'

'Is that bad, Tim?' Paul asked, as he put down his camera. He had joined us in the wheelhouse when the sea had changed.

'We're almost right at the tip of the Llyn Peninsula,' I said, looking at my AA map. 'The girl in the marina chandlery says the peninsula extends thirty miles into the Irish Sea.'

We could now see snowy-white lambs gambolling playfully over crumbling stonewalls on the island.

As if by a pre-arranged signal, Tim and I looked at our watches.

'What time do you make it?' he said.

'Twenty-five to nine,' I replied.

'I don't understand it: we're now entering the sound and have a three-knot tide on our nose; we're right at the tip of the peninsula...'

No one spoke for fifteen minutes. This is how long it took us to travel between the isle known locally as the Island of Twenty Thousand Saints and the tip of the Welsh mainland.

The tide actually turned two hours later as we came into Caernarfon Bay. The early morning sun had given way to a misty haze, the satiny sea the same colour as the duck-egg-blue sky. I sat on the bow of *The Princess Matilda* with a set of binoculars trying to spot our next port of call, Porthdinllaen. We couldn't even pronounce it, never mind find it. Tim had a few goes when he spoke to the coastguard: '*Port-dilian, Porth-dill-ion.*' The mountains of Snowdonia still dominated the misty skyline.

Tim shouted to me from the wheelhouse, 'Can you see the RNLI buoy? We're almost there!'

Cutting through the mist, we had come around another headland and into a horseshoe-shaped sheltered lagoon. There were a couple of small boats at anchor and half a dozen houses on the far shore. 'Look for the RNLI flag!' he yelled once again.

And there it was, flying high above a lonely-looking boathouse.

We had been told to call a chap called Alan, the lifeboat mechanic. I already had his number on speed dial.

'Yes, I can see you,' he assured me. 'That big yellow buoy below the breakwater is ours. Give me another call if you need any help, *carriad*, and the lads want to know if you fancy coming out on the lifeboat this afternoon.'

'We'd love to,' I replied before hanging up.

I waved my arms to attract Tim's attention; he was speaking on camera to Paul.

'There's the buoy, Tim!' I yelled. I don't know how we could have missed it; it was a yard wide and sunlight yellow.

My eyes were drawn to the slate-grey, sheer cliffs to our left that fell vertically into the sea. A small motorboat was crossing the bay. To our right side, barely 200 feet away from our boat, were children playing on a small white beach. They waved to us, then went back to paddling and building sandcastles. The slipway of the lifeboat station cut the sandy shore in half. Three hundred yards ahead of our bow was a crescent of predominately white, two-storey houses backdropped by steep sand dunes. In the middle of the crescent was a red house that stuck out like a throbbing sore thumb. The dunes were enveloped in green brush and butter-cup-yellow gorse. Quaint cottages clustered around another beach. I felt like we had arrived in paradise. The beauty of this tranquil cove was breathtaking, but I had an important job to do before I could relax and enjoy the scenery. I had to get hold of our mooring.

Tim and I were now professionals at getting tied on to these extra-large RNLI emergency buoys. Smaller buoys on offer for recreational craft are just not strong enough to hold our 35 tons. Paul had not witnessed us getting on a swing mooring since Falmouth the previous summer. I think he was pretty impressed that we did this one so effortlessly.

'Well done, Shane,' he said, as I grabbed the float attached to a rope the width of my wrist with the boathook on my first attempt.

The motorboat I had noticed five minutes before had now pulled alongside us and the skipper watched as Tim and I yanked up the slippery black rope that had been lying on the seabed.

'WELCOME TO PORTHDINLLAEN, PRINCESS MATILDA,' he shouted over the noise of his outboard. 'I'VE BEEN WATCHING YOUR PROGRAMME. YOUR BOAT IS FAMOUS.'

I wiped my slimy hands down my clean Image by Vanessa linen trousers and left Tim to finish tying us off.

Our new friend did a full circuit around *The Princess Matilda*. I waited for him to come back before asking, 'How do you say it?'

'PORTH DIN KLINE! DEMI MOORE FILMED HERE…' he yelled, then did another circuit.

'He's definitely not Welsh,' Tim remarked, as we both sat on the gas locker waiting for him to return.

'THERE'S A PUB ON THE BEACH, IT'S CALLED THE TIE COCK INN...'

'That's a funny name for a pub,' Tim shouted, but our friend was already out of earshot again.

After his seventh circuit, Tim, Paul and I had become rather bored and disappeared down into the saloon, closing the curtains.

'The lifeboat mechanic wants to know if we want to go out on exercise with them this afternoon,' I whispered, just in case our new friend was listening to our conversation. Every time he did a circuit, his motorboat grew closer to the barge.

We waited for the sound of his engine to disappear into the distance before locking up and getting in the dinghy.

'Let's go and find the pub on the beach,' Tim said, as we helped Paul aboard. He had a grin like the Cheshire Cat.

Chapter Nine
THE RED HOUSE

The last time Tim and I had been in our dinghy it was a cold damp day in April. We had been drenched as we crossed Fishguard Harbour and had shivered for two hours. But this time the June sun was shining and we had bare arms covered in sun block. We could see to the bottom of the shallow aquamarine sea, and I held on to my hat as Tim steered. The beach where we were headed was not too busy and, once Tim had turned off the outboard so we could run *New Si* into the shallows, we heard music. Paul, Tim and I all jumped out to haul the dinghy above the high-tide mark. The bottom of our trousers were wet and our damp feet heavy from walking through the dry fine sand. We scanned the beach looking for the pub. It wasn't hard to find as it was painted red and had a sign on the gable: TY COCH INN. One of the many people sitting on the beach wall outside the pub was playing a double bass. I suppose the only place we could compare it to was the beach in front of the Ferryboat Inn on Helford Passage. The Helford River is where we had become stranded by the back end of Hurricane Bill the summer before.

'I think this beach and the sand dunes beat even Cornwall, and I can't remember any live music there, can you?' I remarked to Tim as we strolled arm in arm along the sand. 'Wales and Cornwall are totally different countries, hey Tim? But if you and I were blindfolded and taken on a mystery journey we'd know which was which. I don't know how.'

We stamped the sand off our feet and went inside the pub. There was no room at the tables outside. The small whitewashed bar was packed but we managed to push our way through to order a drink. A small woman with sparkling eyes served us. 'Welcome to the Ty Coch, that's Welsh for Red House. I'm so glad you came here; we wondered if you would. We saw *The Princess Matilda* moored out on the bay. She looks lovely! Quick, go and grab that table over there. It's dog eat dog in here on a sunny day. I'll bring your drinks over.'

Tim and I left Paul in the pub after lunch; he said he wanted to get some more shots of the beach.

'Can you give me the number of that bloke from the lifeboat station, Shane? I can meet you there later on,' Paul said.

'He said they would be going down the slipway at five. His name's Alan Parry. Tell him we'll be over about 4.30,' I replied.

'Yes, I need to plan our next passage. I'll be able to ask their advice,' Tim said, as we waved our cameraman goodbye.

Back onboard *The Princess Matilda*, Tim poured us both a drink. He sat at the table with his glass. There were charts and a pilot book in front of him.

'The next bogeyman will be crossing the Caernarfon Bar,' he murmured.

I ignored him and took my drink up to the back deck. I pulled a chair into the shade and watched gentle waves swishing around our stern.

'We could be in Greece or the Bahamas,' I said when I went back inside to get a refill. But Tim was fast asleep. Hardly surprising after our early start. I woke him up with a cup of tea an hour later. 'Come on love, let's get *New Si* over to the lifeboat station. We don't want to keep them waiting.'

Alan met us by the ramp and helped us pull the dinghy onto the beach. There was a buzz of expectation all around us. I am used to my husband being recognized in public, but the kids and their parents weren't looking at him. The ramp had iron rails that led up into the open boathouse. Alan reached down to help me step up. A few more volunteer crew wandered down to meet us. Occasionally, they waved to the tourists on the sand.

'This is like doing a Red Carpet,' I whispered to Tim.

I looked down to the beach; everyone was standing now.

By the time we reached the top of the slipway, our escorts were speaking at once.

'How was your trip through the sound?'

'A lovely day for it.'

'You planning to cross the bar next?'

'How are you feeling about doing the Swellies?'

'Have you been out on a lifeboat before?'

Tim and I didn't know who to answer first, but it didn't seem to bother them. When they weren't asking us questions they were talking ten to the dozen in Welsh.

A small slight man greeted us as we entered the boat-house. 'I'm Robert Jones,' he said, shaking our hands, 'the assistant coxswain, and I'll be taking you out today on *Hetty Rampton*.'

He turned proudly and we all looked up at her. We couldn't miss it, *Hetty* filled the cathedral-like boathouse.

'That's an interesting name for a lifeboat,' Tim said, as we followed him inside.

Robert stood dwarfed under her navy-blue bow.

'The RNLI depend on charitable donations; the money for this lifeboat came from the Trustees of the Estate of Hetty Mabel Rampton. She's a Tyne class and been in service since 1987.' A large man appeared and thrust out his arm. 'And this is Ken Fitzpatrick. As you can tell by his name, he's not a native. He's our operations manager.'

'Nice to meet you, Mr and Mrs Spall,' he said, taking our hands in a bear-like grip. 'Let's get you on the boat, shall we?'

*

I expected to see a ladder, but was relieved to see there were stairs going up into an office with a gantry that went onto the boat. Paul was already in the office-cum-staffroom, drinking tea with the rest of the crew.

Then it was all hands on deck, literally. In seconds everyone was wearing their yellow lifeboat gear and scarlet lifejackets and we were ushered aboard. We couldn't understand a word anyone was saying.

A slim pretty girl came towards me, with blonde hair escaping from her white RNLI helmet.

'*Prynhawn da*,' she said. Then, seeing my look of bafflement, she laughed. 'Good afternoon, I'm Eleri Roberts. Take no notice of this lot, they're not being rude. Even Ken – who you may've gathered is from Liverpool – had to learn. We're the only Welsh-speaking lifeboat crew in the world!' she said proudly.

Tim by this point was standing on the bridge with Robert, but I stayed on the stern with Eleri.

'So are the crew all fishermen?' I asked her.

'Not one of them,' she replied. 'We've got a green keeper from the golf club, a builder, a postman...'

A curly-haired man quietly interrupted her: 'The lads are going to begin winching her down now, so make sure you duck your heads.'

What impressed me most was the lack of shouting; everyone had a job to do and did it without any fuss. A few moments later, *Hetty* grandly inched forwards. I expected us to pick up speed as we shot down the slipway, but as soon as we were clear of the boathouse the lifeboat stopped. In moments, the crew had the tall aerials and the windscreen of the bridge up.

'Blimey, they don't hang about!' I exclaimed to Eleri.

She had taken off her helmet and was running her fingers through her hair.

She laughed. 'Seconds can mean the difference between life and death, but we're in no rush today. Would you and Tim mind if we get some photos for the local paper?'

'Of course not!'

The photographer from the local newspaper wasn't the only person snapping pictures that day. Most people on the beach were doing so too. Robert had been standing next to Tim for the photo call and asked him if he would like to join him on the helm for the launch.

Hetty Rampton began to descend the ramp with Tim at the wheel.

'Don't put her into gear until we're clear of the slipway,' Robert said quietly.

Everyone was now in business mode. The boat hit the water and Tim accelerated. I turned and saw we were being followed by a flotilla of motorboats, all trying desperately to keep up. Eleri had warned me this would happen, as locals and visitors love the thrill of riding over the lifeboat's huge wake. With one hand I hung on to my hat, with the other a grab bar. Eventually, I had to abandon the hat and held it in my teeth as I made my way to the bridge to join Tim and Robert. I was pleased to see Tim had been stood down and the assistant coxswain was now at the helm.

We seemed to be heading towards the cliffs on the other side of the bay, but at the very last minute Robert slowed down. Above us were thousands of nesting guillemots all squawking their displeasure at being disturbed. The cliffs rose above us like battlements from a medieval snow-capped castle, but it became apparent the snow was foul-smelling bird shit. We all had to shout to be heard above the cacophony from the birds.

Twenty-four hours later, Tim and I had to deal with a less pleasant racket.

Chapter Ten
THROW ME THE LINE

Porthdinllaen to Conwy: 48 nautical miles

The Menai Strait separates the Isle of Anglesey from the Welsh mainland. Tim had decided we should take a shortcut instead of heading right out into the Irish Sea. We had left the idyllic cove of Porthdinllaen at lunchtime, and another pod of bottle-nose dolphins joined us as we crossed Caernarfon Bay. I sent a text to Paul Crompton to let him know he had missed them once again. He had been left behind, as he had to make his way back to London on business. It was a great shame he wasn't with us to see the dolphins, or when we entered the lock of Port Dinorwic.

The pilot book told us this was a historic Grade II listed port that was constructed in the nineteenth century to export slate from the local quarries. It lies halfway up the Menai Strait, and for us it was a perfect place to stop off for the night before attempting to go through the infamous Swellies. People on boats love to scare the life out of each other, and we had heard various horror stories over the winter of what might happen in the Swellies if we got the tides wrong.

The locked entrance to Port Dinorwic is only accessible three hours either side of high tide. Tim got the timing right on this occasion and got us there just before high water. I had quite forgotten what it's like to come into a lock with men trying to help. It was a Saturday afternoon and there were lots of them about. By the sound of their distinctive Scouse accents, I suspected most of them were from Liverpool. I felt as if we had accidentally sailed into an episode of *Brookside*, the old Channel 4 soap. Port Dinorwic lock is a small intimate one, more like an elongated boxing ring than a lock. *The Princess Matilda*, Tim and I were sitting ducks. And just like in a boxing ring, we were surrounded by experts, most of them telling me what to do. But, instead of yelling, 'GO ON, HIT HIM,' they squawked, 'Throw me the line throw me the line throw me the line!' I was standing on the bow and looked ahead, then to the left and right. Expectant hands were held out, entreating me, while the chorus of voices became more aggressive. 'Throw me the line throw me the line throw me the line!' But I wasn't sure just who to throw it to.

I needed to establish who was in charge, so I made eye contact with the one squawking the loudest. This man's countenance, I was shocked to find, was one of contemptuous exasperation. 'God help his wife,' I thought, and no doubt he was thinking, 'God help her husband.' Tim and I had come across this type of chap before as we travelled the canals on our narrowboats. The wife would be doing all the throwing and running, while the husband stood bellowing orders.

The lock was a high one, the bollards set back from the side. We have been through locks similar to this on the Thames, but without the shouting. Thames lockkeepers are gentle folk, who bid you 'Good Day' and politely enquire if you need any assistance with your ropes. They never ever roar, 'Throw me the line throw me the line throw me the line!'

In a fit of pique, I chucked my heavy coil, hoping it would hit the gobbiest git – who I had now established was the leader of the pack – in the chops. Everyone went quiet, and then a collective groan ensued. I didn't even come close to hitting the side of the lock, never mind his head. Laughter erupted around me as I began to yank the dripping rope out of the filthy water. As soon as I had it back on the deck, the condescending hilarity ceased and the gang around the boxing ring resumed their mantra: 'Throw me the line throw me the line throw me the line!' Taking a deep breath, I ignored them and climbed up onto the roof, rolling up the sodden rope to throw again. But the chorus had now given way to a single squawk from the ring-leader. 'Throw me the line throw me the line throw me the line!'

'I'll get you this time, matey, and wipe that smug look off your face!' I whispered through gritted teeth.

During this debacle, Tim had brought the boat closer to the other side of the lock. Immediately, I spotted a bollard I could lasso. I wasn't just a deckhand now, I was a cowgirl too. Swiftly, I measured and weighed the rope between my two hands and leaned back, but, before I could take aim, I was stopped in my tracks.

'NO NO NO! NOT LIKE THAT NOT LIKE THAT NOT LIKE THAT!' the ringleader yelled. I turned to face him. His right arm was going backwards and forwards like a one-armed clockwork soldier. 'SWING IT SWING IT SWING IT!'

I shot him a look of disdain and now – completely in my Annie Oakley zone – I hurled out my lariat. It didn't reach its mark, but that was no fault of mine because a hand reached out and caught it.

'Thank you,' I said, as graciously as I could, but inwardly wishing they would leave us alone. I watched my rope being looped around the bollard before it was handed back to me. 'That's very helpful.' I smiled before climbing down to the bow so I could secure the line to the cleat on our foredeck.

A small, smartly dressed woman waved to me and asked if we had had a good trip. But before I could reply the gobby bossy git pushed in front of her and shook his head before walking away. I am sure I heard him say, 'You don't want to be tying it up like that…'

Meanwhile, the barking and squawking had brought people from the inner dock to have a look at what all the fuss was about. I must admit that I was becoming more than annoyed now, especially when someone climbed down the lock ladder and stepped unbidden onto our boat. He had a jolly round face but he ignored me and rushed to the stern. My husband looked as surprised as me. His line was already tied off and he was hanging onto the other end. We both shrugged our shoulders as if to say, 'They must know best.'

Tim and I expected a torrent of water to pour into the lock causing tidal waves and whirlpools to knock us from side to side. This is what happens on the Thames, but the expected torrent was a trickle. *The Princess Matilda* rose a quarter-of-an-inch, which is all it took to make the water level the same as the inner dock.

As the lock gates opened, the yelling began again. This time I decided to completely ignore them all and waited for instructions from Tim, but he was listening to the jolly-faced man who had boarded us.

I waved my arms to get my husband's attention, and having done so had to yell louder than everyone else to be heard. 'TIM! What are we doing?'

Several members of the dawn chorus answered my enquiry, so I couldn't hear Tim's instructions. Eventually, he managed to get a word in edgeways, and pointed to the right-hand side of the narrow inner dock. 'We're going over there!'

Dinorwic has a tiny inner basin and yachts lined the dockside walls, but to the right was a space. Tim signalled with a swirl of his hand that he intended to turn the boat around; the dock master had already informed him over the phone that there was more than enough room to do so. Of course, this exercise would have been much easier if the forward motor that moves our bow had been working, but it had packed up in Swansea. I wasn't worried though; Tim is an expert at turning the fat lump of *The Princess Matilda* about in tight spots without a bow thruster.

Slowly the heavy arse of the boat shifted astern until we were lengthways across the dock at right angles to the far-side wall. I had a fender on the nose, stopping the paint being scraped off our prow. Suddenly, above my head the chorus resumed their chanting: 'Throw me the line throw me the line throw me the line!' I took no notice of them; I was too busy pushing against the wall with my hands. Our boat inched back and I felt Tim giving the engine some revs as he stuck her into reverse. *The Princess Matilda* slowly glided around, as Tim gently put her back into forward gear. This was parallel parking on an epic scale.

With five fingers raised high in the air I indicated how much room we had ahead, four, three, two! Then with the flat of my hand I signalled stop. Meanwhile, echoing around the cave-like port was the chorus manically shouting, 'Throw me the line throw me the line throw me the line!' I disregarded this, intent on keeping our bow clear of a posh plastic boat that was moored in front of our space. Out of the corner of my eye I noticed the woman who had spoken to me on the lock; she was climbing down a ladder. Calmly, without any fuss, she boarded the plastic boat. The chorus was now barking at her too. We both paid them no heed and I politely asked her if she would mind taking my line. Once free of the heavy, black, rugged rope I turned briefly to see how Tim was doing. I could see concentration etched across his face. Alarmingly, I felt my recently abandoned rugged rope being pulled taut across my neck and instinctively I ducked before I lost my head. Someone had come down the ladder and snatched it from the calm lady.

Immediately, I knew who it was, because, while this person was yanking on my bowline, trying to decapitate me, he was also yapping, 'Watch your head watch your head watch your head!'

My new friend, the calm lady, shrugged her shoulders as if to say, 'Sorry about them stealing the rope, but everything's fine down here.' We shared a secret smile of complicity as we pushed our vessels clear.

'I like your boat,' I said, as we drew apart.

'Oh, it's not mine. I just thought I should come down and help you,' she replied.

'That's very kind of you, thanks, we appreciate that,' I said wiping my hands down my trousers.

Shyly, we looked around. The squawking, yelping and barking was still going on. There were men shinning up and down the ladders, stamping over our roof and repositioning my fenders.

'Are they always like this?' I asked her.

She nodded her head.

'Don't you wish they would just fuck off?'

She roared with laughter, pointed towards the gobby man and replied, 'That one's my husband! He means well.'

Tim and I hid away inside *The Princess Matilda* until the cast of *Brookside* disappeared and then sneaked out. I was already in a filthy mood after the circus of our arrival. And now I had to navigate yet another obstacle.

'You have to remember,' Tim admonished me, as he pulled the boat as close as he could to the dock wall, 'that you are now public property. They've seen you on the telly and they think they know you.'

'Shut up!' I answered irritably, pulling myself up onto the rusty ladder. My legs were trembling by the time I reached the top and my temper had not improved.

Now that we had a chance to take in our surroundings,

I could see the boat was moored in a heavily wooded gorge. Tim and I walked to the dock office. Everything was eerily quiet, and there wasn't a soul around, which was a relief.

The office was set back from the lock. Tim knocked and we entered.

'Sorry for all that fuss earlier on, they were only trying to help,' the harbour master said, shaking our hands. 'I'm Steve, we spoke on the phone. You said you were only stopping one night, but pay me tomorrow, you can't go anywhere until…' He stopped and studied a tide table before continuing, '…15.45. You mentioned you needed fuel, you get that in the lock.'

He must have noticed a look of panic on my face. 'Don't worry,' he laughed, 'most of them will've returned to Birkenhead by then!'

Steve then addressed himself to Tim. 'I know you said it all depends on the weather forecast, but, if you do decide to go, let's aim at you getting in the lock at about 15.10, so by the time you've fuelled up it will be time for me to let you out.'

I watched as panic spread over Tim's face now.

'I've seen that look before,' Steve said, laughing. 'But you crossed the Caernarfon Bar to get in the Menai Strait, so I see no reason why you'll have problems with the Swellies.'

Tim rubbed his chin and replied, 'The RNLI crew at Porthdinllaen gave me all the latest information about the buoyage over the bar, but even forewarned I got pushed over by the tide.'

'You would've been,' said Steve, 'there was a bit of wind against tide today and those sandbanks are continuingly shifting.'

'You're telling me!' Tim laughed. 'One of the buoys I was looking for was on the beach. But the Swellies are a different kettle of fish and I've been worrying about this for months.'

'And you'd be a fool if you hadn't,' the harbour master said gravely. 'But I'll wager you've done your homework. Seems to me you've skippered your boat this far, you must be doing something right, Timothy.'

'I dunno, that's the problem, I taught myself, so I never know if I've been doing it right—'

'Obviously you have, Tim,' I said, interrupting them both. 'I don't understand why you doubt yourself so much! Come on, let's find a pub. Got any recommendations, Steve?'

Tim had a bad night tossing and turning, and got out of bed while it was still dark. He woke me up at 7am with a cup of tea. 'I've been working out my passage, and I'm just going to nip to the dock office and see if Steve's put up a new weather forecast.' I turned over and went back to sleep.

'Shane, wake up!' Tim said, giving me a shake a couple of hours later. 'The weather's looking good here, but I'm going to give Conwy Marina a call, see what it's doing over there.'

I covered my head with my pillow and dozed off again.

The vacuum cleaner woke me next time. Tim was Hoovering the bedroom carpet. I pulled the plug out of the socket by my side of the bed.

'I just spoke to Nick at Conwy,' Tim said now he had my full attention.

'Who?' I replied crossly.

'Nick, the manager at the next marina. I've booked us a place, but he reckons it's blowing a force 5 at the other end of the Straits. I don't know what to do!'

I looked at my watch. 'Well, you have a few hours to decide.'

I am used to being around Tim when he is learning lines for a part, but for the next two hours he was memorizing a passage from our pilot book.

'Approach the mainland span of the Britannia Bridge from mid-channel. A white pyramid-shaped beacon stands on the shore. Approach this from mid-point of the span until the two lattice transit beacons on the mainland shore are aligned astern...' And on and on he went.

Fortunately, he had got me a copy of the *Independent on Sunday* while I was asleep, so that kept me busy for half an hour. When I was done with that, I took a look at my AA road atlas.

'Hey, Tim,' I said, interrupting him as he went through his lines. 'On my map it says there's a statue of Lord Nelson by that bridge.'

'Which one?' he asked irritably.

'Britannia,' I replied.

'And why do you think there's a statue of Nelson there?'

I shrugged my shoulders.

'I'll tell you why,' Tim continued. 'The Swellies are between Britannia and the Menai Suspension bridges. Horatio, Lord Nelson himself, described that channel of water, the one that we might navigate soon, as being one of the most treacherous stretches of sea in the world! There's rocks and shoals, whirlpools and tides from hell, so if we get the timing wrong...'

'We won't. Now what do you fancy for lunch?'

'Nothing. You know I can't eat when I'm like this. I'm going to give Nick at Conwy another call.'

After two more conversations with Nick about the sea state in Conwy Bay, Tim decided we should go for it.

There were just a few people around the lock when we went to refuel, but thankfully no yappers issuing instructions. Steve, the Port Dinorwic harbour master, helped Tim fill up our diesel tanks, while I paced up and down the top of *The Princess Matilda*'s flat roof. When I am tense this is what I do, I walk. Tim had passed on his anxiety about our next voyage to me. I even texted my Welsh friend, Miriam Jones, who used to live on the Isle of Anglesey: 'ARE THE SWELLIES DANGEROUS?'

'YES! WHY AM I NOT ABOARD?' was her reply.

I joined Tim in the wheelhouse once we cleared the lock. Welsh speakers know the narrow stretch of water we rejoined as the *afon Manai*, the Menai river. On that June Sunday afternoon, the sky and the water were the same dirty, dingy grey, and my anxiety evaporated because the river felt safe, more like a canal than a tidal seaway. Tim was tapping his various control-panel screens. This is not always a good sign.

'We have a one-and-a-half-knot tide behind us,' Tim said nervously. 'And, according to Steve and my own reckoning, this should be slowing down soon. We've got to hit the Swellies at slack water…'

'And if we don't, then what?' I asked him.

'If the tide's still tipping in?' He checked his watch. 'Then we're in trouble, we could get pushed onto the rocks.'

The river grew wider, opening up to reveal the enormous open-latticed steel-arched Britannia Bridge.

'It looks like toy Meccano from this distance,' Tim said. 'The statue of Nelson should be on the left.' I searched for it through the binoculars, but Tim prodded me and I put them down.

'We have to go through the central arch,' he added, pointing to the photograph of the bridge in his pilot book. We didn't exchange another word until the high-arched spans towered above us.

'Look, look over there,' Tim said with excitement, pointing to something to the right. 'Can you see the white pyramid on the south bank?'

Before I could answer he sharply pulled hard on the steering wheel to change course. Bizarrely, he appeared to be intent on ramming the bank. I knew better than to question his choice of direction, and looked up. Lorries and train carriages were thundering over our heads. Tim meanwhile was now looking behind us and whooped with delight, and once again spun the steering wheel around and changed direction. This was quite a relief, as once again we were heading into open water.

'Can you see them?' he asked me.

'See what?'

'Those two transit beacons on the north bank?' he said, pointing to something behind us. 'Tell me when they are aligned astern.'

'The only thing I can see astern is an Eddie Stobart lorry crossing the bridge.'

'Shut up, Shane!'

Tim's concentration didn't falter. Even I could now see the small white pyramid-shaped navigational aid on the right-hand bank as we passed by. It looked out of place on the muddy shoreline, with only gnarled, knobbly tree roots for company. But Tim was already searching for the next navigational sign.

'That's the south rock marker,' he yelled a few minutes later.

But I was too captivated by the verdant green of the vegetation on the bank to our right to take much notice of what Tim was saying. The water had also changed colour; it was no longer grey, but a deep emerald green, and the shoreline sludge had given way to patches of burnished sand. Beachcombers crept out of secret woodland pathways; a middle-aged couple waved to me and shouted to their teenage children, 'Look, look!' The kids were more interested in rooting around for treasure before it was swept away by the tide, but I was now thinking about the maternity ward of Ysbyty Gwynedd hospital, which I knew was just over the hill.

'We're abeam of the Swelly Rock now, darlin'!' Tim said, grabbing my attention once more. I couldn't see any rocks, just a yellow pole on our left, sticking out of the water with a pointy bit on the top.

'Looks are deceiving,' Tim continued as if he had read my mind. 'There's horrible hazards around here. That pole's the beacon and stands on top of a craggy submerged island. The tide comes in from one end of the Straits as it pours in from the other and swirls around the rocks. Boats have been smashed to pieces here; I think we've timed it perfectly. It won't be as calm as this in an hour from now.'

We both stood quietly holding hands as we drew closer to Thomas Telford's iconic suspension bridge that took the old A5 to Holyhead. I was thinking about a young woman, the one who told her first husband she didn't love him anymore.

'I think the Swellies just about sum up life, don't you? It's all about timing,' I whispered, more to myself than Tim.

I looked down at my road map. We were passing Bangor, where Pascale my eldest daughter had been born – during a heat wave and the worst drought of the twentieth century.

Pascale's birth father was Australian, another unsuitable man I had given my heart to, a year after I had ripped the heart out of my first husband at Aberystwyth Station. I got my come-uppance; the Aussie flew back to Melbourne a few days before my daughter was born. After he left, my parents took me away on holiday to a caravan park off Black Rock Sands, the place as a child I dug around the ankles of my Granny Nance to free her from the sand. The heat that summer of 1976 was relentless, and I was unable to sleep, filled with grief for being left alone and ashamed because I had to return to the care of my mother and father. We sat on the sand, without shade, eating curled-up boiled egg sandwiches, my mother and father sharing secret glances as to how they would cope with me. I stood and walked into the water fully dressed, my gritty sandwich left for the swooping greedy gulls.

The tide was in and I carried on wading, the shock of the cold Irish Sea slapping around my ankles then knees, my mother shouting at my dad to fetch me back.

'Jim, Jim!' she cried, but my dad was getting on and even at 38 weeks pregnant I was quicker than him.

The gentle rolling waves were now up to my thighs and for the first time in months I felt free and unburdened. Then I slipped down a dip in the seabed. As my belly dropped beneath the waves, my baby kicked with such anger at feeling the chill. I knew then that she would be a fighter, just like me.

The next day, Dad drove Mom and me to Conwy to have a look at the castle. This is where I had my first contraction, but I wasn't sure. My mother suspected something was wrong later, at about midnight, when I fell to my knees in the caravan. Dad had been complaining about indigestion all day. For years after it was one of our shared jokes: me being in labour without saying a word and him whinging that the salmon quiche he had had for lunch would be his final demise.

Tim and I, aboard *The Princess Matilda*, arrived at Conwy two bouncy hours after coming through the Swellies. The weather had turned as we came out of the Menai Strait and we had the wind blowing against the tide. Much to my frustration, there wasn't a puffin in sight as we turned right at Puffin Island to cross Conwy Bay.

'That's us for a few days,' Tim said, as we moored in the shelter of Conwy Marina.

'How about I make us a quiche?' I asked him. 'I've got a tin of salmon in the cupboard.'

He looked at me sideways and said, 'But you don't like tinned salmon. Let's find a curry house!'

Chapter Eleven
DAY TRIPPER

There was no curry for us that night. We were told in the marina bar that the closest Indian restaurant was in Llandudno, a cab ride away. We made do with a sandwich; the tinned salmon had passed its sell-by date.

I had been excited when Tim said we were going to be spending a couple of days in Conwy. There is nothing to beat a seaside town with a castle, and in 1976 I was too busy timing contractions to care about its history. The construction began in 1283 during the reign of Edward I, and the castle is now considered to be one of the greatest fortresses of medieval Europe. I had hoped that the marina would be nestling underneath the battlements, but it was quite a way out of the small walled town of Conwy. We didn't get to see much of the town, either. Tim received a call from his agent who asked if he could do a voiceover for a radio commercial.

'It will pay the berthing fees,' Tim laughed in response to the request. Unfortunately, the nearest studio was in Chester.

'It's a shame they couldn't wait for a day or so,' I said to Tim when he hung up. 'We could take *Matilda* up the River Dee, couldn't we?' I showed him where it was on my road atlas. 'Look, it's only round the corner!'

'Let's get the train instead,' he said, slamming my map book shut. 'I've had quite enough of tidal estuaries for a while and the next one we do will be the Mersey into Liverpool.'

Tim was right; it was far more relaxing to let the train take the strain, especially as the station was just a few miles from the marina. From Llandudno Junction you can get a train to Bangor or Holyhead, Shrewsbury or Birmingham, or Manchester via Chester. From Llandudno to Chester the train more or less hugs the coast, the first stop was Rhyl.

The most exciting day of the year when I was a little girl was an annual excursion to the seaside on a green and cream 1950s' coach. The charabanc was organized by the Belt Road Victoria Working Men's Club. I always felt I had a special invitation as the club was next door to my house. To this day, I have not experienced such a fever of anticipation and excitement as the countdown to this outing.

'How many more days, Mom?' I must have driven her crazy. 'Where are we going this year? Blackpool or Rhyl?' I didn't have a preference, both were equally exotic. Billboards promised us: 'Blackpool. Gay and bright, day and night' or 'Sunny Rhyl, The Children's Paradise'. They were both heaven to me.

The trembling of the glass against the frame of my bedroom window would wake me. Calling it 'my bedroom' isn't strictly true as I shared a bed with my three sisters. It was always hard to disentangle myself from the arms and legs to leap out of bed to see what was happening outside. The vibration from half a dozen idling diesel engines shook the whole house. My dad would know without looking just what was out there: 'That's a Bedford 466...' But I was more interested in bagging the backseat of bus No 1 and would dress in seconds, my clothes already laid out ready to wear. Granny Nance would give me sixpence if I managed to elbow the stampede of other kids out of the way. I used to think this was so she could have more legroom, allowing her to sit with her knees open with knitting on her lap. But she had her eyes on more than her clacking needles; nothing happened on our coach without her commentary.

'Look at that Mrs Tranter, who does she think she is? Butter wouldn't melt in her mouth, red hat, no knickers!' But I waited patiently, occasionally fidgeting on the itchy upholstery, for Grandma to announce, 'Vick's coming down the aisle now!'

Vick was the chairman of the club committee who organized the day trip. He gave a bottle of pop and half a crown to every child; there were six in our family, so Grandma palmed fifteen bob, 'For safekeeping.' Fortunately, she wasn't a fan of Vimto, preferring the bottle of warm stout that Vick gave to all the old ladies with a sly wink. The younger women got a Double Diamond and were put on a promise not to tell their husbands. This wasn't a day out for the men; their day trip would be to the races in Chester, not the seaside.

'We can always stop off on the way back,' Tim said when he spotted my wistful face as the train drew out of Rhyl Station.

'No, I'm too big to ride on donkeys now, but you can take me for a posh Chester lunch when you've done your VO!'

Tim and I enjoy trains, just staring out of the window, especially as we travelled that day along the coast. The Irish Sea looked so benign shimmering in the sun, but Tim and I know appearances are deceiving. We sped by with the sea hiding then reappearing behind hills and sand dunes. No sooner had we spotted something, 'Look, look!' than it disappeared from view.

The Princess Matilda with the wind and tide behind her can do about seven miles an hour so we have time to look around, unless we are being tossed about on rolling waves.

'What was that?'

'What?'

'A big white boat on the land!'

'I missed it!' Tim said.

The ticket inspector overheard him. 'That was *The Duke of Lancaster*,' he said, punching our train tickets. 'She used to be a passenger ship, now sits there landlocked like a beached whale. Someone bought her to turn into a hotel, but she's just an old rust bucket now. That's the Dee Estuary out there; it's a wicked stretch of water.

'I'm glad we're not going up the Dee now,' I said, after the conductor left us. 'That stranded old ship looked scary.'

Then my phone beeped. 'I just got a text from Paul. He wants to know if it's OK for Phil Shotton to come and do some filming tomorrow.'

'Ah, Phil, we've not seen him since last September when we left Watchet, in Somerset,' Tim said thoughtfully. 'We've come a long way since then. Do you realize, darlin', that we are now almost north of Manchester?'

'Phil will have an easier commute tomorrow then – he lives in Manchester.'

'Just because Phil's coming, it doesn't mean we're going anywhere—'

'What time would we leave, if we did go?' I said, interrupting him. 'I've already checked the weather, it's looking fine.'

We left a rainy Conwy the following day.

Chapter Twelve
REALLY MAD ABOUT THE BUOYS

Conwy to Liverpool: 45 nautical miles

It must be said that Tim wasn't happy. 'I've not done enough planning.'

'You always say that, Tim.'

He had been up since six, working out the passage on his charts, then putting the route into the autopilot.

'Are you quite sure about the weather forecast?' he asked me once again.

'Yep, slight sea, good visibility. I'm going to put the kettle on. Phil just phoned to say he's in a cab, so as soon as he gets here we'll go, 'cos the tidal flap will be coming back up at ten and we'll be stuck in the marina until tonight!'

'You're just thinking about your belly again,' Tim said, laughing.

'I want a Made in Liverpool vegetable samosa for me dinner, but do you know what? I'm really looking forward to going back to England.'

It had been a year or more since we had left Plymouth, England, to go to Cornwall – the Cornish folk, *m'ansums*, are not part of England and nor are their next-door neighbours, the Welsh.

The heavens opened as we prepared to leave Wales that wet morning and a couple of hospitable Welshmen from the local cruising club helped me with my ropes and fenders. Neither raised his voice or yelled. This is always a bonus. Phil arrived in the nick of time, soaking wet from the walk from the cab to our pontoon.

'Why the rush?' he said breathlessly, as Tim helped him aboard.

'Good question, Phil!' Tim said. 'Shane's got it in her mind we should go to Liverpool today.'

'Hi, Phil,' I joined in. 'We have to go now as the water level in the marina is held in by a tidal flap, and once it comes up we'll be stuck here until the next tide. Give me your coat, I'll hang it to dry.'

'Is that the Great Orme?' Phil asked us ten minutes later, as we crossed a flat calm Conwy Bay.

You can't really miss it; the Orme is a majestic elephant-like limestone headland that separates Conwy and Llandudno Bays.

I nodded. 'Did you used to come to Llandudno for your holidays then, Phil?' I asked him.

He shook his head, while rooting around in his jacket pocket. 'Nah!' he replied, as he began to roll a cigarette. 'Newcastle's east coast, and anyway my old man refused to take us anywhere south of the Tyne. He said North Wales was for soft southern poofs. But the cab driver who picked me up from the station told me you can take a train up to the top of the Orme and on a clear day you can see the Isle of Man. Are you planning to go there?' he asked me.

'No!' was my reply.

'What's that you said about the Isle of Man?' Tim asked. He had been distracted looking at his charts.

Phil repeated what the taxi driver had told him about seeing the Isle of Man from the Orme.

'I'm not surprised,' Tim replied. 'At the moment I think the Orme headland is protecting us from any prevailing winds. I suspect the sea might kick up as we go around it. Hope you're up for a bit of rough, Phil?'

'You know me.' Phil laughed. 'I'm a Geordie, we're always up for a toss about, but I'll just tighten the straps on me life-jacket and have a last tab!'

'There's no rush, we've got twenty minutes to relax before then,' Tim replied.

'And the guys from the cruising club said the cliffs of the Orme are teeming with nesting razorbills, kittiwakes and guillemots,' I added.

Phil is an avid birdwatcher and put his rollup away. In a few seconds, he had his camera zooming in; he wasn't filming anything just looking for razorbills. However, neither Phil nor I had much opportunity to discuss seabirds. Tim was correct with his prediction; our bow was awash with long rolling waves as we came around the headland.

'Just wait until we pass West Constable Bank,' Tim said ominously, as Phil and I held onto the grab bar.

'West Constable's a sandbank?' Phil asked. He had now got his sea legs after coming around Orme Head.

'Yes,' Tim answered. 'If you look through the binoculars you'll see a wind farm. According to my chart we'll come across a few more before the day's out.'

'I suppose it makes sense to build wind farms in shallow water,' Phil replied.

'I'm going to put the kettle on,' I said and disappeared down below.

I had no sooner run the tap than I heard Tim calling, 'Shane, Shane, come up here. Something's gone wrong!'

I rushed up to the wheelhouse. He was pressing switches on his blank control panels. Picking up the binoculars, I searched the horizon for the wind farm. I didn't share the information that it had disappeared in a milky haze of mist. A trickle of cold sweat ran down my neck and I tried to speak as calmly as I could: 'Has the radar gone too?'

'Erm…' Jab jab jab. 'We've lost our position and I don't know what's wrong with this.' He kept manically pushing buttons on his screens.

This wasn't a good sign.

Tim's answer to everything is brute force. He hits the telly with his shoe to get a better signal. I don't know what he did, but that day it worked. All the screens lit up and, as if by a pre-arranged sign, the mist cleared and the wind farm came back into view.

'I think I turned the back lights off by mistake,' he said later, scratching his head.

We were eight miles out on an undulating sea as we crossed Colwyn Bay heading on a course to Liverpool. The sea for once was almost predictable; we could time the waves heading our way. The breaking rollers came in threes, showering the length of the boat with white foaming spume. Then for a few minutes there would be nothing until the next three rolled in, showering splinters of foam-like confetti over the bow. Occasionally, in the lull, we could see the isolated platform of the Douglas oil field.

'Looks grim out there,' I remarked.

My two shipmates nodded their heads in agreement.

'I reckon we have ten miles to go before we get to the mouth of the Mersey,' Tim said, after doing calculations on his chart. 'We're doing 5.4 knots and in about twenty minutes we'll be back in England.'

'Hurrah! But I'm not going to change the Welsh Dragon ensign until we're moored up!' I added.

Since we had left Cardiff in the spring we had hardly come across any other shipping, but as we drew closer to the Mersey we had vessels coming from all directions. And there was another wind farm ahead, the third we had seen that day. The more we saw of them, the less we liked them. Wind turbines are grey and uniformly soulless; they stand to attention in straight, regimented lines. The colossal tri-paddles all revolve in unison. Thwack thwack thwack.

'I suppose most of these ships service the wind farms and gas fields,' Phil said, after he had taken a cigarette break on the back deck. 'There's something coming up behind us, it appeared out of nowhere,' Phil added casually.

Tim and I turned at the same time.

'Fuck me!' Tim groaned. 'It must be doing thirty knots. I hope it's got us on the radar.'

'And I hope it's got that little boat on the radar too!' I said, pointing towards a small vessel to our left. It had 'FISHING CHARTER' emblazoned on the side.

'I'd hope so,' Tim added. 'I've had my eye on that for ages!' He had slowed down so we wouldn't make a wake as we went by. *The Princess Matilda* was passing close enough for me to see the fishermen were sharing a family pack of pork pies and a box of King Edward cigars. They had several six packs of Tennant Super Strong lager on the deck, and they waved to us, each raising a can as if to say, 'Cheers!' I suspected they would suffer from a severe hangover in the morning.

Tim was looking behind us. 'It's the Isle of Man Seacat,' he said, as the ferry drew nearer.

In just a few minutes it left us riding over a tumultuous frothing wake. I am sure I heard one of the fishermen shout, 'FUCKIN' BRING IT ON!'

'I'm definitely going to keep out of the shipping lane,' Tim said after the rocking had stopped. 'It's regularly dredged or it silts up; that's why there's another wind farm out here. But we're a shallow-drafted boat, we won't have any problems.'

Unfortunately, my husband overdid staying out of the shipping lane too much. He had already tuned in on VHF Channel 12 to monitor all ship movements in and out of the estuary.

'All vessels over a certain tonnage and length have to communicate their intention of entering the Queens Channel on the estuary, but we don't have to as we're only 54 feet,' Tim said. 'I'm going to keep outside of the portside buoys.'

I wrote them down in the logbook as we went by. Behind us, but in the shipping lane, were three more ferries.

'I'm glad we're out of their way,' Tim said. 'My charts say we have plenty of water under us on this course…'

'*Princess Matilda, Princess Matilda, Princess Matilda, this is Mersey Radio*,' a disembodied voice crackled over the VHF. '*Do you have any charts onboard?*'

'Mersey Radio, this is *The Princess Matilda*, we have charts and a satellite chart plotter. Over.'

'*Princess Matilda, rejoin the channel between Q3 and Q5 buoys. Over.*'

'I have to turn around and go back?' Tim enquired.

'*Affirmative, turn hard to starboard, keep west of Q3 and Q5.*'

'Starboard?' I repeated. Even I could work out that that meant turn right, and just a few hundred feet away were dozens of swirling grey paddles all facing the wind. Thwack thwack thwack.

'Does he want us to go through this damned wind farm?' I asked Tim.

'I'm not sure, I'm totally confused now! I don't think they are listening to what I am saying. Damned Scousers are like New Yorkers!'

I had heard Tim use this phrase before and wracked my brains.

28th September 1996
Midnight, New York
You had stayed downstairs in the cigar bar with Michael and Bren. We were going to meet them for lunch after your

platelets transfusion. We had spent most of the day together. Poor Bren had such a bad hangover after the Secrets and Lies *premiere party she could hardly speak. We all walked down to the wharf, stopping off at a bar on the way, and had lunch before catching the Circle Line boat around Manhattan, taking in the iconic sights of the Twin Towers, the Statue of Liberty and Ellis Island. Everyone but Bren loved it. I think it made her feel sick and she lay down on a bench on the deck and fell asleep, so she missed it all. Michael kept nipping back to see how she was. You took so many photographs and I worried you might be cold – you were only wearing a thin jacket – but you said you were fine. You told me and Mike Mayhew a story about someone you had met at the after-show party; she was from Liverpool, but now living in New York. You asked if she ever got homesick and she replied, 'No, New Yorkers and Scousers have something in common: they are both sentimental gobshites and they only listen when they are talking!'*

It took us twenty minutes to retrace our steps, so we could enter the Queens Channel at Q5 buoy. Fortunately, we didn't have to play 'In and Out the London Bluebells' with the turbines of the Liverpool wind farm. However, once we were back in the main shipping lane, we had other obstacles to dodge. There were two gas field service boats heading straight at us doing twenty-five knots.

'Hold on!' Tim yelled, as they sped by us.

By the time *The Princess Matilda* had stopped rolling from side to side from the wake, we were back to where we had been sent back by Mersey Radio. Except we were in the shipping lane now, not 50 feet outside it.

'I was just going to rejoin the channel when they called us,' Tim complained.

*

We didn't have much time to appreciate the architecture as we made our way upstream. The Mersey is one of the busiest waterways we had encountered since coming out of Limehouse Marina on the tidal Thames in 2005. After eight hours at sea, Tim and I had become tetchy with each other and our mood didn't improve, as we had to wait for another two hours, going around in circles waiting for the tide to turn.

At low tide, it appeared to us that the mighty Mersey had shrunk to a small river. Wading birds filled the shoreline, looking for fishy morsels to snatch out of the sand. We finally locked through into the inner basin at 8pm. It has an enormous lock and Tim had difficulty bringing us alongside the rising lock pontoon. I would have given my eye teeth to hear someone yell, 'Throw me the line!' But we were on our own.

As is turned out, we left *The Princess Matilda* in Liverpool for almost two weeks. Tim had appointments and the real world called us back down south. Tim and I always feel sad when we leave the boat, but we busy ourselves changing the bed linen and cleaning her from top to bottom ready for our return. We had booked a cab to drive us back to Pwllheli to pick up our car. By road, it is only 70 miles, but to us the distance was immeasurable.

The last words the Scouse driver said to us when he took our bag out of his boot were: 'You must be mad leaving your boat in Liverpool, it'll be on house bricks when you get back!'

Chapter Thirteen
GORMLESS AND LUNY

Liverpool to Glasson Dock: 42 nautical miles

Our exit out of the Mersey passed without any mishap, except we had a helicopter hovering above our heads. Paul, our producer-cameraman, wanted aerial shots for our next series. Unfortunately, I was on the roof of *The Princess Matilda* at the time, adjusting our Union Jack ensign, and felt in danger of being swept overboard by the rotor blades. The helicopter left us, flying slightly north to get some pictures of Antony Gormley's installation 'Another Place' on Crosby beach. Tim had spotted the cast-iron figures as we had come into the Mersey and thought they were real people.

'Look at them,' he had said. 'They're either foolhardy or very robust.'

My sister Jack and her best friend Margaret had joined Tim and me the morning before we left our mooring. They had motored up from Shropshire and drove us to the beach to see the installation. Jacqueline is the eldest of the four girls and two boys in my family. She is eleven years older than me. My earliest memory is snuggling up into the crook of her arm, although she always maintained she was just using me as a human hot-water bottle. There was no central heating when I was young. My three sisters had shared a bed before I was born – the youngest, Jenny, demoted to the bottom when I came along. The day that Jack left home, I felt my heart had been ripped out; for months I cried myself to sleep. She was my Avenging Angel.

I was born between the two boys, my mother's favourite children – in her eyes, they could do no wrong, especially my elder brother. He made my childhood a misery and I would beg my mother not to leave me at home alone with him, but she always did.

'You snivelling ant,' he would admonish me after she had left. 'Now I have to teach you a lesson.' I was made to crawl on my hands and knees to beg for forgiveness then lick his boots and spell out my name thusly, 'T S E T S E'. We had seen a documentary on TV about parasites carried by tsetse flies in Africa and this is the name he called me ever after, that or crawling ant. Every now and again, I would rebel, knowing it would result in a beating, but I would stamp my feet and shout, 'My name's not Tsetse, it's SHANE!' before running on trembling legs until my heart felt like it might burst out of my chest.

One day he chased me around the garden. Like a juvenile Harrison Ford in *Raiders of the Lost Ark*, he was armed with a six-foot whip. My sadistic brother was quite the expert and the end of the whip landed just in front of my next footfall. I knew it was only a matter of time before it came in contact with bare flesh, but then I heard him yell. My sister Jack had come home unexpectedly early from work and got him in a headlock. All of my siblings were afraid of Jack, everyone but me. She told him she would cut off his willy if he ever laid another finger on me. He never did so again.

The iron men on Crosby beach – spread over two miles of sand – didn't impress Jack. 'Why are they all naked? I don't want to see willies!' she complained.

Antony Gormley is famous for creating naked casts of himself. Jack used the shoulder of one of his men as an armrest as she smoked a cigarette. Some of his statues are buried up to the knees in sand. We looked out over the estuary. The wind farms only add to the melancholy of the bleak seascape.

Gormley's iron men are caked with crustaceans; some have only their heads showing above the rippling waves at high tide. All 100 of them point the same way out over the sea. 'Why's it called "Another Place"?' Jack asked me as she lit the end of a new cigarette with an old one. I picked up a discarded coke can for her to use as an ashtray.

'I think the statues represent emigration, people looking towards the New World, a new life. Thousands left Liverpool on ships to New York.'

'Hmmm,' Jack said thoughtfully, 'I think what it says is: "Here I am, I'm looking into the future, but I'm weighed down, I'm heavy, my feet are trapped in the sand. I cannot escape, the sea comes in, the sea goes out, the waves wash over me, the ebbing tide undermines my foundation, the thick grey drifting shoals colour the water brown and grey..."'

I left her to her cigarette and walked along the beach, thinking about that first visit to New York with Tim, when *Secrets and Lies* had opened the New York Film Festival. Returning to the Old World hadn't been easy...Tim and I never did have that lunch with Brenda and Michael after that first platelet transfusion.

4th October 1996
Midnight
Thank God for Bingham Ray and Carin his PA for getting us on Concorde so we could get back to London. A regular flight wouldn't have got you back into UCLH in time for your next bag of antibiotics. (Every eight hours.) There was a car parked outside the Sloan-Kettering hospital waiting for us while your next platelet transfusion and antibiotic drip finished, and then we had to wait for someone to pull

the catheter out of your arm, literally, as we ran down the corridor. Your nurse was so funny. 'I saw Secrets and Lies last night and I stood up and shouted, THAT MAN IS MY PATIENT!'

We both absolutely loved the Concorde lounge. The departure gate was right there, we could see the plane out of the window. Carin had given instructions that we were to be seated last, and we loved that too, we felt like royalty. The plane was full. The only bad moment was when we went through the sound barrier as we'd decided that, if you had not been given enough platelets, that would be when your brain exploded! We tightly held hands. There was a couple of aging New Yorkers behind us who moaned the whole flight, complaining about everything – the flight attendants could do nothing right. The attendants liked us, though, even gave us a couple of bottles of vintage champagne before we got off. (I'm waiting for you to get home before I open one.) Dr Panos was expecting us when we got to UCLH, with that wry smile of his, eyebrow slightly raised. I gave him the photo-copied medical notes which I'd blagged before we left New York. He flicked through them and said, 'Welcome home.'

This morning you were told you could come home as you didn't need a whole course of that antibiotic after all. An appointment has been made to see Dr Goldstone on Monday to talk about cutting what is left of the fungus out of your lung, but that can't happen while your platelets are so low. I wish this was all done with now. At this rate, it will be Christmas before you have your next course of chemo. But we mustn't complain as we thought it was all over, back there in New York. You could have got blood poisoning and organ failure, that's what they were worried about. It shocked us, didn't it, this fine line we are walking between life and death...

'Where you off to next?' Jack asked, once she caught up with me on the beach.

'A place I've never heard of called Glasson Dock. Tim reckons it's about 48 miles north of here. It's on a river called the Lune,' I replied.

'That's what you and Tim are, a couple of lunatics!'

But, barely a day later, *The Princess Matilda* hadn't reached the Lune. Instead she was anchored just outside the Fleetwood shipping lane off Morecambe Bay.

Chapter Fourteen
ALL AT SEA

Mersey to the Lune: 48 nautical miles

We had missed a narrow window of tide to get us a few miles up the River Lune to Glasson Dock. Both Tim and I had been communicating with Brian, the harbour master; Tim by phone and me by email. I had been sent the latest coordinates to get up the tricky channel to Glasson and Tim had spent hours painstakingly plotting the course on his charts. Brian had told us, 'The Lune is notorious for its continuingly changing sandbanks, the buoys are in the wrong order and aren't where they should be, and if you get it wrong you risk running aground.' He warned us, 'I can only lock you through into Glasson three-quarters-of-an-hour before high water…'

Tide and time wait for no man, and *The Princess Matilda* was over two hours late arriving at the mouth of the river at Lune Buoy1. There was an excellent excuse for this.

We had had a wonderful trip along the Lancashire coast and anchored just off Blackpool pleasure beach. 'We're too early to attempt to get up the River Lune just yet,' Tim explained.

I looked at my AA map; I could see the mouth of the river was just a few miles around the corner.

'We have a couple of hours to kill before finding Lune Buoy1 so we might as well put our feet up!' Tim said confidently.

As soon as we upped anchor, I had my binoculars out searching for the buoy.

'That must be it over there!' I said with a great deal of satisfaction. Tim headed for it, but as we drew closer he realized it was the wrong one.

'But it has "Lune" written on it,' I protested. 'How many Lune buoys are there?'

'Two! And this one's Lune Deep. I've got it wrong,' Tim said grimly. He jabbed his chart with his pencil. 'We should be over there. It's miles away.'

'I'm such a tit!' he kept saying, as we raced to catch the tide.

We scanned the horizon, searching for the elusive buoy,

'That's it over there,' Tim said after 45 minutes of breaking the speed limit.

He called Brian on the radio, telling him about our mistake, but that we were now at the river buoy.

'How many knots can you go?' Brian enquired.

'We're going 8.8 knots through the water.'

'You won't make it; sorry you'll have to drop the anchor for the night. There's good holding just east off Lune Buoy1, and you'll be out of the way of the ferries. Give me a call about seven in the morning and we'll take it from there!' Brian advised.

Several factors were in our favour. The sea was an aquamarine serene millpond, our anchor worked, I already had the dinner in the oven, and being midsummer it didn't get dark until just after eleven. The downside was we had a cameraman onboard who needed to get back to his Manchester home. Phil's wife was very understanding: 'That's the best excuse I've ever heard!'

We all sat on the back deck; it was a warm balmy night and we watched a perfect half-crescent luminous moon rise over a clear cloudless sky. The moon cast a silver river of light across the surface of the black satiny sea. To the south was the unmistakable silhouette of Blackpool Tower. Phil reluctantly retired to the spare cabin. 'I want to film the rising sun,' he said before he bade us goodnight. Tim and I stayed up for a nightcap.

'I feel such a tit,' Tim kept saying.

'Well, we knew we'd have to anchor overnight eventually.'

'Let's hope we hold or we'll end up on a sandbank or rammed by a German U-boat,' Tim said pessimistically.

'Oh, we'll be fine!' This is always my response, and besides we didn't have a choice.

Tim set the anchor alarm and we went to bed leaving all the doors open to the wheelhouse. The alarm went off half an hour later; it works with the GPS, the Global Positioning System we use to establish our precise position while at sea. Tim rushed out to check if the anchor was holding firm and returned to bed a few minutes later. 'We've not budged, but I've changed the alarm so it goes off at 200 feet instead of one, so it won't go off now as we swing around the anchor with the tide.'

Between us, we checked our position every two hours. The wind had picked up – I can't say it was the best night's sleep we had ever had, especially with the noise of the waves slurping under the bow. Our bed is at the pointy end of the boat and the sea slopped, slip-slopped, slop-slipped all night long as the tide rushed back in.

Tim called Brian at seven o'clock and was told to up anchor and for us to make our way upstream. So securely was our anchor holding in the sand off Morecambe Bay that it appeared reluctant to leave and stubbornly held firm. We swore and cajoled and bullied it until it came free.

Thoughtfully, Brian had sent his pilot boat downstream to guide us safely up the river – although the word river has nothing to do with what lay ahead. It was more of an open lagoon with water extending for what seemed like miles. The only blot on this idyllic seascape was an ugly concrete squat of a power station that appeared to be moving from port to starboard.

'Don't be tempted to take any shortcuts,' the pilot warned us over the radio. 'It might look like a boating lake but don't be deceived; sandbanks hide just beneath the surface. This is why we keep altering course!'

At times we seemed to be doubling back on ourselves, but we stuck to the pilot boat like a toddler shadowing their mother in a busy supermarket. The power station disappeared and was replaced by remote farmhouses and cottages on a narrowing riparian watercourse.

'Last night at anchor,' Tim said to Phil as he filmed, 'was both fun and horror. Funeror, I've just invented a new word!'

'I slept like a baby,' Phil laughed once he had put down his camera, 'and missed the sun rise!'

The lock to Glasson Dock opened, releasing fresh water into the brackish stream of the Lune. But *The Princess Matilda* had to wait before we entered, as the lock was full of swans that glided gracefully out and were swiftly taken upstream by the force of the tide. The pilot boat had not been so accommodating and had cut straight through the majestic bevy of snowy-white birds. The last time we had seen so many was in Windsor, when we had moored upstream of the castle in 2005. This seemed like a lifetime ago and a million miles away from Glasson Dock.

The dock was built in the eighteenth century because of the hazards of navigating further up the Lune to the port of Lancaster. A canal was cut to join the thriving seaport to the inland waterways via the Lancaster Canal. For old times' sake, once we had moored in the basin, Tim and I took our dinghy up the cut to see what we had been missing.

It felt odd being back on a narrow manmade navigation with banks on either side when we had become so used to the open sea. The canal was bucolic, and serene, the only noise apart from our outboard was the lowing of cows and the gentle rustling of the reeds. Very few boats use this canal and maybe this was why the wildlife was so abundant. We spotted a rare red-necked grebe, playing hide and seek among sunshine-yellow flag irises, and moorhen chicks hopping on and off floating fairy-tale lily pads. It was a shame that Phil the bird watcher wasn't with us, but he had to get back to Manchester. However, Paul had taken his place. We slowly put-putted upstream, not wanting to disturb the waterfowl. Tim stopped under a humpbacked bridge so Paul could get out and film us from the towpath.

'The canals aren't like this where I'm from,' he commented, as he crawled out of the dinghy on his hands and knees.

Paul is a Salford man, and the Glasson Branch that we were exploring has nothing in common with the oily cut where he was born. He ran ahead to get his shot of us emerging from the bridge and when he was satisfied he asked Tim if he could pull over and pick him up.

'Only if you can walk on water, Paul,' was Tim's reply. 'The cut's V-shaped, so really shallow at the sides except under bridges or locks.'

Luckily for Paul, the walk to the lock wasn't too far, and he was excited to discover there was a pub there too.

'In theory,' I said to Paul while we lunched, 'we could go back to London from here on *The Princess Matilda*...'

'We're not going to do that though,' Tim interrupted.

'No, but we could! It's a few miles up the cut to Lancaster, then we could go south, via the newly opened Ribble Link just the other side of Blackpool, onto the Leeds and Liverpool Canal.'

'We'll do it by sea!' Tim said firmly.

We took the dinghy back down the canal and moored it in the canal basin. Tim left Paul and I while he went to find Brian. It was a hot day, so I joined a queue at a busy two-tone stationary burger van to buy a bottle of water. 'The Lock Keepers Rest' was painted on the side.

'It's obviously a popular spot,' Paul commented. Bikers in black leathers sat genteelly drinking tea at picnic tables outside the flower-bedecked van.

'How would we have ever discovered this place without the boat?' Tim said, when he rejoined us.

'By bike?' I said, pointing to the row of Japanese motor-bikes. 'You were quick,' I added.

'I couldn't find Brian; someone told me to go back after two,' Tim replied, 'but across from the lock is a sign that says "Smokehouse", wanna have a look?'

Glasson is a small village and our destination wasn't hard to find. The Smokehouse, we discovered, was also a shop and we bought some vacuum-packed kippers. The governor of the business was called Michael and proudly showed us how the fish was smoked and packed.

'What exactly are kippers?' I asked him.

'Herrings,' he laughed.

'Local herrings?'

'Not anymore,' he replied, 'they were overfished.' Then he called for one of his workers to show us a fresh salmon and a sea trout. 'The trout was caught this morning off Sunderland Point,' he said proudly, 'down by Sambo's Grave.'

He must have seen the look of shock on our faces and quickly added, 'That's not very PC, is it? But it's what it's always been called up here. No one knows his real name. He was just a lad, a slave of a ship's captain, and became ill and died. They wouldn't bury him in consecrated ground as they said he was heathen, but a local clergyman heard about it and placed a cross that said "Sambo's Grave" on the burial site.

You should go and take a look. It's a bit of a drive, although you can walk around there at low tide. Kids decorate the grave with shells and stones.'

'We don't have a car,' Tim said, 'we arrived here ourselves by boat.'

'Oh really?' Michael replied. 'Where you planning on going next?'

'I'm not sure. We were thinking of going to Whitehaven, but thought we should have a look at Piel Island first,' Tim said, rubbing his chin.

'You should definitely go to Piel Island,' Michael said. 'It's on the way and you might meet the new King; he runs the local pub!'

Chapter Fifteen
LONG LIVE KING STEVE

Glasson Dock to Piel Island: 12 nautical miles

When the sea languidly retreats out of Morecambe Bay, it exposes hundreds of golden acres of potentially treacherous sands. But when the tide turns, it does so with deceptive unmerciful undercurrents. The incoming sea sweeps and swirls and, if you are new to the area, picking shells off a beach, you may find yourself on an island with feet sinking into quicksand. The ocean greedily repossesses the area from all sides; these are the rising tides from hell. For hundreds of years the Irish Sea at Morecambe Bay has cut off the unwary; as it did in February 2005, when it claimed the lives of 23 Chinese cockle pickers who had become trapped.

The trip from Glasson to Piel was one of the shortest journeys we had ever made on *The Princess Matilda*; it was also one of the roughest. As we came out of the mouth of the River Lune, it was hard to believe that this was the same place we had dropped anchor a few days before – we had been very lucky. Now, it took us four hours to fight our way across these paltry twelve miles. It was more of a tossing than a crossing.

'I said we shouldn't go, Shane!' the skipper kept saying. 'I said it would be rough, but you wouldn't listen!'

'Well, you're the skipper, so don't put the blame on me!' I shouted back more than once.

Tim spent most of the journey to Piel Island yelling for me to hold on as *The Princess Matilda* was battered by twelve-foot waves. I did my best, but, when I checked everything in our cabin was OK, I was thrown across our bed a couple of times. I witnessed one of the windows in the saloon taking a wave and some of the sneaky dregs managed to slip through a tiny gap where the seal had come loose. It needed immediate attention. The shifty seawater had slopped into a power point and shorted all the electrics in the cabin. I spent half an hour – when I could stand upright – cleaning up the mess of DVDs and pilot books on the floor, after having first plugged the loose seal on the window with J-Cloths.

Neither Tim, Paul nor I was in a good mood when we approached the tip of the Furness Peninsula on the other side of the bay. My husband was still saying we should have stayed in Glasson Dock. Not one of us had had an opportunity to look at any scenery, and we were all rather shell-shocked and grateful to be approaching calm water once more. The tiny island of Piel is protected from the ravages of the Irish Sea and the tides of Morecambe Bay by the mainland peninsula and Walney Island. All we had to do, now we were in this sheltered channel, was find a swing mooring.

This was rubbing salt into the wounds that day. Tim and I had had a barney over the buoy and it didn't help that we were being watched. Phil Shotton had gone ahead to film our approach, and Paul was filming us too. Sometimes, in the making of our television series, I didn't want to play. Frankly, all I wanted to do, once we had finally secured ourselves to a less than sturdy-looking mooring buoy, was have a large gin and watch a bit of crap on the telly. I was no longer interested in making our own TV documentary. However, our television didn't work because our electrics were still recovering from the drenching. Tim and I had a barney about that too; he called me an electric Jonah. Paul tried to make himself scarce, which was difficult on a small boat, but I heard him walking on the roof. He was shouting to Phil who had come alongside *The Princess Matilda* in a boat of his own.

Phil wasn't alone. I put my head out of the window, the one with the J-Cloth, and Phil introduced me to a buxom twenty-something Celtic goddess who was skippering his small open boat.

'This is Princess Nicola,' he said with delight. 'She runs the ferry, looks after the pigs and chickens, and her mum and dad are the King and Queen of Piel!'

'Come on!' shouted Tim, who was already aboard Princess Nicola's ferry. 'Don't bother locking up!'

I put my gin into a plastic cup and stepped down from *The Princess Matilda* and joined the party. Princess Nicola was both regal and down to earth. Her face was ageless; she could have just stepped out of the twelfth century, her dark hair swept back off her beautiful face.

'How do you do, Princess Nicola,' Tim said, bowing.

'You can call me Nick!' she giggled. 'I'm not a proper princess. I'm the daughter of the landlord of The Ship, and it's a tradition around here that whoever runs the pub becomes King of Piel Island.'

'How come?' I asked her.

'My history's not brilliant,' Princess Nicola replied, 'but I think it had something to do with the War of the Roses and some young lad with a name like a cake—'

'Lambert Simnel,' Paul said, interrupting. 'I just googled it on my BlackBerry.'

'That's the one,' the princess continued. 'What else does it say?'

Paul scrolled down his phone. 'The Yorkists tried to pass him off as Edward VI, and had an army of 2,000 German mercenaries behind them. They landed on Piel Island from Dublin, but were defeated at the Battle of Stoke in 1487.'

'The good old days,' Phil laughed. We all looked at him; he was leaning backwards over the side of the boat filming Princess Nicola.

Nicola pretended not to notice. 'Anyway, the tradition of the King of Piel began in the nineteenth century, and is taken very seriously and in the bar is a throne, it's really old. Well, actually, it's more of a chair, but this is where my dad was crowned, wearing an old helmet and holding a sword that are, like, ancient.'

'And do you live in that castle?' Tim asked her, pointing towards a crumbling wreck of a medieval fortification. The characterful grey stone castle dominates the small island.

'No,' she giggled. 'It's seen better days, a bit like my dad.'

Princess Nicola piloted her boat with the ease of someone who had been doing so for decades, and drew alongside the island slipway. She pulled Phil to his feet, before jumping out to help both cameramen with their equipment.

'You're a strong girl,' Paul commented.

'You have to be living here. Can you imagine what it's like when the winter gales blow? My mum and dad are at the pub, you can't miss it,' she said, pointing to the left of the slope. Tim and I walked ahead and looked back to where *The Princess Matilda* was moored in what was, now at low tide, a narrow channel of silky flat water. To our right, almost on the shore of the island, was a small terrace of five houses and a few wind-blown tents. 'The old pilots cottages and the campsite,' Nicola had explained. And to the left at the seaward head of the island was the castle. The pub sits dead centre of the island.

'I'm sure Wembley Stadium is bigger than Piel Island!' Tim exclaimed.

A middle-aged couple was standing outside the handsome whitewashed inn.

'Hello, hello! Welcome to Piel,' they said in unison.

'We're Steve and Sheila Chattaway, the landlords of the pub,' the man added, offering his hand.

'You must be the King and Queen of Piel then?' Tim replied and we introduced ourselves.

'I read in an old book that there wasn't a king here anymore, but someone in Glasson told us you had taken over the pub,' Tim continued, as Queen Sheila led us inside.

'I'll give you a guided tour,' Steve said, 'but I bet you could do with a drink first!'

The bar was handsome, with just enough room for half a dozen small polished tables, each one decorated with a vase of flowers. In pride of place was the throne. Tim immediately sat in it.

'You're lucky there's no one here,' Steve informed him, 'as it's the law that anyone who sits in the throne has to buy everyone on the island a drink!'

'We still live in a caravan,' Sheila explained later, as they showed us around. 'It's taken three years to get the pub up to scratch. A bit like the castle, it was falling to pieces, in a state of disrepair. We've worked like dogs, but touch wood,' she said, looking around, before touching her head, 'we've turned the corner. We even have electricity now the generator's working.'

'You have no mains power?' I asked.

'No,' Steve laughed. 'We do it the hard way, everything including diesel for the gennie has to be brought over from the mainland. I use a tractor to cross the causeway and the ferry at other times, but we wouldn't change anything, we love it here.'

'I'll like it better when we can move out of the caravan,' Sheila added, 'but we've run out of money.'

Suddenly there was noise and laughter coming from outside.

'That'll be our walkers,' Steve said, rushing to the door to welcome them. The bar filled up with excited people, wearing muddy boots, cagoules and rucksacks.

'They come on guided tours over the causeway at low tide. If we get a few more parties like this over the summer,' Sheila said, as she busily began pouring pints, 'we can finish upstairs and I can have a proper bedroom again!'

King Steve was now wearing a chef's hat and taking orders for food.

'Bet you're pleased you didn't sit on the throne when this lot was here!' he said to Tim.

He later put on his ferryman's hat and took us back to the boat, before dropping Phil and Paul off on the mainland.

The wind changed at midnight, just as the tide began to swiftly rush in, slapping, slap, slapping around the hull.

'I hope those walkers crossed the causeway in time,' Tim said.

We sat on the back deck and watched the full moon rise like a beacon over the ruins of the castle; we could hear the wind howling through the old ramparts. In the distance we could see the lifeboat station at Barrow on the mainland. Tim kept saying, 'Let's hope we don't need to call them out. I'm worried this buoy won't hold us.'

'We'll be fine,' was my response, as per usual, before I kissed him goodnight and went to bed. Tim was up every two hours; I slept like a newborn baby.

Chapter Sixteen
ANOTHER HAVEN

Piel Island to Whitehaven: 40 nautical miles

We left our mooring at ten. *The Princess Matilda* had not strayed. King Steve dropped Paul off; our cameramen had spent the night in a local B&B on the mainland.

Tim and I had slowly become aware that our small team of camera crew were enjoying this voyage of discovery as much as we were. Paul had even bought his own AA road map for reference – he showed us the pencilled notes they had made on the Cumbrian page.

'Phil's already on the island,' Paul explained. 'He's going to film you leaving from the top of the castle battlements.'

'With the special permission of the King.' Steve winked. 'I have the only key, but from the top he'll have you in sight for miles. Bon voyage!'

'I think Phil will be very happy up there,' I commented to Paul as we waved Steve goodbye. 'It's a beautiful day and he'll do a bit of birdwatching.'

'I think he'll do a bit more than that if the princess is around,' Paul laughed.

The sea was a glistening pool of undisturbed water, so different from the day before, and Paul climbed on top of the boat to film the Cumbrian mountains.

After a few minutes he put down his camera and lay down.

'Wanna a cuppa, Paul?' I asked him through the open door of the wheelhouse, but he didn't reply.

'Let's hope he doesn't wake up wanting to pee and fall overboard,' Tim laughed.

Paul must have heard me clattering pans as I prepared lunch. He crept up behind me in the galley. He was looking a bit peckish.

'What you making, Shane?' he asked.

'Boiling a few eggs, but if you look out there,' I said, pointing through the open window above the sink, 'you can see Scafell Pike.'

I turned the gas off and ran the eggs under the cold tap. Tim and I hate black sulphurous eggs. Suddenly, we heard *whoooomph*. Paul and I looked at each other and rushed up the steps to the wheelhouse.

'What the hell was that?' Tim asked me.

'I thought it was the toilet seat in the back bathroom falling down...'

Whoooomph.

Tim looked at his charts. 'We're in a firing range!'

Whoooomph.

'I'm calling Liverpool Coastguard!'

Whoooomph.

The coastguard said they would make enquiries and call us back.

BOOOOOM.

'*Princess Matilda*, yes, they are firing live rounds today, but they have you on their radar.'

Whoooomph BOOOOOM.

There were no other ships about, just us.

'Isn't that Sellafield nuclear power station over there?' Paul asked, pointing towards the shore.

'It's a mystery to me why they have firing ranges by nuclear power stations,' I replied, as I looked through my binoculars. 'There's one by Dungeness too.'

*

We arrived in Whitehaven, unscathed by shrapnel, three-and-a-half hours later. Tim on many occasions had said that we would probably winter in Whitehaven, but the autumnal gales that would keep us harbour-bound were months away; we still had half a summer before us.

'How far do you think we'll get this year?' I asked Tim, once we entered the breakwater.

'Edinburgh!' was his reply.

'Are you serious?' I quizzed him. 'You think we'll get to the east coast of Scotland?' But I didn't give him time to answer as I needed to sort out the ropes and fenders.

Chapter Seventeen
LIME TONGUES

A young, highlighted harbour mistress lowered down a bag attached to a rope with details of our mooring as we went through the sea lock into Whitehaven.

'We're here 24/7,' she assured us, 'if you have any problems just call.'

'What a lovely welcome,' I said to her. 'Are you all this friendly?'

The next day I went to do some supermarket shopping, but, when I phoned for a cab to take my groceries back to the marina, there wasn't one available. I phoned Tim and he walked to meet me to help carry the heavy bags. 'I'm standing by a trawler with a "For Sale" sign on it,' I told him.

'That's a sign of the times,' Tim commented when he joined me. The 'For Sale' sign was written on a scrap of card-board nailed to the wheelhouse. 'I bet this harbour used to be full of fishing boats, now they can't make a living.'

It was low tide after we stowed our shopping, and Tim and I walked across the huge sea lock towards the outer sea break; on closer inspection we saw it was made of sandstone. The wind, the rain and the Irish Sea had chiselled out random images into the soft rock of the old harbour wall. Perilous-looking, well-worn steps were cut into the sandstone, and it was easy to imagine generations of women scanning the ocean for the return of their loved ones. Whitehaven had been a colliery town, with mines that run for miles under the sea. The coal was exported to Ireland, but the harbour also imported sugar, limes, tobacco and cotton. The only boats in the harbour now were for recreational use. Two dock piers stick out into the inner harbour, Sugar Tongue Quay and Lime Tongue.

The dock names speak for themselves; ships arriving from the West Indies in the eighteenth century were weighed down with sugar cane that was unloaded at Sugar Tongue. It was distilled by a local family firm, Jefferson's, into rum. The family also owned West Indian sugar plantations. A daily tot of this sugar-based alcoholic beverage was given to all sailors in the Royal Navy and the limes were used to keep away scurvy. Ports from Liverpool to Whitehaven prospered, but the prosperity came at a price. The ships leaving England were laden down with barrels of rum from the distilleries and bales of cloth from the Lancashire mills to barter and trade in Africa. The cargo they took on was human flesh, stored like sardines below the waterline. The poor unfortunates 'lucky' enough to survive the gruelling passage were sold like cattle in the markets in the southern states of the New World, the Caribbean and the West Indies, and forced to work on the sugar, tobacco and cotton plantations. The harvests were then shipped back to Liverpool, Glasson, Whitehaven, Manchester, Bristol and London.

Tim and I were discussing this as we drank our unsweetened tea in the café overlooking the two historic tongues. The sun was dancing across the moored boats in the harbour when suddenly there was a God almighty *BOOOOM*.

We jumped. We both thought the same thing: there's another maniac gunman on the loose! Seagulls soared, squawking their protest into the sky; the air was thick with the smell of cordite.

'Oh, that must be the one o'clock gun,' an elderly lady at the next table said casually, checking her watch. 'They fire it every Friday.'

Once we had calmed ourselves, Tim asked her if it was anything to do with John Paul Jones.

'No, I don't think so. The gun used to be fired at one o'clock every day so passing ships would know the time, but they only do it once a week now here in Whitehaven.' She then put on her glasses and looked very closely at Tim.

'My husband is rather obsessed with John Paul Jones. I thought he was a singer with Led Zeppelin?' I said.

'He is, but the one we're on about,' he said, nodding to the old girl, 'was a Scot and led the only American raid on British soil.'

'April 1778, during the American War of Independence,' the old lady added, as she rooted around absently in her handbag. 'It was the last time England was invaded from the sea. John Paul was captain of an American ship that was anchored a few miles offshore, and under the cover of darkness the sailors rowed two boats into the harbour, planning to burn all our ships. But some of his crew visited a local hostelry and had rather too much to drink and let the cat out of the bag, so the town folk rose up against them!' With a flourish she pulled a packet of sweets out of her leather bag.

I half expected it to be a gun.

'Isn't John Paul Jones considered to be the father of the US Navy?' Tim asked her; she was now digging around in the small packet.

'Yes, he is, but the Yanks have quite a few connections with Whitehaven. The grandmother of George Washington is buried in the local churchyard and there's also an excellent humbug shop!' she said, offering us a choice of confectionery out of her sweetie bag.

'This town is a small friendly community,' she continued after we had taken our pick. 'I know what you thought when you heard the Friday gun. We all know someone that was affected by the shootings. I'm still in shock, but life goes on...'

It began to rain, so we said our goodbyes and went back to *The Princess Matilda*. Everything seemed so 'normal', it was hard to imagine this small town had been fraught with bloodshed.

On the way back to our mooring, we passed the fishing boat, with the 'For Sale' sign on it.

'Do you remember that cab driver that used to pick us up from Fowey and take us to Newquay airport?' I asked Tim, as we increased our speed to get out of the rain. 'He said he used to be a fisherman...' But he wasn't listening. It was really tipping it down now, so we made a run for our boat.

My sister Jenny was due to join us and I met her off her train. She lives near Loch Lomond and had caught a train down to Carlisle, then the branch line to Whitehaven.

'You're getting closer to me,' she laughed. 'I can't wait to get on *The Princess Matilda* and cross the border to Scotland.'

'It's not far. Tim assures me we can see Kirkcudbright from the harbour.'

Jenny looked at me strangely. 'I've never heard of Kirk Cud Bright, do you mean Kirk Coo Brie?'

'Yes, smart arse, but we're not going to Scotland yet because we're off to the Isle of Man!'

'I thought you weren't bothered about visiting the Isle of Man?' she replied.

'No, we weren't. We've kind of got carried away recently, just pushing north for the sake of it, but we've never been to the Isle of Man and Rafe's filming there and it's only 45 miles. Seems silly not to go...'

Our son Rafe is an actor and was filming a TV series, *The Shadow Line*, for BBC2. The Isle of Man has become the new Hollywood of the UK, with two sound stages, unique locations and huge investment in the industry. Since the mid-nineties, over a hundred films and TV programmes have been made there.

'The sea's like a millpond,' my sister said. 'I had a great view out of the train window, so I agree. We should go and visit your son!'

Chapter Eighteen
CELTIC GODS

Whitehaven to Isle of Man: 45 nautical miles

'As my experience increases, my nerves increase exponentially.' This is Tim's new mantra now, each time we set out for our next destination. Mine is: 'I'm going to get some shopping in, just in case, but I'm really looking forward to going somewhere new.'

'That's because you don't have to do any of the planning!' is Tim's answer to that, and to get the last word, my mantra is: 'We'll be fine, and I'll make sure we have emergency rations…'

The day we voyaged to the Isle of Man, the Irish Sea was a magnificent silky-smooth expanse of turquoise tranquillity. It was the farthest we had ever been from the British mainland, but the serenity of this ocean made all the horrid trips we had experienced on our long journey worthwhile. Tim had explained that we were actually going backwards to get to the island, but it would be worth it.

'Really we should've crossed when we left Piel, it's only thirty miles from there; but we didn't know Rafe would be filming then, did we? And do you realize we're surrounded by four other countries? Scotland's just over there,' he said, pointing directly north. 'The tip of Ireland's just about visible over there,' he said, now pointing north-west, 'and England and Wales are behind us!'

'The British Isles,' my sister piped in as she looked up from her knitting to take in the vista. 'How exciting!'

'And the Isle of Man is almost straight ahead. And it's great you were able to join us, Jenny,' I added.

*

During the trip, my sister and I played a few games of Scrabble
– I let her beat me. She is the most competitive person I know;
I think it has something to do with her being relegated to the
bottom of the bed when we were kids. She used to kick up a
storm with her little feet. Out of all my sisters I am perhaps
closest to Jen; where others have judged me for the bad deci-
sions of my youth, she never has.

The Irish Sea may have been benign, but the closer we
drew to the isle, the colder it became. A moody, low-lying,
grey-tinged, fuzzy mackerel sky stopped any sunshine from
filtering through. But the cloud cover was completely dense
over the island. After our game, Jenny and I sat together on
the bow, wrapped in blankets.

'Do you know anything about the Isle of Man?' she
enquired.

'Not much, just the usual. Wasn't it the last place in the
UK to use corporal punishment?' I answered, shuddering,
recalling the fear I had felt when my older brother once tried
to strip skin off me with a whip.

'The story about the last birching was in all the papers,'
Jenny replied thoughtfully. 'It was 1976, the year that Pascale
was born.'

'Ah, yes, I remember it well, the birth not the birching…'
I laughed, making light of it.

'That Australian who left you in the lurch should have
been thrashed!'

'Do you know what, Jenny?' I answered. 'It was the
best day's work that man ever did, getting on that plane at
Heathrow. I wouldn't have met Tim if the Aussie had stayed
in England, would I?'

My sister nodded. She had seen how unhappy I had been
during that long hot summer of 1976, but then she had seen
me really heartbroken in 1996 when I thought Tim might

die. She is more of a best friend than a big sister and neither of us has any truck with feeling sorry for ourselves; certainly not Jenny. She once tripped over a tree root in the middle of nowhere; it took her two hours to hike back to her car, then she drove herself to the local hospital. She had broken her arm.

We sat quietly for a few minutes. Jenny broke the silence. 'See that mist?' she said, pointing towards the island.

'That's not mist, that's fog,' I protested.

'Don't interrupt!' she admonished me, before continuing, 'The mist is the cloak of the Celtic sea god, Manannán mac Lir, who protects the island from invaders.'

'So it hides it so no one can find it?'

'Exactly!'

'How do you know all this?' I asked her.

My big sister put her forefinger on the tip of her nose. I always hated her doing this when I was little. She once told me that I would die because I had stayed in the bath too long so my fingers had become wrinkled. I was only six, but she had me standing on one leg and hopping up and down, assuring me this would save my life.

'I'm going inside,' I told her, as I stood up to walk along the gunwale to the wheelhouse. 'It's cold out here.'

I noticed Tim anxiously watching, as he always does, as I made my way along the side; he almost pulled me in through the wheelhouse door.

'If anything was to happen to you,' he said, putting his hands under my cloak-like blanket, 'I would die!'

'How many times have you fallen in, Tim?' I had once asked him, when he was trying to talk me into swapping our canal boat, for a sea-going one.

'Seven,' was his reply.

'And how many times have I fallen in the cut?'

'Never!'

But he still worried, nevertheless.

The Princess Matilda arrived in Douglas, the Manx capital, at teatime and as a bonus the sun came out too; the Celtic sea god was obviously in a good mood. However, before we could put the kettle on, we had to tie against a high wall. To the other side of the gorge, where we were to moor temporarily, was a main road. Tim knew we would get to this outer dock on an ebbing tide, and the harbour master had instructed us to get between two fishing boats.

'Wait for the tide and I'll get you into the inner harbour about 11.30 tonight.'

This was the time that Rafe was due to finish his day's filming, but Elize, his fiancé, would join us earlier. Tim managed to get us into a gap between the two white Manx fishing vessels next to a flight of stairs, but the base of the stairs stopped at a slimy ledge and a ladder cut into the wall took its place. A couple of heads appeared over the top of the dock.

'Need any help?'

I tied the ends of the two bowlines together and gave them to my sister. 'I love having crew, our Jen. Can I leave you here, while I go help Tim at the back?'

Jenny has a skipper's licence, and she knows what side port and starboard is, while I stick with left or right.

'Of course,' she replied, 'but why have you tied the rope together?'

'The tide's still going out, so we need double the length; we don't want to get hung up on the wall!' I said with a great deal of smug satisfaction.

What I didn't realize, in my rush to help Tim, was that I had actually tied two ends of the same rope together. Jenny never makes a fuss and calmly undid my knot and did the job herself. She still reminds me about it. A security man wearing a high-visibility jacket caught the joined rope as she expertly threw it to him. Fortunately, I did a better job tying up the stern lines, and Tim walked along the gunwale so he could get onto the ladder. Paul was with us filming, and he was already on top of the dock wall. He was only up there for about ten minutes, but, when he came back down the stairs, the concrete steps had morphed into a slimy skating rink. *The Princess Matilda* had also dropped by two feet. I already had the dinner on.

The boat had dropped some more by the time Rafe's girlfriend, Elize, found us; the kindly security men had guided her to us. It is hard to find a boat on a sinking tide and harder still to board one. She navigated the slimy stairs and the rusting ledge and went backwards down the ladder. Either side of her was a dripping glistening blanket of Lincoln-green sea grasses that grew out of the wall. Elize effortlessly climbed from the ladder to the roof of the boat as if this was something she did every day.

'That was fun!' she said, wiping her dirty hands down her trousers. 'And that seaweed stuff looks like an embroidered tapestry.'

Dinner was eaten and the plates washed by the time the tide turned. I sat drinking a G&T on the back deck, while my sister and future daughter-in-law put away the pots. 'Better not have too much of that,' Tim warned me, as I swirled ice around my glass, 'we still have work to do later.'

He climbed onto the roof and lay down for a nap; we had time to kill. During our dinner, several other boats had moored against the wall. It was becoming darker now and the girls joined me in the twilight. We chatted about Elize and Rafe's wedding the following month. We also watched with interest as another vessel, with green and red navigation lights glowing, came alongside us.

'*Princess Matilda*,' the skipper shouted, 'are you mooring here for the night?'

'No, we're waiting for the tidal flap to drop to get in the inner harbour,' I called back.

He rafted against the fishing boat behind us and we all waited patiently for the tide. The tide is the beating heart of the sea, it never fails; two high tides, two low tides, every 24 hours.

When we had arrived, the narrow waterway separating the port and the main port road had been an emptying ditch. The road crosses a lifting bridge to the town and ferry terminal. Once the tide returned, the ditch slowly became a stream, and by 10pm the stream had become a river. The incoming sea swiftly swallowed up the Lincoln-green slimy tapestry on the dock wall, and the tendrils of sea grasses once again floated freely, as if trying to escape.

'All hands on deck!' Tim said when he rejoined us. 'I just got a call from the harbour master, he's dropping the tidal flap.'

The flap keeps the water in the marina, but when it drops the inner basin becomes infused with seawater.

I took charge of the helm; every now and again the skipper allows me to do so, because he cannot be in two places at the same time. Jen and Elize helped Tim get the ropes onboard. Gently, I nudged *Matilda* into reverse to stop her being taken by the force of the tide into the boat ahead of us. Once we were shipshape and everyone was back onboard, I steered towards the road bridge and we all waited for a green light for the bridge to lift to let us through. There is something very satisfying about being on a boat that stops road traffic. Tim took the helm and I joined Jenny and Elize, who were sitting chatting on the gas locker on the bow.

'We don't need any help, thank you,' my sister said, 'we

can manage! Tim says he's going to go hard a starboard as soon as we're through the bridge.'

Chastened, I went back to the stern.

'That boat's been in the wars,' Tim said, pointing to a rusted battered fishing vessel, as we waited for the heavy bridge to open. But we didn't have time to discuss it further, as the red light had turned to green for us to pass through. Tim then took a sharp right once our stern was clear. We were now inside the inner harbour and parallel with the main road. In front of us was another road that skirted the basin. I had a stern line in my hand and was standing dead centre of the gunwale, worrying about climbing a high ladder to tie up.

'Hi, Mum,' a voice said. It was Rafe, he half climbed down the ladder and bent over. 'Pass me that,' he said, taking my rope, 'I'll sort it out. The harbour master was here a minute ago.'

Jenny and Elize managed to get their two lines off the bow without any trouble at all. There were several helpers and in moments we were securely tied off.

We had noticed quite a few boats behind us as we came through the lifted bridge and it became obvious that a large yacht was going to raft against us, so we all helped take their lines and secured them against *Matilda*.

'I thought you hated boats mooring against you,' Jenny said, as she adjusted one of my fenders.

'They asked very politely and it's past midnight.'

These mariners were from Norway, a charming family with three young children. The skipper and his first mate were a young couple, who apologized for disturbing us. Tim and I love good manners, and invited them to cross us if they needed to get ashore; good manners and boating go a long way.

Rafe had the kettle on by the time we went below. I lit the candles to preserve the batteries as we had no shore power.

'The harbour master says he'll fix us up with electricity in the morning,' Tim said, as he poured himself a bucket of Chablis. 'I deserve this!'

'How was your trip?' Rafe enquired, as he got himself comfortable at the saloon table.

'We couldn't have chosen a better day to do it, the sea was flat calm—' but then Tim interrupted me.

'Let's put it this way, the more we do, the more scared I get.'

'Why do you do it then, Dad?' our son asked his father.

'It's a compulsion, going out to sea...'

'Did you see the Tower of Refuge as you came into Douglas? It's built on a reef,' Rafe said, quickly changing the subject. 'They used to keep food in there for shipwrecked sailors. At night it's lit up; we can see it from our hotel room.'

'I missed it!' I said.

'But it's a little castle, Mum. How could you have missed it, you must have sailed right by it!' Rafe responded.

'I saw it,' Tim said, 'but your mother is always looking the wrong way.'

Tim and I found out later that Douglas was the first place in the UK to have a lifeboat and the reef that Rafe mentioned had been the undoing of many ships. Thus, the building of the refuge, with a bell for marooned sailors to ring, to summon help. The present lifeboat is called *Sir William Hillary*, after the man who founded the RNLI in 1824.

Rafe and Elize left us at 1.30am. The ladder was a short climb, as the tide was now in; but the tide, and the extra weight of the yacht rafted against us, had pulled us yards and yards away from the wall. We all heaved on mooring ropes to pull us close enough for them to get off. Elize was flying back to London in a few hours, as she had her wedding to plan; but we arranged to meet Rafe for a late lunch the next day.

Chapter Nineteen
TWO BRIGHT SPARKS

The ropes on the rafting yacht groaned all night long, and once the tide ebbed it sent us crashing against the wall. I suspected our neighbours had a better night's sleep than us, as they were up long before we were. Tim put his head out of the saloon window when he heard, 'Ahoy, *Princess Matilda*, we request permission to cross your ship.'

'Of course you can,' Tim responded. He had hurriedly pulled on a shirt, but was naked from the waist down. Jenny got a shock when she came out of her cabin. I lay in bed and heard the pitter-patter of Norwegian feet going around our bow.

Our neighbours returned an hour later laden down with shopping bags. Jenny and I pulled *The Princess Matilda* as near as we could to the ladder as the flooding tide had once again pushed us away from the wall. I tied a rope to a rung of the ladder to keep us close for a little while to let the crew board us. The three kids, who came down first, put me to shame. The youngest was a girl, no older than six. Her elder sister went just ahead of her, protecting her should she fall. I told them to climb onto our roof, and the bigger girl lifted her sister gently from the ladder and told her to sit and not move. The dad handed the shopping down to his wife, who was halfway down. Jenny took it from her, then the two older children passed it one to the other until the elder one put the shopping onboard their yacht.

'This is team work,' Jenny commented when all the victuals were transferred.

The children stood in a line, bowed and said in unison, '*Tusen takk.*'

Tim had been in the shower while this was going on, but once he was dressed he came up into the wheelhouse so he could listen to the Met Office forecast over the radio. The Norwegian skipper heard it too. 'That sounds good for us, we'll leave on this tide.'

'A bit too fresh for us,' my husband replied.

'I like the name of your ship,' our neighbour added.

Tim explained we had named her after our granddaughter, Matilda, who was born during the construction of our boat.

Paul had stayed the night in a local B&B and had sent a text to ask if we could do a bit of filming around the town. I sent a text back saying I didn't want to climb the ladder, but he was already up by the road bridge waiting for us.

'Oh, you do make a fuss, Shane!' was all I got from my sister, the intrepid mountaineer. She climbed Mera Peak in the Himalayas with a broken foot.

'It's all right for you,' I complained, as I watched her backside disappearing over the rim of the wall. She was carrying my bag as well as her own, and the recycling. Tim offered to tie a rope around my waist and haul me up like a sack of coal.

'Bugger off, Tim,' was my retort. By the time I ascended the damned ladder, with shaking legs, I was hyperventilating.

There was quite a party going on up at the top. A couple of chaps from the marina office had brought us an extra-long hose so we could take on water. The tap was a distance away from where we were moored and so was the shore power; but they had brought along an extension for that too.

'Go and get some lunch,' one of them said. 'We'll have you sorted out by the time you come back. Looks like you're going to be here a while, the wind's picking up!' They also gave us a card to get into the security gate. 'Obviously you don't need it here, but you might want to use the yacht club or the facility block.' They pointed towards the far end of the basin.

Our 'security gate' was the kamikaze ladder and the main road; but the Isle of Man doesn't have choked streets. The only thing holding up the traffic was a man loading a pickup truck with bags of locally caught shellfish that would end up in a Spanish paella in Seville. A bus waited patiently for him to finish. We had lunch with Rafe, who told us he had finished filming and would be flying home the next day. 'But I want to show you something first.'

We walked along the handsome Victorian promenade bent almost double as the wind blew in from the sea, picking up sand and spitting it into our eyes and teeth. Eventually we found a little protection in a bus shelter and Rafe pointed out the Tower of Refuge, a Disney-like mini castle atop treacherous rocks. The fast-rising tide was dumping waves that smashed and crashed over this manmade safe haven and we watched the lifeboat crossing the bay.

'I hope it's not going out after the Norwegians,' Tim and I said at the same time.

A gust of wind blew away my hat, and we all ran along the prom trying to catch it.

'I think we need to get out of the wind,' Rafe suggested, as he stamped on my straw boater. 'I know the perfect place.' He pushed my hat back into shape and handed it to me.

He took us to the Sefton Hotel, one of the many hotels on this Victorian seafront, but this was unique because it had a Norman Wisdom themed-bar. 'He lives on the island, in a nursing home,' Rafe informed us. 'He's ninety-five.' Outside the bar is a bronze statue, with Norman wearing his cheeky-chappy flat cap.

*

Paul and Jenny abandoned ship over the following couple of days, as there were red gale-force warnings all around the British Isles. We went with Jen to the ferry terminal, a two-minute walk from where we were moored. She travelled to Liverpool on the Seacat – the one we dodged as we came into the Mersey. It seemed an age ago, but was barely three weeks. Usually, the crossing over the Irish Sea takes just under three hours, but because of the atrocious conditions it took five. Tim and I resolved to make the most of our time in the Isle of Man and found an excellent restaurant with views over Douglas Bay.

'It looks like we'll be here for a while,' Tim said, as we watched fishing boats battling through the grey rolling waves. 'Those trawlers look so tiny out there and that nor'eastly wind is fuckin' unforgivin'.'

Eventually, Tim used our dinghy *New Si* as my personal ferry in the sheltered haven of the inner harbour; I refused to go up the ladder unless under duress. My ferry ride was about eight minutes, which is how long it took us to cross the inner basin of the marina to the yacht club. We didn't ever go in the club as mostly it was shut, but we could leave the dinghy at their mooring. Of course, this meant a longer walk into the town centre and we often got soaked. It rained a great deal. The inner basin was now littered with leaves, plastic bags, panty liners and bottles that were swept in with the flooding tides. It left behind a storm-strewn sea of detritus. At low water the litter was washed down over the weir of the River Douglas, a backwater behind the yacht club.

The Isle of Man, like Melbourne in Australia, boasts four seasons in one day; in the morning one goes out wearing thermals and boots and at lunchtime the sun comes out and everyone without protection gets sun stroke. I mention this because our granddaughter Matilda, after whom our barge was named, was born in Melbourne. Her dad's family on his father's side had travelled, somewhat unwillingly, as transported convicts from the Isle of Man. I am not sure if the Yarra River in Melbourne has gnats on balmy evenings after the rain, but in Douglas the swarming flying insects wanted to eat us alive. Tim and I swatted them away as we crossed from the yacht club to *The Princess Matilda*.

We made numerous friends during our prolonged stay, one called Roly, an aging hippy from Liverpool with a wispy greying ponytail. He had helped us tie up the night we arrived and made sure our shore power worked. The stern of his vessel was at right angles to our bow and Roly was very accommodating. His boat was an old wooden fishing vessel called *Avail*. The extension from the shore power crossed over his boat, then dropped into the harbour just underneath the surface for about ten feet, before going up and over the roof of *Matilda*.

'Are you sure this is safe?' I said on more than one occasion.

Avail was a work in progress and Roly had two men working for him using electric power tools, which I suspected came from old Czechoslovakia before it split from the Eastern Bloc. Roly assured us the Czech duo could turn their hands to anything. This was good for us, as every time the tide went out our shore power was torn from the socket on our boat. 'Roman will fix it for you,' Roly would say.

Tim and I were walking back to my personal ferry one afternoon and were both shocked as we could not see *The Princess Matilda* as we strode by. There was another yacht rafted against our boat, hiding her from view.

'They've run over our electric cable; it's been dragged under their keel!' Tim said somewhat angrily. I was so annoyed I climbed down the ladder without a second thought. Tim followed close behind.

'I'm going to have to unhook the power lead from our end. Don't touch a thing!' he yelled anxiously.

The crew on the rafting yacht appeared rather shame-faced; all our ropes, fenders and the lethal power line were horribly tangled. Roman came to see what he could do and made a temporary fix to our battered cable.

'I advise you to unplug it if it rainz,' he said solemnly. But with a glint in his cornflower-blue eyes he added, 'As you know, it never rainz in za Isle of Man!'

He promised he would be back the next day to make a better job of it.

True to his word, Roman returned the following morning with his pal Milo. Between them they manhandled what looked like a chainsaw down the ladder. Milo politely asked me if I had something wet to cover the sparks.

'What sparks?' Tim asked him.

'I need to cut a bigger hole to fit a new socket,' Roman said, sinking to his knees in the wheelhouse. 'And the angle grinder,' he said, pointing to the heavy piece of equipment on the deck, 'will spit bits of fire, noozing much.'

'What's an angle grinder, Tim?' I said, as he poured them each a cup of tea, while I ran an old towel under the cold tap.

We both rejoined our new friends in the wheelhouse. Roman had already started cutting away metal; the noise made our ears ring. His friend Milo took the wet towel off me and held it over the sparks as they flew off the grinder. For protection, Roman was wearing a pair of glasses and had a scarf wrapped around his nose and mouth.

'Stop, stop!' I shouted over the noise.

My Ikea wet towel had caught fire. Tim grabbed and stamped on it. Roman removed his scarf and glasses and took a sip of tea. 'Do you have anything thicker than zat towel?' he asked, looking at the charred remains at his knees.

I went below while Tim removed the fire extinguisher above the engine room. 'Just in case!' I returned with two thick damp bath towels and a bucket of water. This time Roman caught the sparks while his mate did the grinding; he didn't bother to use Roman's safety kit of the glasses and scarf.

'Maybe you should take your wife for a walk, Timotia,' Roman said, as steam sizzled in damp clouds above my wet John Lewis towels. It was high tide so I only had three rungs of the ladder to climb, and I was pleased to escape from the butchery.

'Do you think we'll have a boat when we get back, Tim?' I asked, as we strode across the bridge. We turned left and decided to take a look at the rusting boat we had passed the night we had come into the inner harbour. In the daylight it was a desperate-looking vessel, mangled, rusting, bent and a complete wreck.

'Oh my God, look at it,' Tim said with a catch in his throat. 'Look at it!'

Someone was walking on the pavement behind us; the wreck was moored to a wall next to the road. He cleared his throat in such a way that we knew he wanted to speak to us, but was too polite to interrupt. The man had a ruddy-faced, weather-beaten complexion and put out his hand when Tim and I twisted around.

'Sorry to bother you, like.' He was a real Liverpudlian. 'You're off *The Princess Matilda*, aren't you? We waved to you last night when we left the marina. We were going to do a night crossing to the Mersey, but turned back; it was too lumpy for us, like. That's my boat over there on the breakwater.'

'Hopefully it will have calmed down by tomorrow,' Tim said, shaking his hand. 'That's when we're thinking of leaving. We've been here almost two weeks, but after seeing this,' he said, turning towards the wreck, 'we may stay where we are!'

We all rested an arm on the railing overlooking the wreck; we could have climbed over and stepped aboard. At high tide, it is level with the pavement.

'A real tragedy, like,' the ruddy-faced man said. 'It was all over the news about ten years ago…'

'Of course,' Tim responded, 'we thought the name sounded familiar! The *Solway Harvester*, a scallop dredger from Kirkcudbright, she was lost with all hands during a storm…'

'Wasn't there rumours about her being sunk by a submarine?' I asked them both, but they shrugged their shoulders.

I crossed the road and picked some wild flowers that were growing under the cliff and handed some to Tim. We tossed them onto the mangled deck, where once young men's feet had stood. The shape and the structure of the boat was all there, but misshapen, bent and concaved. She had been crewed by nine men; the youngest was only seventeen.

The wreck of this boat was one of the most disturbing sights Tim and I had ever seen; the vessel had been salvaged and the bodies of the dead fishermen recovered.

'Dear God,' Tim said, as we walked slowly back to *The Princess Matilda*. 'The sea is a cruel, cruel mistress!'

We stopped on the bridge and looked back over the wreck of the *Solway Harvester*, then crossed the road and looked down at *The Princess Matilda*. The tide was going out quite quickly. Neither of us spoke for a while, but I knew we were both thinking the same thing.

'Why are we doing this, Tim?'

'I don't know…'

'We can always get her craned out and put on the back of a low-loader and get her ferried back to Liverpool, then use the canals to get her back to London.'

Tim shook his head. 'No, we'll do it under our own steam, one port at a time. I just have to keep my nerve.'

'I think you mean one country at a time. Ireland then Scotland, then we'll be on the home straight, and you will keep your nerve,' I said, patting him on the back. 'All you have to do now is get me down this ladder!'

There was no sign of Roman and Milo when Tim had finished bullying me down the ladder. Two singed bath towels were all that was left, but the shore power was working with a brand-new fitment.

'Well, at least we now know the batteries will all be fully charged before we leave,' Tim said pensively. 'That's one of my worst fears, being out at sea without any power.'

The two Czechs dropped by later, having been caught in a sudden downpour; we invited them inside for a drink and to get dry. They loved *Matilda*. We gave them a guided tour, and they wanted to know where we had been and where we were going to next.

'We only really plan our trips one or two ports at a time,' Tim explained, 'but we've just seen the wreck of the *Solway Harvester*, it made us feel sick.'

'Fishermen risk their lives every time they go to sea,' Roman said thoughtfully 'but you got your boat to ze Isle of Man so you must be doing somezing right, Timotia. Tomorrow I zink you may leave us, ze weather is looking good!'

The sea charts were on the table and the three men gathered around it, as Tim showed them our next passage. Even I showed an interest, as the map of the Isle of Man had been torn out of my AA road atlas.

'It's not too far,' Tim said. 'We're only going to the west side of the island to Peel, then we'll go on to Northern Ireland.'

'Will you take ze inside or outside passage to Peel?' Milo asked Tim.

Roman explained his friend had a Master's Ticket, one of the highest qualification for mariners.

'I'm not sure yet. We had a chat with the coxswain of the lifeboat and he reckons the overfalls at Langness Point will be more of a problem than going through Calf Sound,' he said, pointing to the small peninsula that stuck out like a joke thumb that had been hit with a hammer. Then his forefinger followed the pencilled course through the narrow gap between the small island and the south-west tip of the Isle of Man. 'But if we go around Calf it will add a couple of hours to our passage...'

'It should be OK if you get ze tides right,' Milo said wistfully. 'I envy you, a boat is an adventure, and I miss zat.'

Chapter Twenty
OILY SLICKS

Douglas to Peel: 10 nautical miles (taking the shortcut)

We had an early start. The yacht was still rafted against us, and we had to leave first to get some very precise tidal flows in our favour. Tim had bumped into a local pilot, who advised us to leave one hour before high water so we would benefit from having the tide with us all the way to Peel. 'It will take you through the Calf Sound.'

It is one thing getting your own craft ready to depart, but more complicated when your boat is jammed into a corner. Regrettably, the rafting yacht had had a horrific passage the day it came into Douglas, having crossed in gale-force winds from Holyhead in Wales. Surviving that crossing had been down to fine seamanship, but it was pure luck that the crew had not been electrocuted when they ran over our shore power cable.

The skipper of the rafting yacht was in his mid-fifties and his all-male crew at least three decades younger. Tim and I politely tried to ignore the terse instructions issued from the helm; we sat on our back deck and waited patiently. Unfortunately, it seemed the skipper had not taken the streaming river current that tumbles over a weir from the River Douglas into consideration. We had experienced this fast flow a few times on our dinghy ferry trips to the yacht club. The yacht, once free from us, floundered as it was taken sideways by the current, the skipper fighting to get control. His crew ran in different directions trying to limit the damage to the fibreglass on the high topsides as it came in contact with the bridge. There was a great deal of shouting, but not from us. 'FEND OFF! FEND OFF!' They were more or less trapped as the tidal flap that holds the water in the basin had not yet dropped and the road bridge was still down. All we could do was hold our position; we hadn't yet undone our ropes.

I had time to read up about basking sharks while this was going on, finding out that in perfect conditions this second largest of all the ocean's fish can be spotted around the Isle of Man.

'Tim, it says we have to keep a look out for oily frothy slicks on the surface of the sea.'

'FEND OFF!'

'What?'

'Oily slicks are where the plankton are!'

'FEND OFF!'

'What?'

I looked up from my book; Tim was pressing buttons on his chart plotter.

'The basking sharks are slow moving and have enormous mouths and swim with them open to swallow the plankton, and we have to look out for diving gannets 'cos they love the oily froth.'

'Gannets! Is that all you've got to worry about, Shane?' Tim grumbled, as he started our engine. 'I've been awake since five worrying about tidal streams, eddies, foul ground, Thousla Rock...'

'We'll be fine,' as always was my reply.

The fending-off cries had ceased and the rafting yacht skipper signalled, almost too casually, for us to go first. He was now trapped against a wall, but the tidal flap had dropped.

Half an hour later, we came out from behind the Douglas breakwater, having left the inner harbour to find the bay was still choppy. Hardly surprising after the week of storms, but what was more alarming was the visibility. Dreary low-lying dingy clouds merged with the sea, and we couldn't see any landmarks. Tim called Liverpool Coastguard with our passage details and estimated time of arrival in Peel: '1200 hours.'

'I'm going to turn back,' he said to me as soon as he finished his conversation with the coastguard. 'If it gets any worse, I'm going to turn back.' We both looked behind and the sea looked just as angry as it was ahead.

'Wind against tide,' Tim said, more to himself than to me. 'But once we get around Langness Point it will get better... I hope.'

Not another word was spoken for an hour; we never chat when we are tense. We just stared and held our breath as wave after grey rolling wave hit us, but at least the visibility had improved.

Tim eventually broke the silence. 'That's the east side of the Calf,' he said, pointing to a smoky small dark mass in the distance. 'I'm still not sure which way to go, through or around.'

'What will be quicker?' I asked him.

'Going through the sound, but if I've got the tides wrong...'

'We left an hour before high water so it will be slowing down, right?' I asked him.

Tim studied his watch. It is one he is very proud of, it belonged to his late father. 'If we get to the approach by ten, we should be OK. Ideally, we should only go through within an hour either side of slack water. If we get there much later than ten, we'll miss that window.'

I kept sneaking a peek at my watch too as we drew closer to the Calf of Man.

'This is it,' Tim said twenty minutes later, pulling hard on the steering wheel to change our course. 'We're going to go for it. My hands are shaking, but we are going to go through the sound.' He checked his control panels and I noticed he did indeed have a slight tremor, but his voice sounded more confident when he said, 'We're doing eight-and-a-half knots, that's good. We need more than five if the tide turns.'

I checked my watch; it was five past ten. Then I looked up, and couldn't believe what lay ahead of us. The sky was a rich azure blue, both warm and welcoming, the sea even more so as it was dead flat. Like a pair of meerkats, we turned around to see what was happening to the rear of us. The sea was an ugly maelstrom with storm clouds spitting black shards of rain; we had outrun it and left it behind. Tim and I opened the doors either side of the wheelhouse, and looked from right to left.

'It's not that narrow, this sound, this passage!' I said accusingly. 'And it's really calm.'

Tim meanwhile was looking through the binoculars, then he passed them to me. 'Ahead starboard.' I put the binoculars down.

'Right, look right!' he continued impatiently. 'Those two craggy islets are Kitterland and that white concrete tower to port marks the Thousla Rock.'

I re-focused the binoculars to inspect it closer.

'Bloody hell, Timmy, the sea is swirling around that lighthouse.'

'It's actually a beacon. Can you see the rocks?'

'Not much of them,' I replied.

'Exactly, that's why the sea's churning, but it's what's underneath that matters – and it's going to get rather interesting once we are midway between the islets and the beacon. I have to get a heading of 180 degrees, then change to 140 once we are south of that last Kitterland. If I fuck up, we could be pushed on the rocks.'

'How thrilling! We'll be fine. I'm going to take some photos!'

'You really trust me, don't you, Shane?' Tim said, pulling me towards him then kissing me.

'Of course I do, you know exactly what you are doing.'
I threw my arms around his neck and whispered in his ear, 'I
don't understand why you doubt yourself so much, my love.'

It was exciting, our trip betwixt Thousla Rock and Kitterland.
Tim's navigation was spot on, so once we were clear of the
hazards we were able to relax and enjoy ourselves. For once,
The Princess Matilda, the hot summer sun, the stunning scenery
and the completely calm, cerulean sea were all in harmony.

'This is why we are doing this,' Tim said, with a sweep of
his hand, as we took in the magnificent landscape.

'If only it could always be like this, hey, Tim? I said,
handing him a can of diet coke. 'The coast this side of the
island reminds me of…'

'Cornwall,' Tim finished. 'And I deserve a beer, I've been
up since five.' He handed me back the can and gently smacked
my backside. 'Chop chop!'

I went below to the galley and opened the window above
the sink. A few hundred feet from where I was standing were
sheer cliffs, below which were tiny beaches and secret coves.
The cliffs gave way to lush, grassy, gently sloping hills, a patch-
work of fertile fields sprinkled with grazing fattening beasts.
Whitewashed remote farmsteads looked out over the sea.

I took a chilled bottle of Beck's up to Tim.

'Cheers my darlin'! I bet that tiny bay over there is only
reachable by boat,' he said, pointing out another secret cove.
'And if you look through the binoculars…Oh excuse me –' he
had burped after taking a long drink out of the bottle '– you
might be able to see Peel Castle.'

'Yes, yes, there it is, but no sign of basking sharks or frothy
oily slicks.'

'Oh, I don't know about that.' Tim paused and burped
again. 'That last one was a bit frothy!'

I ducked, but there was no escape. 'And oily after that
Manx kipper you had last night! Thanks, Tim.'

Chapter Twenty-One
PEEL

Peel Castle made the one in Cumbria on Piel Island look like a prefab, but what they both had in common was they had a little island all of their own. Rafe had filmed in Peel and had told us the castle was connected to the town by a causeway. This stately castle was actually first built by the Vikings out of wood in the eleventh century, but had been rebuilt many times over the following centuries. The present structure was built out of sandstone.

'See that round tower,' I said, pointing beyond the walled battlements that were still intact. 'That used to be part of the old Celtic monastery.' We would eventually see the tower and ruins from all sides as we sailed into Peel Harbour.

Tim had booked us a berth inside the marina but, as was the case when we arrived in Douglas, we had to tie up on the wall of the breakwater and wait for the tide. A man called Mark was there to meet us; Tim had spoken to him several times over the phone.

'Hello, *Princess Matilda*,' he called over his VHF mobile radio. 'I'm going to put you by the steps!' He was there in person, the radio now in his pocket, and waved to show us where to go.

'Hello, Mrs Spall,' he said, as I passed him my bow rope. 'I've watched your programme on the telly and know how you hated using the ladder when you moored in Newlyn last year, so I kept this space free just for you!' Then he pointed behind me; the breakwater was filling up with yachts very quickly. 'They can all use the ladders,' he laughed, and then went to help Tim with his lines. Ahead of us were a few fishing boats and a slipway atop of which was the lifeboat station, and the ubiquitous castle.

Tim and I agreed that Peel was one of the prettiest harbours we have ever moored in. Over the little bay was a golden beach. There was even a seal with its nose poking out, as if watching the children building sandcastles and flying kites.

'It's hard to differentiate between the mewing of the seagulls and the screeching of the kids as they run in and out of the sea,' Tim said when he joined me.

I was sitting enveloped in a bubble of contentment on the gas locker on the bow. The two of us sat there quite happily watching as seagulls followed in the fishing boats, but they soon became bored as no fish guts were thrown over the side. These boats, I realized, were only unloading crabs and shell-fish, and the gulls weren't interested in them.

'I'm going to sweep the back deck,' Tim said, bursting my bubble. 'And you should do the same here, your ropes are a disgrace.'

It is true they were covered in grungy weeds that had become trapped, like iron filings to a magnet, in our mooring lines while we had been in Douglas. But over the past two hours the heat of the sun had dried the scummy detritus and a gentle sea breeze was showering our boat with sea grass confetti. I ignored the skipper's instructions and took photographs of the crabbers as they unloaded their catch. One of the larger boats had a lorry with a winch; it was parked high up on the quay, unloading bag after bag of shellfish from the deck. The smaller vessels just landed boxes onto a ledge by the steps where we were moored. A well-built, solid-looking man with a shaved head had been atop the breakwater, and he had been checking us out for a while. He used the excuse of helping one of the crab boats unload his modest catch on the ledge by the steps.

'I'll keep my eye on these,' he said amiably to the skipper of the small crab boat. 'You get off to your mooring. I'll still be here when you get back with your pickup.'

The box of crabs was shielded from the sun by wet rags.

The shaven-headed man looked up as the crabber reversed away from the landing stage, and acted as if he was surprised to see me sitting perched on my gas locker high above him.

'Oh, hello, hello,' he said in a soft Scottish burr, 'that's a lovely craft you have there. Is it sea goin'?'

'We're in trouble if it's not,' I replied, slightly irritated by his condescending manner.

He realized immediately that he had pissed me off. 'Do you like Queenies?' he said, changing the subject swiftly before I could take even more umbrage.

'Queenies?' I asked. I didn't want to be, but I was now intrigued; I thought it might be something to do with the castle. I shielded my eyes from the sun half expecting a queen to appear above the battlements.

'My name's Alistair,' he continued with a voice full of treacle. 'The Isle of Man is famous for Queen Scallops, not as big I am sure as the big plump ones you and your husband are used to.'

I may have been mistaken, but I am sure he gave me a sleazy wink when he said plump.

'I'll be back,' he said, running up the steps.

He had abandoned the crabs and I felt duty bound now to guard them, so I jumped off the boat and stood there.

'What are you doing?' Tim asked me a few minutes later; he had a broom in his hands. 'Have you cleaned that foredeck yet?'

'No, I'm watching the crabs for the man. He's gone to get us some Queenies.'

Tim jumped down too, with the broom, which he handed to me, but we both stared at the writhing box of crabs.

'Those are mine!' someone said accusingly. It was the crab man with his van at the top of the dock.

'Och, it's fine,' the treacle voice of the Scotsman said, as he sauntered back down to us. 'Your crabs are fine, man!'

The crab man picked up his box and ascended the steps.

'Here's your Manx Queenies. They're clean, dressed, fresh out the sea not more than an hour ago,' the Scot said, taking the broom off me and giving it back to Tim.

I was handed a battered old plastic three-litre ice-cream carton of something pale and heavy. 'Fry a cupful of those for a couple of minutes with a knob of butter and a squeeze of lemon juice. Beautiful, Rick Stein loves them!'

'How much do we owe you?' Tim asked him.

'You wouldn't have a chilled beer on this marvellous ship of yours for a very thirsty man?' he replied. 'That's all the payment I need. It must be at least 30 degrees today.'

There was a slick patina of oily sweat on his forehead.

Tim invited him to come aboard.

Alistair made himself at home on our back deck; there was something about him that we couldn't help liking. Tim got him a beer while I stared at the ice cream carton.

'Where did you get them from, Alistair?'

'I'm the island's seafood development officer, and I just got those from the local fish processing plant.'

'There's rather a lot of them,' I said. He had taken the plastic cover off. The tub was full of small round pink lumps of flesh. I was extremely pleased that the contents were dead; I am a vegetarian with a conscience.

Tim had come back up with a bottle of beer. 'Here you go, mate.'

Alistair thanked him and took a dainty sip.

'Shall I get you a glass?' I asked him.

'Yes please,' he replied, 'but you want to get those Queenies in the fridge ASAP. I'd take some out for your dinner and freeze the rest.'

Later, Tim would eat some and say, 'Mmmm cor...' Which I think meant, 'How simply delicious.'

Alistair stayed aboard with us for a couple of hours, sprawled on a director's chair in the shade under the awning. He nursed his beer refusing a top-up, unusual for a Scot. He reminded us of Telly Savalas and we almost expected him to pull out a lollipop and say, 'Who loves ya, baby?' to the fishermen as they went by. Each of them seemed to know him. We discovered that he had a boat of his own and was planning to sail it to Scotland in a couple of weeks.

'I'll look out for you,' he said when he left.

I suspect he may have stayed the night except we got a call over the radio from Martin.

'*Princess Matilda*, if you still want to take on some fuel, there's enough water in the East Quay now.'

Unfortunately, Tim suffered a minor tragedy when we did this, in his rush to secure us to the pontoon. This is hard to do with an incoming tide, and he lost his father's watch in the drink. Tim was mortified; his mother had given him the watch shortly after his father Joe had died. It had sat in a drawer for years, and every now and again Tim would take it out and say, 'All it needs is a new strap and a service.' We eventually had this done in a little shop overlooking the fishing fleet in Weymouth, when our boat was wintered there the year before last. 'I should have left it in the drawer,' Tim said sadly.

Chapter Twenty-Two
CHARISMA

Peel to Bangor: 46.3 nautical miles

'This trip to Ireland's going to be a real milestone,' Tim said when we left Peel the following morning, leaving the red-stone ramparts of the castle behind us. On this voyage we had no land to head for; we were too far away from our destination to see where we were going. This made me feel uneasy; this was going to be one of our longest trips.

'But we have fair weather,' Tim said to allay my anxiety. We now take it in turns to pacify the other.

With our heads together we had listened to the Met Office forecast over the VHF radio, but for the first time this was given by the Belfast Coastguard. This change in the coast-guard station is always a morale boost for us and makes us realize how far we have travelled. Recently we had recognized certain voices as we had given our routine passage, but now the voice was Northern Irish, replacing the lady from Liverpool. Our Liver girl had sounded quite sad when she advised us to let Belfast know when we arrived in Peel.

'We are in another country, and heading to one more,' Tim had said when he had done so.

We have two VHF radios aboard *The Princess Matilda* and one is always set to Channel 16, as it is the international distress frequency. The coastguards monitor it 24 hours a day. It is also used to call up ships or shore stations, and, after an initial response, the call is switched to another channel to keep 16 free. Three hours into our journey to Ireland, we thought we heard a faint crackly voice transmitting, but not from the coastguard. '*Princess Matilda, Princess Matilda, Princess Matilda, this is...crackle crackle crackle...Over.*'

It was a faint signal, but there is a protocol with VHF radio transmissions. Tim replied, 'Station. Station. Station. This is *The Princess Matilda*, over.' We listened carefully for a reply. 'Station' can be any vessel in the vicinity.

'*Princess Matilda, this is Yacht Charisma, change to 6, change to 6 please.*'

Tim quickly tuned our second radio to Channel 6. 'Hello, *Charisma, The Princess Matilda* here, over.'

For the next few minutes, we chatted to a yacht that was also crossing to Ireland. We could no longer see the Isle of Man and the Emerald Isle was still far away. The skipper said that they had seen us as we had come out of the Menai Strait in June. '*It's a small world, but it's rather lonely out here, isn't it, Matilda?*'

'It certainly is,' Tim responded.

'*It won't stay like this, there's a busy shipping lane ahead. There's huge factory trawlers coming out of Belfast Lough and watch out for the Belfast to Birkenhead ferries, they don't take prisoners either!*'

'We will, thanks,' Tim replied. Sadly we were too far-off to give *Charisma* a wave.

Halfway across the Irish Sea our phones went back to Orange – we had been on roaming on the Isle of Man. We still had Manx currency.

'Hope they take Manx pounds in Belfast,' Tim commented.

'I thought we were mooring in Irish Bangor?'

'We are, but I have a voiceover in Belfast tomorrow. My agent says it's only about fifteen minutes from Bangor Marina; all I have to do is get us there safely.' He turned around and looked at our wake. It was a white scar of frothing foam left on the surface of the flat blue sea, although I wasn't aware just how deep it was until Tim said, 'The sea's 75 fathoms back there.'

I shuddered; I like to believe the sea is only knee high, but even I know a fathom equals six feet. 'What time do you think we'll get there, Tim?' I asked him, relieved we could now see a faint shadow of land once again, albeit through strong binoculars.

'We'll be pushing a bit of tide soon, so that'll slow us down, but about five. My main worry is Donaghadee Sound, so'east of Belfast Lough. The chart says it shouldn't be attempted on spring tides by crafts unable to do more than ten knots...'

I interrupted him: 'But we can't go that fast!'

'If you'd just let me finish! I was about to say we're on neaps, so we should be OK.'

He noticed the blank look on my face. 'How many times do I have to tell you these things, Shane? A neap tide occurs during the first and third quarters of the moon cycle, so there is less of a gravitation pull. In other words, we'll be fine.'

'That's my line!' I complained. 'You've got me worried now, all this deep water, and *Charisma* is right,' I said, looking around us, 'it is lonely out here.'

'Not any more – we've got a massive tanker coming up behind us!'

We kept our eye on the tanker that quickly overtook us, leaving us bobbing around like a tiny rubber duck in a children's paddling pool. No sooner had we recovered from this tidal wave than Tim pulled back on the revs; there was a fast ferry crossing ahead of us. He let that go by. Trawlers the size of cruise ships appeared out of nowhere; a washed-out fluttering blur of seagulls surrounded one, so they must have had the nets out. The granite-grey peaks of Ulster's highest mountain range, the Mournes, were now clearly visible to the naked eye. I found them on my AA map too.

'Ireland, where the sea, sky and mountains meet,' Tim said reflectively. 'Shame the sun's gone in.'

The sun and blue sky had been left far behind us, so it had become chilly in our wheelhouse. I shut all the doors and put on a wrap. Above us were dreary, drooping clouds and it began to drizzle, what the Irish call soft rain, and our Manx ensign began to flap as the wind had changed. Matt David was waiting to film us as we came into Bangor and I hoped he was wearing warm clothes. I reminded Tim of this. 'He'll have a long wait,' he said. 'We've still got two more hours before we get there. It looks like we've left the good weather in the Isle of Man.'

The sea, one minute grizzly grey, then emerald green and in some places raven-wing black. A gentle froth of half-hearted white horses threatened but fizzled out before they reached us. Tim put on the windscreen wipers; the drizzle had turned into torrential rain.

An hour later, we had the three tiny isles of Copeland, Lighthouse and Mew before us and the mainland of Northern Ireland to our left, but we didn't have time to take in the scenery.

'That's the sound ahead, isn't it, Tim?' I asked.

The half-hearted pussycat white horses had turned into stampeding stallions that were now intent on flattening us if we were stupid enough to get in their way.

'Hold on, darlin', hold on!' Tim cried, as we both braced our legs.

To tell the truth, after the Calf of Man I had begun to take Tim's warnings about the perils of headlands, narrow sounds and tidal races with a pinch of salt.

SPLASH, we were showered with spume. I hung on to the hatch above the steps to our saloon with both hands – SPLASH SHUDDER SPLASH – bending my knees as *The Princess Matilda* rode roughshod over the stallion waves. Tim and I remained silent for the next five minutes, dealing with each furious rabid horse as it leapt over our bow.

'That's Deputy Reef buoy to starboard,' Tim said, although I could hardly hear him over the clatter of the rain beating down on the tin roof of the wheelhouse. The white horses had completely disappeared but we were now surrounded by little swirls of whirlpools about the size of a dustbin lid on an otherwise flat calm satiny sea. Tim pointed ahead to another buoy, but this one was green, the others were red. 'Look through the binoculars, that should be the Foreland Spit buoy.'

'Yes it is!' I said with excitement.

'I have to leave that to port. I can't believe those whirlpools, look at 'em! If we were to lose power now we'd be spun around; no wonder the pilot book says you need a big engine to push through this!'

Matt David was waiting for us; he joined us for a curry in the Bokhara Indian restaurant just off Bangor High Street. First, however, we stopped off at TK Maxx to get him dry clothes and a waterproof jacket. Matt is skinny and his rain-soaked T-shirt was sticking to his rib cage, he was also wearing shorts. 'It's summer, I didn't think I'd need warm clothes,' he had said through chattering teeth.

We all felt shabby the following morning – what the Irish call soft shabby – but we had felt a celebration was in order. 'It's not every day a man gets to skipper his own boat to Ireland,' Tim said, as we all downed another Jameson's.

*

We arranged to meet Matt at an iconic pub called The Crown in Belfast at noon, but first Tim had to do his voiceover. His agent had arranged a cab to take us to the studio that was actually in Holywood, on the Holywood Road just outside the city. Tim had the address on his iPhone and we drove up and down the busy street several times. Many of the buildings had no numbers.

'For sure people were afraid to have a number on their doors during The Troubles,' the driver said with a shake of his head. 'Belfast is a different place now, thank God. And you'll be having your dinner in The Crown, I hear. Everyone knows The Crown, some great craic and a fine glass of porter to be had there.'

Tim had sunk pints of porter in The Crown Liquor Saloon in the 1980s during the height of The Troubles. At the time, our families had thought he was foolish to go to Northern Ireland, but he had been invited by the Belfast Film Festival. 'I'm an actor, I'll be fine,' he said, as if this would save him from Provisional IRA bombs. He had stayed at the Europa Hotel, which is just across the road from the most spectacular gin palace in the whole wide world.

'It's hard to imagine it now,' Tim said, as we stood outside the ugly-looking 1970s hotel, 'that it was surrounded by barbed wire and we had to go through army check points to get to reception.' Then he lowered his voice, and looked around just in case anyone was eavesdropping: 'It was one of the most bombed hotels in the world. But just look at that bar,' he said, pointing across the street. 'That's what I call a pub.'

Written above the pub was: 'SPIRIT – LIQUOR * THE CROWN * SALOON – VAULTS'. 'Come on in, have a drink!' the golden-tiled façade of the gin palace called out to us.

Tim grabbed my hand and we dodged hooting, swearing traffic to get to the other side of the road and entered the bar between two marble Corinthian columns.

The Crown is a time capsule of opulent Victoriana, with mirrors and gothic ceilings swathed in swirls of ruby-red and the floor an intricate pattern of mosaic tiles. It was lovingly renovated in 2007. Tim had been promising to buy me a drink in there for 25 years, so this was a special occasion.

The saloon was dark, as all atmospheric bars should be; the illumination came from the hissing white light orbs of gas lamps as well as diffused daylight filtered through large windows.

'They remind me of stained-glass windows in a church,' Matt whispered.

And much like windows over an altar, the glass was red, green, blue and gold. But The Crown panes didn't feature saints or martyrs, but fairies, fleur-de-lis and shells. The day we were there it was drab outside, but even so the crystal-cut mirrors reflected the gaslight and changed the greyness of the weather outside into a kaleidoscope of rich colours.

'I'm sure if the sun was shining then the whole bar would blaze,' I commented, as we navigated our way towards the red granite-topped bar. It ran the whole length of the gilded room. There was a waitress at the end of the bar, and while Tim ordered us a drink I asked her if we could have lunch. I followed her like a chorister walking through a cathedral, because this is what it felt like, but with carved golden pineapples instead of angels. She knocked on what appeared to be one of many confessional booths and opened the door for me to step inside.

'Take a seat, then when you're ready ring the bell and I'll come and get your order.'

Tim and Matt joined me; we had room to spread across the sumptuous leather seats, room enough for eight, but this was our own secret haven. Tim gave me a glass of the black stuff; I cannot tell you how much I love Irish Guinness. It takes an age to draw a perfect pint and requires a bartender with patience.

This is something that is never rushed in Ireland. The three-quarter-filled glass is left to settle for a few minutes before the final creamy headed top-up. If you are careless as you drink it, you are left with a white moustache.

'Cheers, darlin',' my husband said, clinking his glass of silky smooth porter against mine. 'Here we are in The Crown, and we came here on our boat!'

'Yep,' I replied, 'you navigated us to Ireland.' I threw my arms around him and gave him a kiss. 'I think we can go anywhere now!'

The saloon outside our confessional box filled up quickly and heads appeared over the neck-high booth to see if it was free.

''Tis the Yanks,' the waitress explained when she came with a refill and our lunch. 'There's a cruise ship in the port; they take photos of everything, every piece of graffiti scrawled into the panels, every carved piece of wood. You see how much Belfast has changed since the end of The Troubles? Please God, we keep the peace now,' she said making the sign of the cross. 'Every time they tried to blow up the Europa, we were damaged too!'

Tim and I lived in London during the seventies, when certain members of the IRA saw civilians as a 'legitimate target'. As 'civilians', Timothy and I could have been shopping in Selfridges in August 1975 when a bomb injured several people, or been at the Tower of London in July 1974, that left one dead and 41 injured. My boyfriend at the time, 'the' Australian, had bought a VW Beetle from an Irishman in Athens. The Aussie was very proud of his Irish registration plates until the car crossed Westminster Bridge and was surrounded by armed Special Branch. I was sitting on someone's lap on the back seat, but they had everyone out of the car and lying on the footpath in seconds. The car was thoroughly searched before they told us we could stand up and drive away. My Aussie couldn't get over the fact that the plain-clothes coppers had found a bag of hash but left it in the glove box. In the car, besides my Aussie and me, were a couple of other Australians doing what is now called the 'overseas experience'. One of them had a girlfriend with a newborn baby; he left a few weeks later and went back to Oz; the writing was on the wall.

Chapter Twenty-Three
LEADING MARKS

Bangor to Portpatrick: 22.5 nautical miles

Tim, Matt and I left Bangor Marina at eight the next morning, steering clear of trawling fishing fleets, fast ferries and tankers. At first, the sea was kind to us; just a hint of a gentle swell in the green-grey sea as *The Princess Matilda* and her merry crew of three set forth towards the Firth of Clyde. Then a couple of hours later everything changed. This is the story of our life.

'Hang on!' Tim yelled down to me.

I was in the galley making tea. Quickly turning off the gas, I put the kettle out of harm's way in the sink; it had just come to the boil. I sat down on one of our tethered chairs – we lash them to the radiator when we are at sea – and braced myself. I keep the TV tuned in to our boat's own web cam, the one that Dangerous Dick Dynamite had fitted on our bow in Penarth Marina. On the screen everything looked fine, but the next moment I was almost thrown out of my perch and all the books and detritus from the shelf behind my head shot forward. Our copy of the Oxford dictionary hit me – it may have been concise but it almost gave me concussion. I watched as our granddaughter's Lego model of an airplane picked up speed and crashed into the bulkhead and shattered.

I was too surprised to feel any pain from the dictionary as *Matilda* began to roll. In a split second the sky disappeared and all I could see out of the saloon windows was swirling briny water. I held my breath, hoping the window would not shatter as it became submerged. There is only so far a boat like ours can roll before it goes the whole hog and capsizes, and for me there would be no means of escape. I thought, 'This is my metaphor for life.'

From the corner of my eye, I noticed the web cam on the telly had gone into freeze-frame as if shocked by the prolonged drenching.

'Shane, Shane, are you OK?' Tim yelled.

The freeze-frame speeded up and I could see the horizon on the TV once more as *Matilda* righted herself. I knew I only had seconds before the next wave smacked us, so I made a dash to the wheelhouse.

'I'm fine, I'm fine!' I shouted to Tim, who had a face greyer than the sea. I hung on to the hatch above the steps.

'I'm going to call you Jonah, from now on, Matt!' Tim managed to say, as another wave dumped tons of water to shove us over.

'It's not quite as rough as when we went around St David's Head!' Matt yelled back, after *Matilda* once again righted herself from another 45-degree dip.

These uncomfortable conditions only lasted for twenty minutes, but it seemed an age before the sea calmed once more.

'I think that was rather more than wind against tide,' Tim said, zooming in on his electronic chart plotter. 'We just crossed over a two-mile-wide trench called Beaufort's Dyke, which is about a thousand feet deep and about thirty miles long!'

'A thousand feet deep? That's like two Blackpool Towers,' I said incredulously.

I went below and picked up the remains of the shattered Lego airplane and found a new home for the dangerous dictionary. I could not help but think what might have happened had *The Princess Matilda* turned over; she has a ballast of twenty tons of concrete in her hold. We would have ended up on the bottom just like the *Solway Harvester*, with me trapped inside.

Tim's new iPad had also fallen on the floor and I was pleased to see the screen had not shattered. I googled Beaufort's Dyke and called up to Matt and Tim in the wheelhouse.

'Did you know that we just crossed over the UK's largest offshore dumpsite for World War Two explosives? There's over three million tons of munitions down there!'

I poured myself a tiny G&T, even though it was only ten in the morning, and knocked it back – medicinally – in one go.

'It felt like a couple of tons exploded,' Tim responded, 'but we have another hazard ahead.' The Irish Sea pilot book was open before him and he read me a passage about the approach to Portpatrick. '"On the hill beyond the town there is a radio mast…" That's it over there,' he said, pointing ahead. It was clearly visible as we were only a couple of miles away from our destination.

'Oh, it looks a really pretty place…' I said, but he didn't let me finish.

'Listen, this is important!' And he carried on reading from the book. '"Once the entrance has been identified."' Once again, he stopped and pointed. 'Look, can you see that sea wall under the town?'

I used the binoculars and replied, 'Yes, looks like there's a nice pub there too!'

'Bugger the pub, can you see an orange mark on the wall?' he asked me anxiously.

'About one o'clock from the windscreen wiper,' I answered, pointing so he could find it.

'Yes, I can see it now,' Tim said, peering through his set of binoculars.

'That orange stripe on the wall has to be aligned with one on a house on the street running down to the harbour. Can you see that one, darlin'?'

'Yes, it's across the road from the pub!' I answered with

excitement, as if I had won a line at bingo. Both orange stripes were visible, as were the goats nibbling away on roots on a rocky crag.

A few minutes later, Tim said, 'Give the harbour master a call, let him know we'll be in the harbour in about ten minutes. I'm going to take this slowly, very slowly. It's ridiculous,' he continued, as he handed me his mobile, 'that, with all this technical equipment, I have to line up two orange lines, on a wall and a house, to get into port! I have to keep clear of that buoy over there, it marks the Half Tide Rock,' he said, with a sweep of his hand.

'That number's ringing out,' I interrupted, giving him back his phone.

I picked up the pilot book and saw a picture of the buoy and the inner harbour.

'You didn't say there'd be ladders!'

Tim didn't answer me; he seemed to be intent on crashing us into the sea wall to the left of the pub. I saw the orange stripes were now perfectly aligned, and then he spun the steering wheel and took a sharp left. I could now see the real ladders, I didn't need a photograph. The craggy goaty outcrop had hid the inner harbour from sight, and the large red buoy marked the Scottish rocks hiding beneath the surface. This was it: we had made it to Scotland – a whole other country.

'Hurrah! I'm going to text our Jen,' I said a few minutes later, as *The Princess Matilda* arrived safely in Portpatrick Harbour.

Tim cheered too, 'We did it! We got to Scotland!'

I stood behind him as he steered and put my arms around his waist. In our living room at home is an old framed map of Scotland, I can stare at it for hours. On the left going from the top to the bottom is written 'ATLANTIC OCEAN' and on the right 'NORTH SEA'. The county borders are brightly coloured in greens, yellows and pinks. Across the border Northumberland and Cumberland are an unexciting smudge of beige. If this was the only map I had ever seen in my life, then Eyemouth on the east coast and Gretna Green in the west would be the last posts of civilization. The Scottish west coast is a jigsaw puzzle of pink- and yellow-tinged islands, most, according to the old map, served by a steamer route. *The Princess Matilda* had just completed one of these routes; this was a huge milestone in our journey.

We had not 'planned' to go to the Isle of Man, if Rafe had not been filming there when we were in Whitehaven we would have given it a miss, and so too Ireland. I suppose this is what Tim and I love most about our maritime quest, we are able to do things on a caprice, weather and tides allowing. We are blessed with over 6,000 miles of coastline, but even idiots like us know we need to find a safe harbour. And even safe harbours such as Portpatrick are tricky to get into.

'You'd better get the fenders dropped, darlin', before you do any texting,' Tim said with a satisfied grin lighting up his face. 'And I'm going to turn her around so we'll be pointing in the right direction in case we leave tomorrow.'

This gave me more than enough time to do all my jobs before climbing onto the roof. Both Tim and I had noticed a smartly dressed solid-looking harbour master indicating where he wanted us to moor.

'At least the tide is high,' I said to him, before throwing him my rope. 'I've been told I'm a rubbish chucker!'

There was a safety barrier with people watching as other boats came in with the tide.

'Nothing wrong with your chucking, my lass,' the harbour master said, laughing as he caught my rope. 'Your skipper did a good job getting in here. My name's Paul and, as you can hear, I'm a Yorkshireman not a Scot!' And quickly he handed me back the end of my rope to tie up on the bow. 'I've left you a lot of slack for when you drop and, look, you even have a welcoming party,' he said, pointing to three black funny-looking birds with tiny red flat feet on the roof of our boat. 'Those are black guillemots; they're very rare, and people come from all over the country to see them!'

We got to know the black guillemots well, as we had a nest all to ourselves in a cranny in the wall where we were moored. They may have had tiny feet but, as we sat inside the saloon after tying up, they sounded like they were wearing Doc Martens. But we didn't hang around to hear the birds do their clog dance, as Tim was keen to get me up the ladder before the tide turned.

Portpatrick is nestled between two cliffs and, according to a leaflet we picked up from the pub – the one I had spotted through the binoculars – the small town benefits from 'the famously mild Gulf Stream climate'. But as soon as we had finished our lunch it began to rain, what the Scots call drizzle.

Matt had to get back to London; he later told us it took him many hours to do so on public transport. But Tim also had a transport problem, getting me back onboard *The Princess Matilda*. It was my own fault, as we had spent a couple of hours exploring the pretty unspoilt town, so, by the time we returned to our mooring, our boat was at the bottom of a long ladder.

Tim did his very best to entice me to climb down, and I understood he would soon begin to swear, but Paul the harbour master was walking by and offered me a ride on his punt. What girl can refuse an offer like that? There was a group of people watching us over the railings, as Paul rowed me to *The Princess Matilda*. One I noticed was deep in conversation with Tim, nothing unusual in that. But my husband told me, after he climbed down the ladder to help me out of the punt, that the man he had been speaking to was the ex-coxswain of the lifeboat.

'We were discussing the tides for tomorrow to get us up to Troon. The old boy said, "It's going to be wet, but there'll be little wind." That will do us! Now I'm going to have a kip. What are you going to do, darlin'?'

'Guillemot watch!' was my reply. 'I'm not going to climb the ladder.'

Guillemots are clean birds; they put their bottoms out of the hole in the wall to evacuate their tiny little bowels. The nest was now fifteen feet above us and the poo decorated our paint-work. By the time Tim woke up, we had quite a mess of it. I was sitting in the wheelhouse when Tim joined me; he was carrying a bucket of hot soapy water.

'I'm going to clean up the crap,' he said, and climbed onto the roof so he could throw the water over the bird droppings. I went below to make sure all the windows were shut, but I was too late.

'You've just flushed guillemot shit all over our telly!' I hissed. It took me twenty minutes to clean it up.

'Those wood pigeons disturb me,' Tim said, when I joined him in the wheelhouse. He had a mop in his hand that he was waving at the pigeons.

'Every time the guillemot hen leaves the chick, they make a beeline for the nest. I think they want to eat them!' The chick was squawking but still shitting and so were the cannibalistic woodies.

'You stand guard and scare them away,' he said, giving me the mop, 'while I go and do our passage to Troon tomorrow.'

The tide had turned and the little harbour was filling up with vessels of all kinds and sizes, until there was just one boat left without anything rafted against it; fortunately, this was

The Princess Matilda. Tim and I disappeared inside the saloon to draw the curtains when we saw a predatory yacht heading our way.

'Give me the guillemots walking on the roof any day of the week,' I moaned ten minutes later.

We now had tossed ropes and size tens stamping above our heads. The yacht had already tied onto us, but terse instructions were issued from the skipper to a crewmember on the harbour wall. My hackles rose as I heard someone else yell, 'Throw me the line throw me the line throw me the line.'

'Don't get so annoyed, darlin',' Tim said. He had gone out to see if he could help. The crew declined any assistance.

'I am annoyed!' I said, before stomping up the steps to see what was going on. There were half a dozen different ropes over our roof and they were getting tangled around our mast, radar, aerials and spare anchor.

'What are you doing?' I snapped at a skinny, goatee-bearded man who was hurling more ropes across us.

'It'll be all right, love,' he said patronizingly.

'Don't you dare 'love' me!' I retorted with mounting anger.

Then his companion, wearing the size tens, climbed down the ladder and back onto our roof.

'Oi!' I shouted, 'Please don't do that, this is our home!'

They all walked sheepishly around the gunwale when they left to go to the pub.

Tim spent an hour or so in the wheelhouse while they were gone, putting our next passage into the autopilot, while I read my bird book.

'Look, quick,' he said quietly, taking my book out of my hands and indicating that I should stand. There on our roof was the guillemot hen with a fish in her beak that drooped like a *Viva Zapata!* moustache. She was sitting almost casually on top of one of our life rings as if pretending that nothing of interest was going to happen. A few moments later, she slowly drew her sooty-black head into her chest, before nonchalantly flapping her black and white wings. She then stretched out her long elegant neck.

'It's like she's just woken up from a long sleep,' I whispered to Tim. Then we watched as she jumped off the ring and waddled clip clop clip, on her little red feet, towards the nest in the wall. The famished chick was screeching for food, so the little hen jumped onto a spare sausage-shaped fender we had on the roof. It rolled a little bit, but with the expertize of a circus performer she went with it until it stopped. Tim and I observed all of this without speaking, or moving or breathing; then suddenly she threw herself at the hole in the wall and missed by two inches. *BANG* she slammed into the rock and fell into the water. This happened five more times; she had the same *Viva Zapata!*-shaped droopy fish in her beak but we could tell she was becoming exhausted.

'I know we're not supposed to mess with nature, genetics and Darwinism and all that,' I whispered to Tim, 'but can't we give the poor little mother hen a hand, especially after that last Kamikaze attempt?'

Tim gently placed one of our boat hooks into the hole, just a tiny way in; we were level now with the nest, but the boat moved and it fell into the harbour. It took Tim a few minutes to retrieve it and we watched the panting hen have another attempt. *BANG* she went once again into the wall, before falling like a rock into the water. Over and over again she tried, as her defenceless chick screeched for food.

'I'm going to have another go,' Tim mouthed, and ever so carefully he put the boat hook back into the hole. Then we waited; this time the hen flew up to the roof of the wheel-house, clip clop, clip clop, clip clop, back and forth she went, then jumped down onto the fender. We willed her to jump onto the pole, but she didn't, she flew straight into the hole.

'Phew! I think she needs glasses,' I said with relief.

'And after its feed the chick will reward us with more projectile shit,' Tim replied.

The next morning, I spent half an hour with a scrubbing brush getting rid of the guillemots' dinner.

Chapter Twenty-Four
WAR SHIPS AND CATS

Portpatrick to Troon: 45 nautical miles

We left Portpatrick Harbour at 11.30 the following day with a stowaway guillemot chick.

All morning, the hen had been bringing it food as it squawked and crapped on the roof of *The Princess Matilda*. These seabirds only have one chick and our one had made a break from its hole in the harbour wall as we slept.

'Look,' Tim had said, as we watched the mother fishing, 'these birds fly better underwater than they do in the air.'

It was true and we decided this was the reason the hen had such a problem the previous night. The birds come out of the sea and run along the surface like manic sprinters doing the hundred-yard dash. When they get enough speed they barely manage to get airborne, skimming inches across the surface of the water before swooping upwards to get into their craggy holes in the cliffs or in our case the wall.

'We were in the way,' Tim commented, as we were leaving the harbour, 'but I hope that fledgling chick can fly better than the mother or it will end up miles away from home!'

The chick made a run for it, fluttered then dropped like a stone into the harbour as we turned right, heading north. We both held our breath, willing it to remerge but were now too far away to see if it had survived.

'I'm going to put the washing up away,' I said, sighing, 'just in case. We don't want any more broken crockery.'

While I was inside the galley Tim called Clyde Coastguard to give them details of our next passage.

'He asked me to look out for a large yellow buoy that's become adrift in the channel. Let's hope the visibility stays good; we don't want to be crashing into it!'

The perfect visibility lasted exactly 75 minutes, but we were heartened that we could see a flashing light on the headland.

'That must be Corsewall Lighthouse, just south-east of Loch Ryan,' Tim said, after a quick look at his chart.

I had a peek in my road atlas and told him, 'All those years of looking at that lovely Scottish map at home and now we're going around that funny-looking hammer head of Scotland. It's called the Rhins of Galloway. Why didn't we go into Luce Bay at the south of it? It looks like it's got a nice beach.'

Tim looked at where I was pointing on my AA map, and laughed. 'Good idea, then we could have put *Matilda* on a lorry and driven about six miles on the A75 to Stranraer on Loch Ryan, but we're going the long way round and going straight over that sea loch,' he said, indicating the indent of Loch Ryan. 'I can't believe we've got all this equipment and I'm commenting on your bloody road atlas – put it away!'

'It's a lovely sea though, isn't it, Tim?' I said, after shoving my map behind my chair. 'I love this smooth wallowing motion, my favourite kind of sea. It's like watching an enormous silk sheet gently drying in the wind.'

Tim wasn't listening, as he was pressing things on the radar monitor. 'There's something large moving up behind us at a considerable speed. I suspect it might be the Belfast Stena Line Seacat heading into Stranraer! I'm going to slow right down to let her pass, and we'll get the usual bouncing around from her wake. Is everything put away downstairs?'

'All shipshape,' I answered, and we both kept a look out behind us to see who could spot the leviathan ferry first.

'I'm going to get closer into the shore,' Tim said about five minutes later, taking *Matilda* off the autopilot and turning the steering wheel manually. 'Make sure we're well clear.'

We had moored close to a Seacat in Weymouth in 2009; she could have sailed right over us and we could have passed easily between her two hulls.

'Good idea!' I replied.

The catamaran emerged out of the mist like a ghost ship, and she was by us in seconds.

'Hold on, Shane!' Tim said, but I didn't need to be told, as he steered us so we would cross over the spume of her twin wakes. Then the ferry disappeared back into the mist as quickly as she had appeared.

'Thank God we had the radar fitted,' Tim said a few minutes later when the rocking and rolling had stopped. 'And hopefully we've missed that errant yellow buoy!'

We picked up another birdie hitchhiker a couple of hours later. A lazy fat lump of a gull, with just a hint of sea breeze ruffling its feathers, was sitting quite happily atop our spare anchor.

'I think it wants a lift to Ailsa Craig; we're about six-and-a-half miles due south of it, and if the visibility was better we should be able to see it by now,' the skipper said.

I knew all about this Craig – most birdwatchers do, as the high granite cliffs of the sheer-faced plug of an extinct volcano is home to colonies of seabirds. Tim had read all about it in the *Reeds* and a sailing club guide given to us by a Manx mariner in the Isle of Man.

'According to your guide, it's 340 metres high and two miles in circumference,' I said to Tim, as I scanned the grey, bleak ocean through binoculars. I put them down and went back to Tim's new guide. 'I do hate it when metric measures are used. How high is 340 metres in real money?'

Tim then went into some long complicated monologue

about how to convert metres into feet, but I had beaten him to it using his iPad. 'One thousand one hundred and fifteen point five feet!' I said. 'So why can't we see it?'

Just then our VHF radio sparked into life: '*This is the War Ship Scarborough, War Ship Scarborough, War Ship Scarborough informing all ships we shall be commencing shooting practice... crackle crackle crackle...north of Ailsa Craig...crackle crackle...*'

'War Ship!' we both said at the same time.

'*Crackle crackle...55 degrees 08 minutes decimal point... crackle crackle...590 north...crackle...005...crackle minutes decimal point...crackle...west.*'

'We really must get a better radio,' Tim said. He had obviously understood more of the crackles than me, because he took out his brass dividers and measured something on his paper chart.

'It will be a couple of hours before we get there,' he said, searching the horizon. I thought he was looking for the war ship.

'No,' he said, 'that's miles away. I'm still looking for the volcanic butt plug, but I'll check with the coastguard in about half an hour just to make sure. Meantime, we have a calm sea, I just wish this mist would clear. Ailsa Craig is supposed to be the distinctive leading mark into the Firth of Clyde.'

'Paddy's Milestone,' I added. I was feeling more at ease now that we weren't going to be blown to smithereens.

'Paddy's what? That's hardly PC, is it?'

'Well, it's halfway between Ireland and Scotland,' I said, bluffing it, 'but that's what it's called in my bird book, diving gannets and...' Then I stopped, pulling a sharper focus on my binoculars. The mist had cleared. 'I think I can see it, Timmy! It looks like a giant Christmas pudding!'

Tim peered through his binoculars too. 'I can't see it...oh yes, yes, I've got it now. We'll pass it four miles to port and according to my chart it's where the Irish Sea ends, but I think she might have one last go at giving us a nasty ride!'

Tim was correct, as the sea surrounding the granite mound slopped and backwashed, causing us to bounce from side to side.

'Give me the ground swell of the Cornish Atlantic, or the race of the British Channel any day of the week, rather than that spiteful Irish Sea,' I said, once the sea calmed down as we cleared the channel.

I patted Tim on the back, and said, 'Congratulations, you clever old thing.'

'What for?' he replied.

'Navigating us all the way to Scotland.'

The gull stayed with us for another ten miles. It obviously wasn't bothered about visiting the Craig.

We soon discovered we had more than the odd gull and Seacat stalking us, but this didn't show up on the radar. Tim was standing on the back deck, and I joined him, putting my arms around his waist. We were on autopilot and had left Ailsa far behind us. We were too far away and bobbing about too much as we passed to see any diving gannets.

'My God, what's that?' Tim said, pointing to the left-hand side of our snowy-white wake. 'It's a fin!'

'Too big for a dolphin,' we both said at the same time.

'It's black, gotta be three feet high. It's a whale!' I yelped, but then it disappeared.

'How much further do we have to go?' I asked my husband once our excitement at seeing a whale had died down.

'About twenty miles and we'll be pushing some tide soon, hopefully in the opposite direction to the war ship.' Tim was back by the steering wheel, checking his charts. I sat and put my feet up and read my book. Tim never sits down when we are at sea. He was on his feet for eight hours that day.

We moored in Troon Marina with the sun shining for the first time since we left Peel in the Isle of Man. Phil, our

Geordie cameraman, was there to meet us; he phoned me and said he had got us 'a dead good mooring'. Tim and I were too knackered to take much notice of our surroundings and shared a tin of tomato soup before falling into bed.

Chapter Twenty-Five
WOOD

Troon to Ardrossan: 8 nautical miles

Tim and I awoke to a familiar rumble of a noise. Rather earlier than planned, we both lay in bed listening, without speaking, then fell back to sleep. I used earplugs, but the noise infiltrated the wax again at about eight and I thought it sounded like a ferry. I made breakfast for Tim and went back to bed to read my book. Almost at the same moment, we both said, 'Sheerness!' In October 2005, we had been rescued by a pilot boat after losing our steering on our way to Rochester on the Medway. The following morning we awoke to the same noise of a timber boat offloading. We put on our dressing gowns and went up to the wheelhouse to investigate. Sure enough, a few yards in front of our mooring were a couple of cranes taking timber off a boat. The two cranes danced and worked in perfect harmony, one removing the cargo, and tidily laying it in piles, the other taking it from the piles and loading it onto huge big wagons. 'We must thank Phil for finding us this pitch,' I said to Tim, as I followed him down the steps to the saloon.

'Let's have a lazy morning,' Tim suggested, after he had showered. 'The weather forecast's pretty bad, we don't want to be moving today. What's Phil up to?'

'Filming the timber boats, I expect, but I told him to meet us for lunch in that restaurant by the marina office.'

Phil joined us for coffee; he was soaked to the skin.

'You'll get your death of cold sitting around in those wet things, Phil,' I nagged him.

'No, I'm a Geordie – we don't get colds!'

We all sat chatting, enjoying a drink and watching the crane cabaret through the picture windows.

'Troon has one of the biggest wood-processing plants in Europe,' Phil commented. 'Did it keep you awake, like? It operates 24 hours a day according to some aud gadgie I met yesterday when I was waiting to film you coming in.'

Tim and I laughed and said we loved living on top of a timber yard, listening to bark being stripped and planks being cut, ready to be sent to builders yards and Wickes.

It wasn't only cranes, lorries and heavy machinery that kept us awake that evening. The wind was screeching and several yachts had ropes – or, as they are known to the sailing community, halyards – slapping around the masts. *Flapflapflapflapflapbang-bangbangflap...* But the wind had died down considerably by the time the cranes woke us again the following morning.

'Well,' Tim said, when he returned from paying our mooring fee, 'the ancient wind-o-meter in the marina office says it's blowing west nor'west force 3. What does it say on your laptop?'

I had the page open. I use a website called XC Weather. It provides real-time weather maps and wind strength in any given area, and we find it reliable.

'Blowing eight to nine miles westerly,' I answered.

'Right then,' Tim said, 'I think we shouldn't have a problem if we leave today; it's only eight miles, a short hop to Ardrossan. I think it will be rather pleasant! We'll get some fuel and leave at quarter past one.'

'Oh, good,' I replied, 'that'll give me time to get some shopping in – we're low on everything.'

I put all of my shopping away carefully, not making the same mistake I had made a couple of years before, when we had left

Brixham. This came to mind half an hour after our departure from Troon, while I was hanging on to the grab bar as *Matilda* rolled perilously close to capsizing. That trip from Brixham to Dartmouth in 2009 had been a short hop too; but on that occasion I had not shut the doors to the cupboards properly. Smash went crockery, cups, glasses and food as we were tossed unmercifully from side to side.

'Here we go again,' I thought, as Tim, Phil and I watched an elegant yacht under sail leading the charge.

'Great conditions for them, they must be doing six knots,' Tim said, as he wrestled with our steering wheel. 'Look at it, heeling over!'

We waved goodbye to the yacht forty-five battered minutes later as she set a course towards the Isle of Arran; and we headed towards our next port of call that was tantalizingly close. I was on the back deck sorting out the mooring lines.

'Typical,' Tim said angrily, 'now I have to hold off.'

I put down the ropes and staggered back inside the wheel-house just as the skipper put *Matilda* into neutral.

A boat in choppy water without propulsion is a bit like riding one of those rodeo horses in a Western-themed bar. Backwards, forwards, forwards and back at the same time as careening from side to side. We all watched a ferry heading our way and it appeared obvious we wouldn't be able to get into Ardrossan Harbour before it did.

'That must be the Arran ferry,' I said, as I tried to change position; I had cramp in my calf from all the bouncing about.

'Yes,' Tim said, 'and that's bloody Eagle Rock about a cable to starboard. I'm going to have to circle and wait for the ferry to go first.'

He turned us in a full circle, not once but twice.

'I should have just gone for it,' he said with annoyance, 'we'd have had more than enough time to go first...oh I'm a bit...FUCK!' And he spun the wheel around and shoved *The Princess Matilda* into reverse gear.

'I was a bit too close to that port hand buoy over there,' he said, pointing behind us, as we once again headed away from the security of the harbour. 'That denotes a covered rock, which needs to be avoided at high tide!'

'Is it high tide now, then, Tim?' Phil asked him.

Tim nodded.

What I like about all our cameramen is they never flap, having as much trust in Tim's skippering abilities as I do. We all discussed this later over a beer, once we were safely moored in the marina. But all Tim would say was: 'Sometimes this bamboozling briny can turn the sanest of men into a loony, especially someone like me who's already halfway around the bend. Why is it I'm driven to the very edge of the precipice with self-doubt and the screaming abdabs?'

'You doubt yourself too much, Timmy, but I'd rather your abdabs than your maniacal loose cannon rocking the boat!'

'I was a bit crazy when we left Cardiff, wasn't I?' he asked me.

'Not half!'

It was a pair of icy feet that woke me up the following day, not raucous cranes offloading lumber.

'I think we need another blanket on the bed,' Tim complained, cuddling up to me seeking warmth.

'Your turn to make the tea,' I replied, giving him a gentle nudge as encouragement.

He put on his UGGs to warm his toes and I pulled up the duvet so I could read my book. Tim shivered and piled on jumpers and said, 'Well, we're in Scotland, what do we expect?'

'Clouds and drizzle,' was my response.

'Well, we're not going anywhere for a couple of days and I'm off to Glasgow to do a voiceover this afternoon. Do you want to come?'

'How far is it by car from here?' I asked him.

'According to my agent, about twenty-seven miles.'

'I'm sad we're not going up the Clyde. We could have taken the shortcut, couldn't we, Tim?'

'To the Firth of Forth?' he replied.

'Too many Firths,' I answered, 'I get confused. Will you get the road atlas so I can have a look, darling, please?'

Tim tutted but delivered the AA map with my cup of tea.

'Yuk, it's curdled, the milk's gone off!' I protested. I put the cup down on the bedside shelf and looked at the 'key to map' pages at the front of the road atlas. 'Did you think we'd get this far, when we left Penarth in the spring?' I asked him as he fished for a carton of long-life milk in the emergency ration cupboard.

'Good lord, no, and it's only July!' he replied, but he was obviously concentrating on things closer to home. 'I thought you did a shop yesterday; we need more long-life,' he added.

'I'll make a shopping list and go out later,' I said, still looking at the map key. 'Glasgow and Edinburgh are so close together, but, if we were to go through the Forth and Clyde Canal to the east coast, that would be cheating though, wouldn't it?'

'We're going to cheat one way or the other. We ain't going around the top of Scotland via the Hebrides or the Orkneys!' Tim said firmly. 'It's too dangerous and wild; it would be suicide to do it in our boat.'

I laughed and said, 'Just seeing how far north it is on my road atlas is enough for me!' We might be daft, but we are not stupid.

'And then what?' I said, turning to page 71.

There seemed to be so many ways we could go.

'You know when we watch the weather forecast on the telly and we always comment on the willy bit of Scotland?'

I laughed. 'That's the Kintyre Peninsula – will we go there?'

'Only to the very tip of it,' Tim replied, laughing too, 'but not the knob end.' He was about to fry some sausages and came into the cabin, threatening me with one.

'Stop it, that's disgusting, Tim, and that frying pan's too hot.'

He went back into the galley and turned off the gas. 'You cook them then. I'm the skipper and you're the galley slave.'

I put on my dressing gown and handed him the atlas, while I washed my hands. He put it on the table and said, 'We could go via the Kyles of Bute, but we have to get back to London soon for Rafe and Elize's wedding, so I'm thinking the Sound of Bute to East Loch Tarbert, that's the isthmus that joins the mainland, then through the Crinan Canal…'

'Where Jen can meet us. I'm going to text her now!' I said, interrupting him.

'Cook my sausages first, slave, and if you speak to her ask her if Alison and Fred are free. I'd like to pick their brains about the route to Oban.'

Freddy and Alison Moore and their two kids are Jenny's close friends and live, as does my sister, on Loch Long, near Loch Lomond. The Moores have a yacht that they keep in Helensburgh on the Clyde.

'Now do you want to come to Glasgow or not?' Tim said, watching me greedily as I turned his sausages.

'No, I need to do some washing and get that shopping in. From what I know of the Highlands of Scotland, the shops will be getting harder to find.'

Tim left me in Asda to replenish our emergency supplies. There are some things you don't want to run out of, like toilet paper, teabags, sausages, firelighters and gin. Tim came back about 7pm, and we wrapped up and took a walk to the end of the harbour. The wind was howling. We looked at the sea and both shook our heads.

'We're definitely not going anywhere tomorrow.'

'Not many starlings around tonight,' I said to Tim. 'I was looking forward to seeing them again.' The night before we had had dinner in an Italian restaurant on the marina front, and we had watched as several flocks of starlings joined up on their pre-roosting dance over the harbour. 'Do you remember what they were like when we moored in Brighton? Millions of them.'

'Not quite that many,' Tim laughed, 'but that does seem so long ago.'

'June 2008. How intrepid we thought we were getting there. You thought we were going by Beachy Head and it was Hastings!'

'Can you remember every single place we've been to?' Tim said, quickly changing the subject. The port game is one we often play, but the list was getting longer and harder to remember. We would argue and squabble about what came first, but as always I began my rote of ports of call.

'Limehouse, Rochester, Chatham, Ramsgate, Dover, Eastbourne, Brighton, Gosport...erm...Lymington, Isle of Wight, Poole, Weymouth...'

Then Tim took over, adding, 'Torquay, Brixham, Dartmouth, Salcombe, Plymouth...erm...'

Then we both took up the chant: 'Fowey, Falmouth, Helford, Newlyn, St Ives, Padstow, Ilfracombe, Watchet and Cardiff.' We held hands as we walked along the pontoon back to the boat. 'I'm going to light a fire!' I said, as I put my free hand in my pocket.

We noticed a group of sea cadets in boats rowing around the marina. 'They must be freezing,' I said, as we went inside the boat.

'Pull pull pull!' we heard the cox shouting as they were put through their paces. Then it all went quiet. Twenty minutes later, the cadets were standing on the pontoon trying their best not to stare through the windows. Tim was in our cabin on the phone so I went up into the wheelhouse and opened the door. They were very young, all smartly dressed in uniform, not one of them over twelve. The sea cadet lady apologized for disturbing us; they just wanted the cadets to see *The Princess Matilda*.

'We've seen her on the telly,' one of them said, 'and your husband's in Harry Potter.'

'Do you think we can have a picture please?' another requested politely.

Tim popped his head out of the window to see what was going on. 'Can we get a photo please?' an excited chorus of youthful Scottish voices chirped.

'It will be my pleasure,' Tim replied, and joined them on the pontoon.

'And you too, Mrs Spall, if you don't mind.' A tall man in uniform introduced himself: 'I'm John McDonald, chief petty officer of the sea cadets here in Ardrossan.'

Then he introduced a youngster who was older than all the rest: 'This is Able Seaman Daniel Small, he was a cadet for six years,' he said proudly. 'And he joined the navy in January 2009.'

'I'm off to America in a couple of months,' Able Seaman Small said, shaking us both by the hand.

'Will you be taking *The Princess Matilda* over to Arran?' he asked us.

'A bit too blowy for us at the moment, but we're going to get the ferry over tomorrow,' I replied.

'Well, you won't have far to go to get that,' the chief petty officer said. We all turned as the ferry, a couple of hundred yards from where we were standing, sounded her deep throaty horn.

Tim checking we are ship shape
before leaving in Pwllheli
(Photo Paul Crompton)

Tim and I in our dinghy *New Si* on the Glasson Canal
(Photo Paul Crompton)

I hate ladders generally, but this one in Fishguard was especially daunting

My big sister Jen and I on a flat calm sea going to the Isle of Man

(Photo Paul Crompton)

Rafe, Tim and Norman Wisdom in Douglas

The wreck of the
Solway Harvester in Douglas

Our Scottish flag is doused by spray
as a wave crashes over the bows

Tim and I happy to be in Portpatrick,
our first Scottish port of call
(Photo Matt David)

Enjoying the scenery on the Crinan Canal

Sadie and her father shirking on the Crinan Canal

The Princess Matilda
moored in Crinan Basin

(Photo Paul Crompton)

The old Clyde puffer
filling up with coal,
Crinan lock

Matilda with her sherbert dip keeping an eye on her granddad

Matilda and I on top of Kerrera looking out across Loch Linnhe

Cyrus after an Atlantic salmon. Luckily we weren't relying on him for our dinner!

The Princess Matilda awaiting the Buckie-wood make over!

In the snow in Banff. We always try to spend New Year with *Matilda*

(Photo Andrew Taylor, Banff)

Team *Matilda*: With the cameramen who had filmed us over the course of our long voyage after we arrived back in Chatham. From l-r, Phil, Matt, me, our friend Frances Barber, Tim and Paul

It was getting on for 10pm when they left us.

'See, not all kids are on crack and breaking windows. Did you see how they all looked up to that able seaman?' I said to Tim, as we waved them goodbye.

'I did, his parents must be very proud of him.'

Tim has a soft spot for the services – he had been an army cadet, and if he hadn't become an actor he had planned to join the Tank Regiment.

'Too late to make a fire now. Do you want a glass of champagne?' Tim asked me, as he opened the fridge. 'I see you've got enough in to last a fortnight.'

'It was on special offer at Asda, and Sadie is staying with Jenny. They are going to drive over and meet us when we get to the Crinan Canal, and they will guzzle the lot.'

'Our little Sadie, the married woman.' Tim smiled. 'I do miss the kids.'

We went to bed listening to the lullaby of groaning ropes.

Chapter Twenty-Six
IT'S A FAMILY AFFAIR

Ardrossan to Loch Crinan: 43 nautical miles

We returned from a ferry outing to Arran with a carrier bag full of local cheese, which we had for lunch a few days later, sharing it with my sister Jen, our youngest daughter Sadie and the Moore family. They had joined us at Ardrishaig, which lies at the head of Loch Gilp – a mini loch that comes off the better-known Loch Fyne. We were moored above the sea loch on the southern end of the Crinan Canal. Tim and I had spent the night before in Tarbert on the Kintyre Peninsula, with Paul Crompton who had stayed the night in a B&B; but we had all literally run away on the next tide. There was a funfair 50 feet away from where we were tied up; they cranked the music up at eleven and it didn't stop until past one in the morning.

'If this was Lewisham,' I had complained, 'they would have had that sound system confiscated!'

The Moores have two teenage children, Lucy and Nicky, and they – like their parents and Jenny – had brought their bikes with them. (They didn't cycle all the way from Loch Long; the bikes had been transported in the back of a four by four.)

'Here comes the cavalry,' Jenny had shouted, as they appeared over the bridge of the sea lock. One, two, three, four, five of them on mountain bikes. Sadie was at the rear, walking carefully in handmade leather boots.

'I hope you're not expecting me to do any of those beastly locks,' she said, as she climbed aboard *The Princess Matilda*.

Just ahead of us was the first of the fifteen locks of the manmade nine-mile-long shortcut to the Sound of Jura.

Jenny was already aboard pouring tea for Fred. Nick and Lucy had been sent back to the car to collect a picnic basket.

'Stop moaning, Sadie,' her aunty Jenny gently admonished her. 'It's a beautiful day and you can help the skipper with the ropes.'

'I'm not touching those filthy things either,' she replied. 'And Alison says to tell you she's getting the lock ready.'

Tim and I have known Alison for years; she works for the same Highland Hotel group that Jenny does. They are both hard working, but they can party hard too and never miss dancing a Scottish reel at a ceilidh. Alison's husband, Fred, skippers sightseeing boats on Loch Lomond and is the king of the reels – he likes nothing better than spinning women off their feet. I left him with Tim who was regaling him with stories of high seas and mountainous waves.

I joined Alison at the lock to help her empty it of water. She was using what is known as a windlass to open the paddles to let the water out.

'Golly, Alison,' I said, as I used my light aluminium lock key, 'where did you get that heavy old lump of iron from?'

'They keep them on the lock,' she replied, as sweat trickled down her neck. It was a warm sunny day. 'I'd much rather use yours. Where did you get it?'

I was standing on the other side of the lock, winding away. 'A relic from our narrowboating days. I knew it would come in handy one day.'

Then we had nothing to do but wait as thousands of gallons of water poured through the open sluices. I climbed over the gates and we sat on the balance bar and chatted.

'How was your trip up to East Loch Tarbert?' Alison asked me.

'Wet, misty, damp, wet!' I answered.

'Welcome to Scotland,' Alison laughed, 'but it's a shame you didn't do it on a day like this; the scenery around lower Loch Fyne is amazing. On a clear day, you can see for miles.'

'I bet,' I replied.

'And Jenny says you had a horrible night in Tarbert, because of the Glasgow Fair?' She obviously saw a look of bafflement on my face – we were miles from Glasgow.

'It's what they call it. In England, it used to be known as Industrial Fortnight, when all the factories shut. Up here it was the Clyde shipyards and the engineering works and the Glaswegians flocked out of the city to the fairs.'

'Even in the rain?' I questioned her.

'Mostly in the rain, but all the kids from miles around still look forward to that fair. It's the most exciting time of the year, except for Hogmanay.'

'I can imagine. And thanks for coming to help us today, Alison.'

'My pleasure, it makes a nice change to be helping someone on their boat instead of having Fred yelling at everyone to fend off on our yacht. At least yours is made of steel.'

'Do you always come this way?' I asked her, as we both craned our necks to see if the level of the water in the lock was the same as that in the canal.

'Aye,' she replied. 'We always go sailing in the Western Isles and the canal saves us a passage of about 200 miles around the Mull of Kintyre. It gets really nasty out there. Oh, I think this lock's ready!'

I quickly re-crossed to my side of the lock.

We both positioned ourselves so we could use the whole of our weight to push open the heavy lock gates.

'I'd forgotten what hard work this is,' I grunted, trying to get a firm foothold.

'It will be worth it, I promise,' Alison replied, as she put her back against her bar. 'So many flowers in bloom this time of year and you'll see forests, mountains and sea lochs,' she panted, before standing up and rubbing her back. 'Nick and Lucy will be here soon to help you. I'll cycle along and get the next one ready.'

I walked to the head of the lock and crossed the gates and handed her my aluminium windlass.

'Oh, thanks, Shane!' she said gratefully. 'I hate those iron things.' Then she looked ahead and noticed someone filming us.

'Hi, Matt,' I said, waving. 'Where did you come from?'

He walked over and I introduced him to Alison.

'We don't usually have two cameramen with us, do we, Matt?'

'No,' he laughed, 'but Paul wants me to get some general views as he's read the canal is the most beautiful in the world. I'm in a hire car so I'm going to be going ahead. I just met Fred and he showed me a couple of places on the AA map where I can get you high up from down below, if that makes any sense?'

'Oh, I know where he means,' Alison said. 'We'll cross over a high embankment, by a football pitch, so it will look like we're floating in the air!'

'That's the one,' Matt replied. 'I hope I can find it.'

'I think Shane should sit on a chair on the roof – she'll look like Cleopatra sailing up the Nile,' Alison laughed.

We all watched as the not-so-royal barge *The Princess Matilda* made her entrance into the lock.

King Freddy was sitting on the gas locker with my bow rope in his hand, ready to tie up in the lock.

'I'd better go, or I'll be in shot,' Matt said, breaking into a run. Paul was on deck filming.

'Me too,' Alison said, climbing on her bike, 'and by the way, just to warn you, you can't turn over in bed up here without everyone knowing your business, so beware of the towpath grapevine.'

We moored up a few locks later by a conveniently placed pub; my sister said that they were probably expecting us. Jen and I had unanimously insisted that everyone else should go in for a pint. We had been preparing our lunch while the locks were being done, but it wasn't quite ready.

'We'll join you soon,' we said, with our heads poking out of the saloon windows, and we watched 'Team Matilda' chattering away as they walked along the picturesque towpath.

I had already taken the ice-cream container of Alistair's Manx Queenies out of the freezer. It was a warm balmy day, so they would defrost quickly; Jenny had brought her own picnic of food.

'Fresh bread, I made it this morning,' she said proudly, removing a snow-white ironed tea towel from on top of her basket. 'And a roast chicken...'

'A chicken,' I interrupted her, 'they'll all get food poisoning. You should have put it in the fridge!'

'Oh, it will be fine – it's been in the shade on the back deck. And anyway, *we* won't eat it!'

Jenny, like me, is a vegetarian.

'I'm all right Jack.' We giggled in unison. As children, our elder sister Jacqueline always got first pick of everything, so this was a family joke.

My mobile went – it was Sadie wanting to know how long we would be.

'I'll cook the Queenies to order when we get back,' I said to Jen, 'but that chicken is going in the fridge!'

We drew the curtains to keep the saloon cool and covered our culinary collation with fly nets. I had the keys in my hand, and Jenny said, 'You won't need to lock the boat.'

I ignored her and put the padlock on the wheelhouse door.

'What about all your bikes?' I asked her. They had been left on the grass by the visitor mooring pontoon. Only Fred's bike was on the roof of the barge – he was the only one of our visitors not to have used his to ride ahead to get the locks ready.

'Mrs Spall, I'm a skipper and just like your husband,' he had said winking, as he enjoyed a glass of lager with Tim, 'we both have wives and children to do this for us.'

'The bikes will be fine,' Jenny said. 'No one locks anything around here.'

'Hmmm, well I've locked the boat. Paul's got all his equipment in the back cabin.'

Jenny and I walked arm in arm along the towpath, picking the odd wild flower and enjoying the sunshine.

'Have you been to that café on the barge moored on the wall in East Loch Tarbert?' I asked her.

'Not yet, but if you say it's good I'll give it a go next time I'm passing through,' Jenny replied.

'A great selection of veggie food – we ate there before we ran away from the fair.'

'I'm sure it wasn't there the last time I drove through,' my sister said. 'You know we drive miles for something decent to eat. Come to think of it, we drive miles to get to a supermarket, which is something I did this morning because your daughter wanted roast chicken.'

We stopped to admire a canal-side garden before we crossed the Cairnbaan swing bridge to go to the pub of the same name. There was a woman who was cutting a bunch of Michaelmas daisies, and she came over to us and we chatted for a few minutes, mainly about the weather.

'We have to make the most of the sunshine, don't we?' my sister said to the lady.

'Aye, we do, we don't get many days like this in Scotland, but this fine weather after all the rain will bring out the adders. At twilight, my lawn is a slithering snake highway.'

'Snakes?' I said anxiously, looking across her manicured lawn.

She laughed at my discomfort. 'You'll be fine; they are more scared of us than us of them. They live in my compost heap, and there's lots of babbies at the moment,' she replied, pointing to a steaming heap of grass cuttings at the bottom of her garden.

'They lay eggs in your compost?' I asked, unable to disguise an involuntary shudder.

'Oh no,' she said matter-of-factly, 'they keep their eggs inside their bodies and give birth to live young. I've got a couple sunbathing on my patio making the most of the sun. Would you like to take a look?'

I grabbed Jenny's hand, before she could say 'yes please', and dragged her away, and we found Paul was at the bar of the nasturtium-festooned pub.

'What can I get you?' he asked us. 'I'm just ordering some food for me and Matt.'

'Why? We've got a bloody barge full of food!' I said rather more sharply than I had meant to.

'We don't want to intrude,' he replied almost shyly.

'Don't be so daft, Paul, you and Matt feel like family now!' I answered. 'We've got Arran cheeses, egg mayonnaise, Loch Fyne smoked salmon, Manx Queenies and a roast chicken, but I'd go for my food not my sister's!'

I could see Paul was salivating.

'I'll just have a tonic water, thanks, Paul,' my sister said, giving me a kick. 'I'm the designated driver.'

13th October 1996
Midnight
You had a Full Blood Count (FBC) on Friday and your
platelets were 19. The last transfusion had been on the 3rd

in New York before we flew on Concorde. This is the longest you have gone. At first it was every other day, then every five and today is eleven days. Looks like they are coming back. We saw Mr Wilf Pugsley (you refer to him as Pitchfork Pugsley) the thorax surgeon on Wednesday and he explained about cutting the section of the fungal infection out of your lung, if it's still there when the platelets come back. Apparently he will pull the ribs apart and take away the top half of your left lung and within two weeks you will be fit for more chemo. He made it sound so easy, IF the platelets come back and they pass 120, all steam ahead…but none of it is easy, is it? Selfish old me, all I can think about is what I go through, but I know what you go through too.

I'm alone in our bedroom now, as I write my mad midnight notes to keep my sanity, but I know eventually you will go back into hospital for more treatment and then I really will be sleeping completely alone again, all night alone. When I was a child our Jenny used to say, 'Make the most of it!' I wish I had learnt how to do it, but I haven't. You are watching TV downstairs and when you come to bed I'll be asleep, and I'll get the kids up in the morning and do the school run and life will go on, but for how long? You keep telling me that you don't want to go to St Christopher's Hospice if you relapse. We are both afraid this will happen as you've only had the two courses of chemo. Four or five will 'guarantee', not that there is a fucking guarantee…and you want to change your will and leave your mother £20,000. I want nothing but you, not money, or silly cars, or holidays or big houses. You are my life.

14th October 1996.
Midnight
We saw your consultant Dr Goldstone today; he says a bone marrow transplant may be in order – a cure. You are

depressed about this, I think because you think it's a last resort
– which it's not! What can we do but trust his judgement?
I suggested a second opinion but you say no. According to
Panos, there are nine or ten experts who have been discussing
your case. Tomorrow you have another bone marrow biopsy.
You tell me you wish you could reproduce a clone of yourself
so you could stay home and send the clone to be treated. 'I just
want to go back to work,' you added.

Brenda Blethyn came back from the States yesterday;
she's been away for three weeks publicizing Secrets and
Lies. *She came around with Mike and I cooked an organic*
chicken for our tea and she asked you if you would like a glass
of Chablis. You declined. I spoke to Jen who's coming for our
anniversary on Wednesday. I don't want it to be our last.
You and I, I can't help it sometimes. I only have this file on
my laptop and my midnight notebook. You still think I am
writing up my thesis, which I don't give a damn about. Life
without you would kill me. I watched the video today of my
dad, the one I made in Spain before he came home to die. My
dad…I miss him so much.

16th October 1996
Midnight
You were filming on location in Hitchin doing Home
Sweet Home *with Mike Leigh. You've known Mike as long*
as you've been married to me, longer.

Me and little Pas went to stay with you in Langford after
the school broke up, in that little terraced house. Stayed the
whole six weeks, but then we had to go back to Wolverhampton
in September, when the school holidays were over, and you
missed us so much after we'd gone that you phoned me and
said, 'Will you marry me?' We fell in love 31st May 1981,
and you asked me to marry you 12 weeks later. WE WERE

*STRANGERS and got married on a special licence as soon
as you had finished the job. It was at the wrap party that I
met Frances Barber for the first time, dear darling Frank.
You told me, 'You'll like her, she's from Wolverhampton.' I
don't know how I would manage without Frank, Miriam or
my sister Jen. They are my rocks.*

17 October 1996
Midnight
*Our fifteenth wedding anniversary yesterday and Jen came
down from Scotland; we had a lovely party with all of our close
friends. You lost your thumbnail, which had been chemo-fried,
as you were closing the curtains. When people were arriving
I was tearing up an old silk shirt to use as a bandage. Your
platelets are still low, so we were anxious to stop the bleeding.
It really hurt you and I was cooking and distracted, and
Jonny Sessions made a toast, deliciously mushy, and you said
how much you loved me and got a bit drunk (first time since
May), but your thumb woke you up when we went to bed. The
pain was dreadful – 'Been through two lots of chemo and lung
infections and this is the worst pain I've suffered,' you said.
We saw Dr Goldstone at 10am. A transplant is now definitely
on the cards. Scary and I fear, oh how I fear, for the future;
I want things to stay as they are because you are now reasonably fit and well and at home and according to the biopsy
still in complete remission. You could be cured, but you might
relapse; doctors don't let you off the hook, do they? Goldstone
says you should have more chemo, but you can't because of
your low platelets, and new research published last week indi-
cates you should now have a bone marrow transplant, but it's
dangerous because of your lung infection…and you could
have rejection and I'm scared and want to stop all this now.
I'm tired. I don't want you to go back into hospital.*

Team Matilda had become rather rowdy by the time we reached the end of the Crinan Canal. The Queenies and even the chicken had been eaten; the Arran cheese relished and most of my emergency supply of champagne had been quaffed. Tim and Fred were the most raucous of us all, and after we spent half an hour getting moored on a bend in the Crinan Basin we all sat on the grassy-banked hill enjoying the last of the sun.

'We never get weather like this, do we, Freddy, when we bring our boat through?' Alison said, as she and Jen began to offload the bikes from the roof of our barge. They had put them there at the penultimate lock as there was a long gap before the final one, and now they were getting ready to cycle back the nine miles of the canal.

Fred and Tim stood up to help them. Being moored on a bend meant the boat only touched the side at the bow and the stern. Naturally, the bikes were all in the middle and the two men almost slipped into the basin a couple of times.

'No, my darling, it always rains for us,' Fred eventually answered his wife, 'but, if you and the lassies want to start cycling back to the car, me and Nick will catch you up. You know we're faster than you, and Tim's just opened that bottle of Single Malt that Jen had hidden in her picnic basket.'

'How am I getting back?' Sadie said, as she took a dainty sip out of her plastic champagne flute.

'Me and Matt will drop you off,' Paul piped up, before quickly adding, 'well, Matt will, he's driving!' Tim had handed Paul a cut-glass tumbler of whiskey too.

'Where did you get that from?' I asked my husband. All my best glass-wear had been bubble-wrapped and put away to save them from stormy seas.

'I found them, and I've borrowed a couple of outfits out of your wardrobe – I knew you wouldn't mind,' my sister said, winking at me. Her rucksack was overflowing.

'I hope it was something from Image by Vanessa,' Tim laughed.

'How clever you are, Tim,' Jenny replied, but looked confused when Tim cheered, 'Hurrah!'

'Take no notice of him, Jen,' I said. We often swap clothes.

'I'll let you have them back when you drop off my picnic basket,' she said. Then, climbing astride her bike, she turned to Lucy, her goddaughter: 'Come on then, Lucy.'

'I'm getting a lift with Sadie.' Lucy hiccupped as she took a long swallow out of her plastic champagne flute. 'Do you have room in your boot for my bike, Matt?'

'We'll make room,' Matt replied. 'I wouldn't fancy riding a bike back there either!'

'I think you've had enough of that champagne now, Lucy,' her mother admonished her, as she too climbed onto her cycle.

'And watch you don't fall in!' Freddy shouted, as Jen and her best friend set out along the lumpy towpath.

'Bye, thanks for the help,' Tim and I yelled over the top of Freddy's laughter, as we all stood waving them goodbye.

It had just gone ten when Fred and Nick set out, but it was still light.

'One of the perks of living in the north-wesht is the shummer twilight shlingers,' Fred purred, as he tried to get his leg over the bar of his bike – three times.

'Come on, Dad,' a grumpy Nick commanded him. 'You go first, I don't trust you!'

Sadie, Lucy, Matt and Paul left us half an hour later.

'I've had a lovely day,' Sadie commented, as we kissed her goodbye.

'Far more fun than I have on Mum and Dad's yacht!' Lucy said, pretending to be thoroughly sober.

'A brilliant day,' Paul agreed.

'I wouldn't have missed it for all the world; those Queenies were amazing,' Matt joined in. 'This is the best job I've ever done – it doesn't feel like work.'

Then it was just Tim and me left sitting on the grassy, now dew-laden bank.

'I can't believe we are here,' we both said at the same time.

'A shame Pascale and Tilda couldn't make it,' I added. 'But they're visiting Jen after Rafe's wedding, so maybe they can all join us when we do the Caledonian Canal.'

The sky now was a shimmer of cobalt threatening blackness, as we watched our last four visitors walking around the basin towards the car park. They quickly merged into the shadows of the trees, which stood out against the backdrop of the purpling sky like cut-outs from a Victorian silhouette slide show. But we could still hear Sadie and Lucy's laughter and the slamming of car doors.

'Come on, let's go for a walk before it becomes completely dark,' Tim said, pulling me up from the damp grass. He assured me there would be no snakes.

We walked up the bank and there before us was Loch Crinan, a plate of black satin, that seemed to whisper, 'Come on in, the water is lovely.'

'Not tonight,' Tim said, taking my hand as if he had heard it too.

'I love you, Timmy.'

'I know. Come on, let's light that fire; it's turned chilly and we can finish off Fred's whiskey.'

We found out later that Nick became annoyed waiting for his father to keep up and arrived back at the car twenty minutes before Freddy. Jen and Alison had taken all the bikes to pieces to fit in the boot by the time Fred wobbled precariously out of the darkness.

Chapter Twenty-Seven
BOYS' TOYS AND CAULDRONS

Loch Crinan to Loch Shuna: 10 nautical miles

The following morning, a loud husky *TOOT TOOT* woke us. I quickly dressed to see where the noise had come from, leaving Tim in bed nursing a hangover. In the basin was an old steam tug with black sooty clouds bellowing out of its red and black smokestack. *TOOT TOOT* it went again.

'Come and have a look, Tim,' I shouted down to him from the wheelhouse.

We spent the rest of the morning sitting on a park bench outside a café watching the comings and goings in the busy basin. The star attraction was the tug; an old Clyde Puffer called VIC *32*.

'I think it plans to do the Crinan Canal backwards,' I said, as we watched the skipper reverse the raven-black and canary-yellow tug into the lock.

'No, I think they are taking on coal,' Tim said, pointing towards half a dozen middle-aged men with wheelbarrows.

It took them a good hour to do the work, and the more coal that was loaded the more the tug listed. *TOOT TOOT* the tug hooted, as it slowly lurched out of the lock. *TOOT TOOT* warning everyone to keep out of the way. Every time the whistle blew, more smoke bellowed from the smokestack. It was a smell that took me back to my childhood; I can still remember steam trains.

There was a skinny, nervous man in a tiny yacht by the basin café, and he became noticeably more fidgety as the tug was heading his way, but at the last moment the skipper put the mighty tugboat into reverse gear and she drew away. It took the master twenty minutes of tight manoeuvring before he turned the tug around and then headed back into the lock, pointy end first this time. *TOOT TOOT* she went, to let people know it was safe to move their craft, but there was nowhere anyone could go. The sea lock to the loch was on a lunch break and the greedy tug was hogging the canal lock. The men with the wheelbarrows were now stripped to the waist, as they loaded coal into the other hold, until the tug was once again level.

The waitress in the café had informed us that the men doing all the hard graft were paying passengers. 'The Puffers were used during the war, now they are toys for big boys to play with,' she had laughed.

We went back outside and chatted to the nervous man. It appeared he was an expert on the tug too.

'VIC stands for victualling inshore craft; they were used to move stores to larger ships. There's only a few of them left now. My name's Christopher,' he said, climbing out of his teeny yacht.

Tim and I spoke with him for a while. I don't know why, but I felt quite sorry for him. His clothes were scruffy and he looked unkempt. He told us he was a chaplain from the University of Greenwich and was doing a charity solo circum-navigation going clockwise.

We told him we were doing the same but in the opposite direction to him.

'How long has it taken you to get here?' I asked him.

'Three weeks – how about you?' he replied.

'About five years,' I laughed. I began to explain to him why we were doing it, 'It all began in 1996', but his eyes glazed over and I could see he wasn't interested.

18th October 1996
Midnight
Jenny went back to Scotland today. She told me all about her Kilimanjaro trip, which I had to pull out of because of your treatments. She's glad she went. I'd have hated it as it was all uphill! We took her to Heathrow and you and I just had enough time for a sandwich before the scan on your lung. Panos was there to tell the radiographer exactly where to take the X-ray so you weren't given any more radiation than necessary. We had a good laugh about that in the corridor, the amount of toxins you've had with the chemo!

What Is at Stake
You are reasonably well now, although your platelets are low, but they are coming back. If you don't have any more treatment of any kind, what could happen?

1) *Nothing, you'll be fine because you are 'cured'.*
2) *But could relapse at any time and will need more chemo or have a transplant. This could happen next week/month/year/decade.*
3) *However, if you have the transplant when you are really really well, this will be more favourable because you will be stronger.*
4) *If you do relapse, it will be harder to 'cure', but what are the guarantees that the transplant will be successful?*
5) *Should we get a second opinion?*
6) *Where would we get it from?*
7) *Let's just let it stay as it is now. No more treatment?*
8) *My instinct tells me this is the best course of action!*
9) *WHAT THE FUCK DO I KNOW?*

Tim had nipped back to the barge and returned with one of our windlasses, not the aluminium one, but a heavy iron one.

just in case our new friend needed it going through the canal. The lone sailor took it and thanked us. 'I could always use it as an anchor,' he laughed, before stepping down in his boat.

The tug had left the lock, fully laden with fuel, *TOOT TOOT*. We helped Christopher with his lines and walked around the basin and watched him going into the lock.

'Good luck,' we shouted, 'and fair weather!'

The Princess Matilda was moored almost next to the lock and we saw a man in a uniform giving her a look.

'Hi, Tim,' he said, putting out his hand as we approached him. 'Do you remember me? We used to sit at the same table at Butlins in the sixties. I'm Lee.'

They swapped nostalgic childhood recollections, before Lee said his lunch break was over. We walked the few steps back to the lock with him. We were just in time to see Christopher's yacht exiting the top gate.

'Did you hear what happened to him?' Lee asked us.

'No, what?'

'Well, people think he can't afford mooring fees so anchors overnight, and he got a real drenching off Holy Island in a force 6. He reckons he almost sank!'

'No wonder he looked so nervous!' Tim replied. 'Poor man, I feel for him; the sea is a cruel mistress.' I saw Tim shudder as if a dark cloud had swamped him.

The lockkeeper didn't seem to notice, but repeated what Tim had just said. 'A cruel mistress, I like that!' before changing the subject. 'Do you remember when everyone at Butlins used to cheer when a waitress dropped a tray?'

'Yes, I do,' Tim said, laughing, 'and on that note we're going to get shipshape; we're going through the sea lock at 1pm!'

'Where you heading?' Lee asked Tim.

'Loch Shuna to a marina with an unpronounceable name,' Tim replied, 'but it's only ten nautical miles.'

'You've got a great day for it. Just keep well clear of the Corryvreckan whirlpool; they say at high tide you can hear the roar of it from ten miles away!'

'What's he on about?' I questioned Tim, as we prepared to leave the basin.

'Corryvreckan?' Tim said with a hint of apprehension in his voice. 'It's one of the largest whirlpools in the world; tides from the east and west meet off the northern tip of Jura, even the Royal Navy stay clear.'

'We're not going that way, though, are we?' I looked at him, seeking assurance.

'No, darlin', I wouldn't put your life at risk, not for all the tea in China…we just have to contend with tiny whirlpools as we go through Dorus Mor.'

'How tiny?' I said anxiously.

'Hopefully no bigger than the ones we encountered in Northern Ireland…'

'And how far away will we be from Corryvreckan?'

'Far enough,' Tim replied.

The sea lock was a tight squeeze. A yacht had foolishly gone in before us; we had expected them to hold off, to let us in first. This was the sensible thing to do. *The Princess Matilda* is a potential crushing machine and they soon realized their mistake; there was a look of terror on the crew's faces as we barged in. There was the usual manic shouting: 'Fend off, fend off!' But this time it came from us; we had all our fenders on the wrong side, so there was a slight hint of panic as my fingers untied the knots. Tim and I had become used to having Jenny and the Moores crew for us and it came as a shock to realize it was just the two of us once more.

People enjoy standing around locks, as they are such potentially hazardous places because so many things can go wrong. Crews have been known to fall in and boats with a bow too far forward might be sunk as the lock chamber fills, the water pouring into the boat and not the lock. This particular lock, with a backdrop of Highland mountains, is a popular spot for spectators, who are known by the canal fraternity as gongoozlers.

Many of the spectators, including us, had gongoozlered around the sea lock when the VIC *32* tug went through. The coal carriers had become sweaty stokers, covered in rivulets of sooty sweat from feeding the boiler. Standing on the deck were their long-suffering wives, trying to keep out of the way of the men who were playing deckhands, casually tossing ropes to the lockkeepers as if this was something they did every day of their lives. There was no need to move fenders as tractor tyres protected the hull. Many of the gongoozlers had streaming eyes from the smokestack as the water level rose, but I heard no complaints. There was plenty of time for conversations between spectators and passengers; it takes a while to fill a large lock with water.

'Where are you going?'

'Loch Sween and the Fairy Isles.'

'Craighouse, Jura.'

We'd all watched as the tug *TOOT TOOTED*, setting out on the cruise of a lifetime. The bellowing clouds had been visible for miles.

Beside the lock is a hotchpotch of a hotel that had been added to over the decades. It stands out like a sore thumb amid the beauty of the Crinan Basin and the sea lock. Jenny said it had a fine reputation for good food and hospitality. Tim and I can vouch for this, because, while we were waiting for the lock to fill for us, a smartly dressed man in a cravat gave Tim a loaf of freshly made bread. Tim later told me he was the owner of the hotel and they had met earlier in the day. I waved my thanks from the bow, as it was *The Princess Matilda*'s turn to exit the lock; I was rewarded by thirty pairs of waving hands from our gongoozling friends.

Tim and I had only really seen Loch Crinan by night, but in the daylight we realized the lumps of black velvet we had seen the night before were actually small islands.

'And a castle!' I shouted, pointing to a craggy outcrop on the headland as we came out of the lock into the loch. The thick emerald loch-side forests were reflected in the silky water, as were the purple-topped mountains.

'This really is glorious,' Tim said, when I joined him back in the wheelhouse.

'Even the hotel looks better from the water,' I replied. 'Jen said that Princess Anne goes in there; she keeps a yacht some-where around here.'

'On a day like today, I wouldn't want to be anywhere else,' Tim said, with a sweep of his hand. 'Not a ripple, no wonder people come to Argyll and Bute for their holidays.'

There wasn't a cloud in the sky as we headed out of Loch Crinan. The tiny, uninhabited, crumpled-velvet islands were dwarfed by the majestic mountainous might of Jura.

'I'm staying well clear of the Gulf of Corryvreckan,' Tim said, snapping me out of my reverie. 'Then we're going to wend our way through those islets off the Craignish Penin-sula,' he said, pointing towards a headland.

My AA map was open, and, after a quick peep, I commented, 'It doesn't even have a main road.'

'Neither does Cruve Haven where we're heading.'

I flicked through the atlas index. 'There's no such place as Cruve Haven on my map. It must be isolated.'

'It's spelt C R A O B H, but the bloke in the marina office says it's pronounced Cruve.'

'Opposite the Isle of Shuna?' I asked him.

'That's the one,' Tim said.

'There are so many islands,' I remarked after another glance at my map.

I still had a tourist pamphlet that I'd got the day we had gone to Arran from Ardrossan on the ferry. It seemed so long ago, but it had only been a few days. I already knew from the pamphlet that Jura is the third largest of Argyll's Atlantic islands, at its widest it measures 8 miles and is 28 miles long. The highest mountains are the Paps of Jura, but the ones we could see was Cruach na Seilcheig. My mountain-climbing sister Jen had told me it was actually a 'Marilyn' – a hill of over 150 metres. I took her word for it, but the Marilyn on the other island towered above its neighbour. They looked like they wanted to have a fight.

'Stunning,' Tim said.

'Awe inspiring,' I answered. 'It's like something from *Lord of the Rings*. Hey, Tim? Do you think Tolkien came up here?'

'If you remember,' Tim said, 'Tolkien used to spend his holidays in Bournemouth; we've got a photo somewhere of us below that blue plaque.'

'When we were moored in Poole – bloody hell, that was two summers ago. Did you ever think we'd get this far, Tim?'

'No, darlin', but I think it's time we both re-read some Orwell,' he replied.

'Of course, he lived on Jura. I bet he didn't get many days like this when he locked himself away to write his books.'

I used binoculars to get a closer look at the rugged larger island behind us.

'I'm sure he didn't, but he must've had one hell of a view outside his bedroom window. Apparently he almost drowned when he got too close to the Corryvreckan whirlpool, but was rescued by a fisherman,' Tim said. 'Thank goodness it's all so calm today, and we have the tides right.'

'I think he wrote *1984* on Jura—'

'Why's that yacht stopped?' Tim said, interrupting me.

For the last hour we had been following the yacht that had been in the sea lock with us. It had sails out, but they had told us they had planned to motor through Dorus Mor, which is on the edge of the Gulf of Corryvreckan. Our satiny sea now resembled a fast-flowing, shallow brook that was running over pebbles.

'I think they're in trouble,' Tim said anxiously. 'They are right in the middle of Dorus Mor; they must have lost their engine.'

On top of the ripples were angry spiteful twirling whirl-pools, the size of the tyres on the Puffer. The stranded yacht began to tremble and shake. Tim gave *The Princess Matilda* some more speed, while I found a long rope, just in case we needed to give them a tow. Fortunately, we had no problem going over the malicious mini-vortexes. As soon as we were close enough, Tim shouted, 'Is everything OK?'

He got a thumbs up from the crew – they had got the spare outboard working.

'I'll go make some sandwiches with the bread that man gave you,' I said to Tim once the drama was over. Once again we were on a silky sea. I returned with our lunch and a couple of DVDs that we had got free with a Sunday paper; every now and again they reissue old 1940s classics. We had already watched one of them, *A Matter of Life and Death* – a romantic fantasy film by Pressburger and Powell, starring David Niven and Roger Livesey. Actually, we had watched it several times, but for some reason the other DVD, *I Know Where I'm Going*, was still unplayed.

'We'll watch this one tonight, Tim,' I said. 'Another Press-burger and Powell, starring Wendy Hiller and Roger Livesey – according to the cover, she's a head-strong heroine, that's me, and he's the local laird and naval officer, that's you, and it's all set around the islands.'

I could sense Tim was about to do his husky-voiced Roger Livesey impersonation, so I attempted to nip it in the bud. 'And I just googled Corryvreckan, on your iPad; do you know what it means?'

'*Aaaah, Corryvreckan, my dear,*' Tim replied – it was the theatrical throaty devil-may-care Livesey impression, '*is the Gaelic word for cauldron.*'

I laughed, and said, 'I can't wait to see the real thing – I mean Roger, not the cauldron. I may even light the fire again.'

'*I think you should, my dear, I can smell rain in the air. I fear this may be the end of our Scottish summer.*'

'That's enough of that, you'll hurt your throat. How much further?'

It had begun to drizzle and a smoky mist was smothering the colour out of the deciduous forests on the mainland. But behind us the majestic Marilyns of Scarba and Jura were topped with a crown of blushing schoolgirl pink.

'*Shuna to port and the wee isle of Eilean Arsa to starboard, you will soon spot the sheltered entrance to Craobh Marina three cables to starboard.*'

I realized we had picked up another passenger. Roger would be with us for the rest of the day.

We moored in torrential rain but didn't bother locking up the wheelhouse before walking up the long pontoons to go to the marina office. There wasn't anyone aboard any other boats.

'*There's no one here,*' Tim/Roger said.

'Nor a signal on my laptop dongle or my mobile either,' I replied.

The manager of the marina said we could use his landline, before he left for the night. 'Sometimes if the wind's blowing in the right direction, you might be able to pick up Wi-Fi by the refuse bins. The trouble is,' he said by way of an explanation, 'we've got the mountains of the Lunga Estate behind us and that stops the mobile signals, and this isn't helped much because the marina was created by linking that hilly island to the right with that island to your left, so you won't get a TV reception either unless you have a booster.'

'We'll manage; we'd planned to watch a DVD,' Tim replied, 'but we've a more pressing problem because I need to get to Oban tomorrow. Is it far?'

'About twenty-odd miles.'

We didn't get round to watching the DVD, as one of our toilets had become blocked. Tim left me to it. 'I need to call my agent from the public phone box, find out where that sound studio is tomorrow and book a cab. My voiceover agent is a saint.'

'So am I,' I replied, as I snapped on a pair of rubber gloves to attack the lavatory.

Tim came back just as I was throwing the rubber gloves in the bin.

'After using the phone box I had a bit of a walk to see if I could get a signal on my mobile. The only place with a half-decent signal was by a war memorial,' he said, showing me a photograph on his iPhone.

'That's so sad,' I said, after reading the inscription on the grey weather-worn slab.

'It made me cry too,' Tim said.

The inscription was for just two members of the same clan, who had died during the Great War. The younger one was a Captain Iain MacDougall who died aged 27 on 1st September 1914, and the other his father, Lieutenant Colonel Stewart MacDougall who fell at Vermelles, aged 61, 21st July 1915.

'You are a long time dead,' I said.

'Yes, that's why we have to make the most of every single day,' Tim replied, giving me a hug. 'I almost didn't make it, did I?'

Chapter Twenty-Eight
HIRSUTE AND WILD

The Oban cab Tim's agent had booked had a driver called Dougal, and he was waiting for us by the marina office. 'Oban, where you are wanting to go today,' he said with a booming voice, 'or, as the Gaelic speakers among us say, *An t-Òban,*' before booming even more loudly, so that seagulls scattered as his voice ricocheted around the amphitheatre-like marina, 'is the gateway to the Isles. *An t-Òban* is the seafood capital of Scotland and means little bay.'

He ceremoniously opened the rear passenger doors for us to get into his spotless car.

'I hear you are away back to the great metropolis soon? I hear you plan to get a taxi to Loch Long, and then an airplane to *Londinium* from Glasgow, as you have a son getting married, is that correct?'

I wondered if he had been hiding when I had rung my sister Jen from the red phone box. He looked at me through his rearview mirror for confirmation.

I gave him the briefest of nods.

'I can give you a very good fare to Loch Long, and as you can see I have a very nice car, room to spread out, and we could take the drover's old road. "Great stalwart hirsute men, shaggy and uncultured and wild, who look like bears…" That's when men were men and the bonny lassies were all grateful,' he said, laughing at his own joke. 'The Highland drovers left more than cattle dung behind them as they drove their beasts to England.' He guffawed.

We were now at the junction of the A816, having come off the unmetalled track. Dougal opened his glove box and took out a business card and gave it to Tim.

'A very good price – you won't get anyone better than me,' he boomed, as he put on a pair of beige kid-leather driving gloves, smoothing them so the holes were aligned perfectly across his knuckles. He flexed his fingers several times, before switching on his indicator lights; he checked his rearview mirror, looked left, then right, then left, then right, before turning left towards Oban. His gloves stayed at ten to two for the whole twenty minutes as he pushed and pulled on the steering wheel. I asked him to drop us off at the Caledonian Hotel. Tim's saintly agent had said the studio was close by. Tim paid Dougal the whole fare and put the cab number in the nearest bin.

When Tim had finished his voiceover we walked into the town. It wasn't far; Oban is a small compact place with handsome seafront shops selling postcards, tartan scarves, kilts, haggis, shortbread, umbrellas, pocket mackintoshes and miniature bottles of single malt whiskey; not in every shop, just most of them. The others sold ice cream. The A816 ends more or less at the port, and from there you can drive your car onto a Caledonian MacBrayne ferry, or, as they are known to the locals, the CalMacs. That is if you want to visit any of the Western Isles. My sister Jen and her friends the Moores often go to Coll, a small island west of Mull in the Inner Hebrides. It has a population of 164, except when the Moores et al visit. Sometimes, the weather is so atrocious that the CalMac is unable to dock, and islanders and visitors have to wait for the gales to die down before they can get off the island. This can be difficult if you have a sick relative on the mainland, but the coastguard will send out a helicopter for any medical emergencies.

Tim and I saw more than the CalMacs and the local fishing boats as we had our lunch in a harbour-side restaurant. A few feet away from us was an elegant small cruise liner called the *Hebridean Princess*. It looked like it had just had a paint job, the white of the top decks sparkled in the sun, contrasting with the deep royal blue of the rustless hull. Around the blue of the hull was a band of gold. Through the newly washed grand windows, Tim and I were able to spy on what was happening in the premier cabins. It was obvious that the occupants were not passengers, but a posse of tartan-clad chars busily vacuuming and dusting.

'That's a handsome-looking ship,' Tim said to the sulky-faced waitress who had come to take our order.

'Oh aye,' she said, without looking up, 'the royal family have just come back off their annual holidays around the Western Isles; the Queen always uses the *Hebridean Princess*.'

With that, she moped away.

'She must have just fallen out with her boyfriend,' I observed.

'Bet she would've smiled at Prince William,' Tim laughed.

'It's certainly a busy harbour,' Tim said as we walked off our lunch with a stroll around the wharf.

'And the view of the town is better from here too,' I remarked.

The town sits beneath a wooded hill on top of which is an arched Roman amphitheatre.

'*That must be McCaig's Tower*,' Tim said, doing a boom-voiced impersonation of the cab driver. '*Mr McCaig was a philanthropist and an admirer of the Coliseum in Rome; the building of the tower saved a local stonemason from starving during the long winter months.*'

'Oh stop it,' I said, laughing. 'He's obviously proud of the place.'

'And I'm freezing cold,' said Tim. He was only wearing a thin jacket and a foldaway mac. Everyone else was wrapped up in tartan scarves and fleeces.

'Do you know, you are starting to look like one of those hirsute old drovers?' I said, running my hands around his chin. 'I think we should go into one of the Highland tourist shops and get you some grey shaggy tweed and a kilt.'

He had begun to grow his whiskers for a film, but as with most UK film projects the producers were still trying to raise the money. Tim hung onto his beard, just in case. 'I know as soon as I shave it off, they'll get the green light.'

'Let's go and have a drink in the Caledonian Hotel,' Tim said, pulling me through crowds of puffer jacket-wearing tourists, not so much promenading as bracing themselves against the sea breeze.

'It's worse than Oxford Street during the sales, but with a wind machine,' I said breathlessly.

The grand Victorian, turreted hotel dominates the seafront and is steps away from the ferry port and the station.

'There's no doubting that Oban is on the tourist trail,' I said, as we escaped the day-tripping hordes that were deposited daily by the 'executive coach' load.

Tim led the way into the hotel reception, where several manicured Polish receptionists ignored us and we followed the green plastic sign that pointed the way to the bar and lounge.

'Oh, it's a bit disappointing inside, the outside promised so much,' I remarked, as I followed Tim into the bar. I had his iPad in my bag, hoping to get onto the hotel's Wi-Fi. I also had a charger. I looked around to see if there was a free table with an electric socket – I am always stealing electricity. In the past I have unplugged six-foot-high standard lamps to charge a phone or a laptop; once I accidently dimmed half an illuminated Christmas tree.

Tim came back with the drinks, just in time to hear me muttering under my breath. I had moved a pretend palm tree out of the way; it had soggy-looking crisps, a couple of bendy straws and three empty sachets of salad cream in the plastic terracotta pot.

'What are you doing?' he asked me.

'The sockets have been blocked with Mothercare socket covers. Health and safety my foot. More likely just tight-fisted Scottish buggers,' I complained.

'I'm going to the loo, then we'll find somewhere you can charge that damned iPad and get online!'

Tim was back from his 'comfort break' swifter than usual.

'Gordon Bennett, that's the most disgusting gents I've ever been in; there was poop all over the shop. Let's get a cab back to Craobh! They must have Wi-Fi in that pub at the marina, and hopefully a clean lavatory.'

3rd November 1996
Midnight
Shit happens…Another month, how long has it been since this nightmare began? May, June, July, August, September, October. Pam, the head nurse, told me, 'The next six months are going to be the hardest of your life.' The bad times are not over yet. We are in limbo. Dr Goldstone wants to see you again in two weeks. He wants to wait, your platelets are still not back, although you don't need transfusions as often. You have only had one lot since we got back from New York.

5th November 1996
Midnight
Your mother's birthday, we had a bit of a do and built a small bonfire. I have spent days preparing the garden for winter, cutting and pruning, planting out bulbs for next

spring; how little I knew what the future would bring when I planted out the sweetpeas earlier this year. I pulled them up yesterday to burn. A season passed. I prepare the ground, digging in the compost, thinking next year, next year. The wind is blowing fiercely. We moved the shed to the bottom of the garden yesterday. Next year, next year, I chanted as I dug with my spade. My plans for the garden are for next year. An incantation.

Our bonfire party was made up of Brenda, Michael, Sylvia, Maff, Tony the runner from Outside Edge, Miranda Richardson, Sadie, her friend Beatrice and Rafe. You light the fireworks. What a daft, thrilling thing to do when you have low platelets. I have to go inside, I can't bear to watch.

14th November 1996
Midnight
Platelets gone up by two, we see Goldstone tomorrow. We know something has to happen soon. You are so fit, you even did a day's filming on Sunday. The last time you left the house to film you didn't come home for three months. I'm back to researching my PhD at Goldsmiths most mornings, until lunchtime. You drop me off and pick me up, the porter always lifts the barrier so you can drive in through the gates. He doesn't do that for anyone else!

27th November 1996
Midnight
I've not written for a while, your platelets have dropped by one. We saw Rafe and Sadie's school drama festival last night and were impressed with Rafe. 'Very naturalistic, son,' you told him, and he beamed with delight. Sadie was a narrator. A big girl stood in front of her so we couldn't see her, but she read well. You had another CT scan on Monday

to see how the fungal infection is doing in your lung. Panos
did a biopsy and it all looks 'good'. Whatever that means. We
had lunch in the Italian, we call it the bone marrow restau-
rant, I don't know what the waiter thinks as you stagger in
there like a drunken sailor, as you are always so dopey from
the anaesthetic. Any other doctor than Panos would insist
you stay in bed for two hours, but he knows I look after you. I
order you the lamb chops and by the time they are cooked you
are back to normal.

It's my birthday on Tuesday. I shall be 43, but I feel
50. My hair is falling out in clumps and my skin is grey
and pallid.

I was in the garden yesterday. I was digging up the
clematis when you called for me. It was so upsetting. A
neighbour had come around to tell us the Siamese kitten had
been run over. So upsetting, that poor little creature with
the life gone out of her. We buried her in the garden after
taking her to the vets (just in case). I shovelled in the earth
on top of her little body, which we'd wrapped in a pillow slip.
Death, final, gone. We put stones over her so she wouldn't
be found by the foxes. The kids are inconsolable. Sadie put a
note on our pillow, when we went to bed, in her large childish
scrawl: 'MUM AND DAD I LOVE CLEO SO MUCH I
REALLY MISS HER PLEASE COME BACK CLEO. WE
ALL LOVE YOU.' She's still only a little girl.

There was a young woman in the loch-side marina pub trying
to entice two highchair-bound toddlers to eat. Strapped to her
chest was a tiny baby. With a weary countenance, she watched
me as I found an electric socket to charge Tim's iPad.

'Are you off *The Princess Matilda?*' she asked me, as she
re-scooped regurgitated mush back into the mouths of her
two older children.

'Yes I am,' I replied. 'How old are your kids?'

'Three, two and three months,' she answered. 'I hope they didn't wake you in the night? We're on the yacht on the pontoon next to you. We must've been asleep when you arrived. I catch up when I can, but the baby wakes the others. I see dawn break every morning.'

'We didn't hear a thing, did we, Tim?' I said, as my husband brought over our drinks.

'Is it just you and the kids on the boat then?' I asked her, trying not to wince from Tim's kick under the table.

'At the moment. My husband was called back to Edinburgh on business a couple of days ago. We're supposed to be on holiday…'

'You're not having much of a break,' I said, rubbing my shin.

'What did you kick me for?' I later asked Tim.

'Don't exaggerate, it was only a tap, and you shouldn't be nosey, asking personal questions like that. She could've been a single mother…'

'On benefits? I don't think so. Have you seen the size of that yacht? It looks brand spanking new, and, as for the husband's important business back in Edinburgh, he obviously just wanted a rest! Poor Christine.'

We had walked back to the boat with her; she had the toddlers in lifejackets, holding each one by the hand. Tim helped her get them back onboard the yacht – there were safety nets everywhere.

'If there's anything we can do to help, just give us a knock,' Tim said to her. 'We're not going out again tonight.'

Christine took us up on Tim's offer, and tapped on the saloon window a couple of hours later. Tim and I paused the DVD we had been watching.

'The little ones are in their cots fast asleep,' she said, the baby still strapped to her chest, 'and I've locked the door from the outside, so you can get in, but they can't escape. I hate to impose, but would you just keep an ear open? I need to get my washing out of the machine or they'll have nothing clean to wear tomorrow.'

'Of course,' Tim and I answered together.

'I was going to hose the boat down anyway,' Tim added. 'And Shane was going to help, so we'll both be on the pontoon and if we hear a peep we'll run to the utility block and find you.'

She gave us a look of such gratitude that it was almost too painful to see; her face was etched grey with tiredness. 'Thank you so much,' she said, as she turned to walk up the long pontoon.

I looked through the open saloon window of *The Princess Matilda* and saw the DVD, *I Know Where I'm Going*, had been paused on the scene where the boat had lost its engine and was heading towards the maelstrom of the Corryvreckan whirlpool.

'Pressburger and Powell, what wonderful film makers. There was no CGI special effects in those days,' Tim said, peering over my shoulder. The frozen shot was the boat about to be sucked into the watery equivalent of Dante's Inferno.

'I hope they make it,' I replied, straightening up and stepping two paces to peer through the porthole of the yacht to check for the ninth time that the toddlers had not stirred.

'*I'm sure our leading characters will make it, my dear, I'm sure they will,*' Tim said, doing his Roger Livesey, sexy but rakishly dependable, impression for the ninth time. '*Now be a good wee lassie and close all the windows so I can give this heavy old bitch a good wash so she'll be nice and clean when we get back from London.*'

*

The next morning I packed all the food from our defrosting fridge into carrier bags and tapped on Christine's yacht. She ducked beneath a makeshift clothesline of children's clothes, her baby still strapped to her chest and the toddlers in life-jackets hanging onto her skirts.

'Tim said you wouldn't want any of this,' I said, offering up our leftovers, 'but I hate to throw good food away. There's half a loaf of bread, cheese, milk, some tomatoes, fruit—'

She didn't let me finish. 'Shane, you are an angel. I'm running low on supplies and my husband won't be here till five and now I can make sandwiches.'

Tim had our roller bag on the pontoon and was holding a three-quarter-full bottle of Chablis in his hand.

'Would this be any use to you?'

'I'm in heaven! Thank you both so much,' she said, bending to reach for the wine. 'It's been so long I've forgotten what it tastes like. My husband and I will share this tonight. He's promised to cook me some lamb chops, if he remembers to go to the butchers. When will you be back?'

'A couple of weeks,' we both replied.

'We might still be here,' Christine said, as she waved us goodbye. 'And we'll keep our eye on *The Princess Matilda*...'

Chapter Twenty-Nine
WEDDINGS AND MONSTER MUNCH

Craobh to London and back: approximately 1,000 miles

We had two celebrations while in London, Sadie's 25th birthday and, shortly afterwards, Rafe and Elize's marriage. There had been lashings of rain on the morning of the wedding, but the kilted Highland piper who welcomed the guests to the Berkshire churchyard didn't miss a soggy note. The sun came out just as the radiant bride arrived with her father at the flower-festooned church. This was the second Spall wedding of the year, but Tim had been spared making the father-of-the-bride reception speech. Instead, he gave a reading from the apse of the tiny church, of a poem he had written especially for the occasion.

As love is as the sea so is the sea as love,
Oft smooth and calm, betimes rough and angry,
Off high and low tides, one quick the other sluggish,
'neath the surface sharp rocks and lovely creatures
Conflict in meetings and turbulent confusions,
Wind sped passions crashing in glorious union,
Cruel and wonderful as the power of The Cosmos,
Bountiful and nourishing as the horn of plenty,
Soothing and warm as the breath of cherubim,
Cold and wicked as the eyes of evil,
Yet ever constant continuous and true,

The elemental liquid womb of the giver of all,
The moving blood of God the everlasting truth.

After the wedding, we flew back to Scotland with our five-year-old granddaughter Matilda, or, as she likes to be known, Tilda or Til. My sister Jenny was there to meet us, wearing one of my Image by Vanessa outfits. Her house on Loch Long is about a forty-minute drive from Glasgow airport. The Moores invited us for dinner and we caught up with all their news and they with ours.

'I envy you your next journey,' Fred said to us. 'It's supposed to be incredible that passage from Craobh to Kerrera. We've not done it yet, but my brother Jeremy has a boat in Oban and says it's pretty amazing, even when the mountain peaks are thick with pelts of cloud—'

'And scary too if I get it wrong,' Tim said, interrupting. 'I know it's only seventeen nautical miles, but I've been going to bed with my *Reeds* every night, we're definitely not doing anything dangerous with Tilda onboard.'

'Aye,' Fred replied, 'of course you won't, Timothy, but if you do your homework and get the tides right...'

'The thing is, Fred, you are a trained skipper, but no one has taught me if I'm doing it properly.'

Fred laughed and refilled Tim's glass and said, 'You are one of the few sailors I know who works out his passage on a paper chart; most folk rely on electronics.'

'You doubt yourself too much, Timmy,' as always was my response.

One of the Highland Hotels that Jenny oversees as executive manager is in Fort William, which is north of Oban, and she was going to drop us off at Craobh 'on the way'.

'The scenery is so beautiful, this is why I love it,' Jenny said, 'except when landslides close the Arrochar Alps on the A83, which necessitates a sixty-mile-plus detour around the western shore of Loch Fyne.'

Jenny had proposed we should have an early dinner at the Loch Fyne seafood restaurant, even though my sister and I are vegetarians. The Loch Fyne Oyster Bar chain of restaurants always has a reasonable selection of fishless food; we both fortunately love chips and mushy peas.

'Can I have calamari?' my granddaughter had piped up. She has been a regular at Loch Fyne since she was six months old, although she then got her dinner through a circuitous route.

'Of course you can, Matilda,' her great-aunty Jenny replied. 'Then we can stop off in Inveraray so you can all go to the Co-op and get in some groceries and wine...'

'And some more Hello Kitty DVDs and a Swizzel Candy Whistle?' Tilda asked hopefully.

Her granddad promised we would try. 'You're on your holidays now, Til!'

The original Loch Fyne restaurant began life as a roadside shed selling local oysters, before moving into an old cow byre close to the head of the loch. This was before Tilda's time, although she refuses to believe it. Our family has visited the restaurant and delicatessen many times over the years while visiting my sister.

After parking her car we all stopped to admire the astonishing panoramic views over the longest of Scotland's sea lochs. Loch Fyne extends out forty-odd miles into the Sound of Bute, where we had come into the Crinan Canal. The loch was formed millions of years ago when the glaciers that carved out the deep U-shaped valley had retreated and the rising sea had rushed in forming a lake. Beneath the surface of the gunmetal-grey still waters of the loch are mysteries that are best concealed. At least the cauldron of the Corryvreckan whirlpool is predictable, governed by the moon and the tides. Illness is not.

Tim theatrically drew in deep breaths of pure air. It was times like these that reminded me how ill my husband had been in 1996. After his second course of aggressive chemotherapy, when his immune system had been flattened, a part of his lung had been invaded with spores. Because of this, a fungal infection had spread like mould through a ripening blue cheese. This was something that had worried me more than it had Tim. He wasn't really aware, or chose not to be, how life threatening this had been. As long as he had been 'well', in remission, this pocket of disease was contained, held in check by his antibodies that had built a protective dam around the rotten small core of his lung. But all it would take to break through the weakest membrane of this protective shield was a dodgy immune system; a relapse would probably kill him.

'We now know where this tidal lagoon pours out to,' Tim said, after taking half a dozen more breaths of the fine unpolluted air. 'All these years coming to this restaurant with my sister-in-law,' he continued as he took her arm, 'and just a couple of weeks ago we had *The Princess Matilda* at the brink end of this very loch.'

'Yes and I did most of the locks to Crinan Basin,' Jenny laughed.

The restaurant was almost empty; at lunchtimes customers have to queue for a table. We congratulated ourselves on arriving at 6.30 not 8pm.

'Have you booked?' a jolly-faced Scottish waitress asked us.

'But you don't take reservations?' my sister quizzed her.

'No, not for lunch, but we do in the evenings during the summer,' the waitress answered, tapping away on a computer, 'and we can't fit you in.'

'But you've twenty empty tables and my sister-in-law is almost a local,' Tim said 'and we eat really quickly.' He shot her a charming smile.

'Aye, but it would take us too long to turn a reserved table around,' the waitress replied. The jolly face had been replaced with one that would curdle cream.

'Can't we have that one?' I asked hopefully.

'No, it's booked.'

'How about the tables back there by the toilets?' my sister asked. 'I come here all the time when I have visitors.'

We all waited for the computer to say no, but Jenny played her trump card. 'We've got a little one here, and she's very hungry,' she said, patting Matilda on the head, hoping that would get us an in.

'No.'

We left the cavernous empty cow byre not wanting to ruin a splendid day. Jenny and I are from the Midlands and can turn, when faced with adversity, into downright nasty cows, but we keep it in check. Our father reared us on tales of women stripping down to their stays and punching the 'lights' out of each other. We have often wondered whether this reference to the innards of livestock, i.e. the lungs, is one of the reasons we don't eat meat.

'It's not like we can just nip to a bloody McDonald's,' Jenny said with annoyance as we fastened our seatbelts. 'We're in the bloody middle of bloody nowhere... Oh, Tilda,' she grimaced as she looked over her shoulder at her great-niece on her booster seat. 'I am so sorry for swearing. Your aunty

Jenny is very naughty but I'm very hungry and that makes me bad tempered.'

Matilda rooted around in her pink spotted Hello Kitty rucksack and brought out a bag of Monster Munch. 'It's OK, my bloody mummy swears too. Would you like one of these, Aunty Jenny?' she asked, offering her the bag.

The four of us shared the jumbo bag of Monster Munch and a stale packet of crisps that I had discovered, along with four mouldy cherries, in a bag of rubbish on Jenny's back seat. For the next half an hour, as my sister did hairpin bends, we laughed so much we had to stop for a comfort break behind a lichen-encrusted heritage stone wall.

We had an excellent dinner at eight in the welcoming candlelit bar of the George Hotel, in the royal burgh of Inveraray, the ancestral home of the dukes of Argyll. Even our five-year-old admired the Georgian whitewashed buildings with the black window casings that Inveraray is famous for, but after our feast she had her eye on the traditional black and white building that housed the Co-operative supermarket, and she wasn't interested in the dividend.

'Inveraray is the county town of Argyll,' Jenny tried to inform Tilda as she helped her choose from a display of Hello Kitty DVDs. 'The duke was the head of the powerful Clan Campbell—' But Tilda interrupted the history lesson because Tim had unwrapped a Swizzel Candy Whistle. She pursed her lips and blew *TOOT TOOT*.

Chapter Thirty
SMALL ISLANDS

Craobh to Kerrera: 17 nautical miles

It was late, chilly and damp by the time we arrived in Craobh and waved Jenny goodbye. Tilda insisted we bring along a scooter that she keeps at Jen's house. The scooter was placed on the roof of one princess, and the other princess was tucked into her bunk with a hot-water bottle.

The Princess Matilda was now all alone at the end of the long lonely pontoon. Christine and the babies had left Craobh on their yacht. We had told Til about the toddlers and she had been looking forward to making their acquaintance. However, the next day Tilda would make new friends as we lunched outside the loch-side pub.

'Besides,' Tim had said, 'we want a perfect day when we go. I know it's been sunny the past couple of days, but it's been a bit too breezy and even the lesser bullying breeze can turn into something larger. I'm not taking any risks with Til onboard. I want to make sure I've got our next passage thoroughly worked out, it's going to be tricky.'

Matilda and I left him to his homework while we explored the little self-catering holiday village. There wasn't a great deal to see, one shop, one pub and a chandlery, but there was always a number of children on the pontoon by the gantry and Tilda shyly chatted to a couple of boys with crab lines. The water was so clear that the crabs were sitting ducks, and didn't have much of a chance to escape until they were unceremoniously tossed out of the buckets back into the loch. Tilda made do with a fishing net but mostly caught weeds.

'Come on, let's go and see what your granddad is doing,' I said on the final afternoon. Tilda had been with us now for four days, although the boat had been moored there for over two weeks. We stopped and chatted to a few people; it must have been the sunshine that had folks rushing from Glasgow and Edinburgh to use their boats.

'Your husband says you're away tomorrow,' a melodic lady from Wales updated me. 'My husband's been telling him about the best time to get through Cuan Sound.'

'Don't tell me what happens if we go through it at the wrong time,' I laughed.

'Oh, you'll be like a champagne cork popping out of a bottle,' she replied, winking at Tilda who was pulling at my hand.

'You're a long way from home,' I remarked. 'We wintered our boat in Wales last winter.'

'So I hear. Me and my old man came up here for a holiday twenty years ago and never went back. I think your daughter wants to go.'

'She's my chum not my mummy,' Tilda piped up.

'My daughters call me Mum-Chum, and my granddaughter has picked up the name too,' I explained.

'We all have to be so careful nowadays, women having babies in their sixties. I didn't want to put my foot in it,' our Welsh friend said, bidding us goodbye.

I wasn't sure if that was a compliment.

Tim was sitting in the dinghy when we got back to our pontoon. 'Do you want to come for a ride, Til?' he asked her.

'Yes please,' she said, happily abandoning her fishing net next to the scooter.

We had established the ground rules on the first morning

that she was only allowed to scoot when supervised and had to wear her lifejacket at all times. I had bought it for her in Cardiff during the winter half-term break. She had long outgrown her baby one that she had last worn when we anchored off Sandbanks for the Bournemouth airshow during the summer of 2008. I quickly grabbed a couple of grown-up lifejackets out of the wheelhouse and threw one to Tim. 'I want to see what's going on on that little craggy island over there,' I said, pointing towards the one by the manmade causeway that keeps the marina safe. Tim and I had become quite territorial and had seen at least two people coming and going from the mainland.

Tim rowed, not wanting to disturb the tranquillity of the afternoon by using the outboard. Tilda wasn't quite as considerate as she enjoyed scaring the waterfowl by blowing the emergency whistle on her lifejacket. She had been given instructions on what to do should she fall in, and blowing the whistle was part of her man-overboard training.

'What do you do if you fall in and we can't see you, Til?'

TOOOOOOOOOT.

We left the haven of Craobh reluctantly at twelve the following day. 'This has to be the loveliest marina in the country,' I said to Tim as he stood on the pontoon by the bow. He handed me my bowline and Tilda, my little shipmate, helped me roll it up and put it out of the way. The two of us cautiously made our way along the gunwale back to the wheelhouse. My granddaughter is careful and follows my instructions to the letter: 'Keep hold of the grab rail at all times.' The weather was perfect for our next voyage; the gentlest of warm summer breezes smoothed the waters within the marina, so all it reflected was the blue of the sky.

'I'm going to take my time, take it slowly; we're barely doing three knots,' Tim explained as we left the shelter of the marina's breakwater. 'I have to go through Cuan Sound on the floodtide. I don't want to get there too soon.'

Over the years, my husband and I have travelled all over the world, but the scenery we experienced that day was truly awe-inspiring. The distant majestic mountain ranges of the Scottish Highlands were smudged in a shimmering purple bruise of a psychedelic haze. But closer to home, Loch Shuna sparkled in the sunlight like a blue-tinged slab of marble that had been decorated with randomly tossed pies, but the pies were feathery fern-topped little islands

'Are you going slowly so we can enjoy the scenery?' I asked Tim. But I didn't await a reply, as there was too much to see. 'Look over there, Til,' I said, as I picked her up for a bird's eye view. 'There's a Billy Goat Gruff on that island.' I had to put her down; she takes after her father and is a longshanks.

Tim and I both laughed as we watched her peering through a small pair of binoculars that we had given to her that morning. She was very proud of them and had practised her fine-focusing techniques.

'He's got curly horns, Chum. Do you think he can swim?'

'That's a good question,' I replied. 'It's a shame that Matt is meeting us in Kerrera and not with us for this voyage today. The scenery really is stunning.'

'Who's Matt?' Tilda quizzed me.

'Oh, he films us sometimes,' I answered.

'Well, I don't want to be filmed,' Tilda said firmly.

'You don't have to do anything you don't want to do,' Tim assured her.

There were so many small islands. 'Do they all have names, Tim?' I asked, changing the subject. 'I mean the islands, not the goats?' The skipper had slowed our speed down so the Perkins engine was hardly ticking over.

'That one over there to port is Eilean Gamhna,' he said, pointing towards one of the larger ones.

'You sound like you're clearing your throat. Say it again,' I interjected innocently, before ducking so he couldn't spit in my face this time. He pinched me instead and glanced at his speedometer.

'We're punching a bit of tide now because we're crossing the entrance of Loch Melfort,' he said, pointing to another glistening mountain-locked lagoon to our right. Both Tilda and I looked through our binoculars.

'That's quite a big loch,' I commented, before Tilda drew my attention away from Melfort and back to the goat island.

'On second thoughts, I think they are sheep, Tilda, and they don't look like they go hungry.'

'So are these both islands?' I asked Tim, as *The Princess Matilda* entered a narrowing between the two.

'No, to our starboard side with all those crags and woods, is the mainland, Degnish Point and the Seil Sound will get narrower, even too narrow for us, so we're not going that way,' he said, pointing ahead. 'Fred says there's a humpback bridge at the top of the sound, so you can drive onto the Isle of Seil, but we're going to come out onto the Firth of Lorne around the other side of the island and that's where it will be really interesting.'

'Cuan Sound?' I asked tentatively.

Tim nodded. 'But for the moment,' he said, pulling hard on the steering wheel, 'we're going to go north of this little beauty, hard to port and hug the shore, so it'll feel like we're doubling back on ourselves. The *Reeds* calls it the dogleg shortcut.'

'Oh, I should have my AA map up here, but I don't want to miss anything,' I said with excitement. 'It feels like we're the first people ever to have done this.'

Tilda interrupted me, waving her arms at something to our left. 'I can see cows, Chum.'

'The cows are on the island of Torsa and the larger island behind it is Luing, and if you had your map book in front of you, you would be able to see where the B road stops at Cuan and you have to get a ferry over to Luing,' Tim informed me.

Tim and I love a B road. He and my father used to spend hours discussing favoured routes around the countryside. 'I never imagined we would ever see Scotland this way,' I said thoughtfully. 'I'm so proud of you, Tim.'

'Tell me that in an hour from now…'

I could almost smell the wild flowers on Torsa, we were that close. 'Are you sure there's no rocks hiding beneath the loch?' I quizzed him.

'The only rock we have to worry about at the moment is that one with the navigational marker,' he said gravely as he pointed to a tiny island that had what I thought was a fence post on it. 'That's Cleit Rock.' Then he nodded towards our granddaughter, who was dipping her fingers into a sherbet lemon; the nod was our pre-arranged signal.

'I think it might be best if you go inside now, Til,' I said. 'Do you want to watch Hello Kitty?' Kitty had woken us up for the last two mornings.

I went down the steps with her, the DVD was on pause. 'I want you to sit on that chair and don't move. Granddad says it might become a bit choppy soon, so make sure you hold on to the side of the chair with two hands.' The chair was strapped to the radiator and would not move.

'OK,' she replied happily, and put her sherbet dipper on the marble work-surface, licked her sticky fingers so she had two hands free and settled down for an hour of Kitty.

By the time I rejoined Tim, *The Princess Matilda* was looking as if she was about to go right over Cleit Rock, but at the very last moment he spun the steering wheel, mumbling, 'This is the 90-degree dogleg.' He took a quick look at his watch. 'Should be on floodtide now,' he said with some urgency.

Then we heard a roar that made us almost jump out of our skin. From out of nowhere, a speedboat had appeared.

'Great, that will help,' Tim said angrily, as the wake of the powerful engine sent us rocking from side to side.

'Are you OK, Til?' I shouted down into the saloon, bending so I could see what she was doing. She smiled and nodded, oblivious to the rocking of the barge.

Tim had *The Princess Matilda* on full throttle now. I thought for a moment he was trying to keep up with the speedboat, but realized he wanted to get us through this treacherous waterway as swiftly as possible.

To the left of us on Luing were a few spread-out houses and to the right on Seil half a dozen snot-green static caravans.

'Can you see if that ferry is coming or going?' Tim asked me. 'That must be Cuan village ahead to starboard.'

'I think the ferry's dropping off – there's a few cars waiting to get on,' I replied, trying to remember if starboard was right or left.

'Where the ferry crosses is the narrowest part of the sound, about 200 yards, and that's where we'll feel the eddies, so I hope to God we get through before that ferry turns around, 'cos I don't want to slow down,' Tim said, with concentration etched across his hirsute face. 'Is Til OK?' I nodded.

'This is almost biblical,' I whispered, more to myself than Tim. I wasn't concerned about going through the choppy sound; on the contrary, I was looking forward to the challenge. I trusted Tim and I trusted *The Princess Matilda*. It occurred to me that there could be no turning back; we could not change our minds. Mother Nature and the power of the Atlantic Ocean had taken over. In the far distance, on the Isle of Mull, were mountains so high that I was afraid to look up at in case I got vertigo. My imagination took over, and the remark the Welsh woman in Craobh had made about a champagne cork erupting out of a bottle now made sense.

The angry spiteful wake-waves from the speedboat were splashing and hitting against the rocks of the two islands, sweeping back and forth. I can only liken them to a swimming-pool surfing experience where everyone whoops and rides the waves, but Tim and I didn't whoop as we were in the way. The rebounding surf rumbled under and over us. I took an opportunity betwixt the twisters to check on Tilda. My granddaughter looked at me guiltily; she was sitting at the table with a colouring book. I fell onto her recently vacated 'safe chair' as the ricocheting speedboat wake-waves re-hit us. The remote control was under my bum, so I switched the TV to scart, the channel that works with our web cam.

'What do you think about what's on the telly, Til?' I asked her.

'Wow,' was her reply, before she chose a blue felt tip out of her pencil case, putting out the tip of her tongue so she could concentrate on the job in hand. She was filling in the sky. The sky that I could see on the TV screen was coloured pearl grey, and the narrow sound we had to pass through was churning with white-tipped ripples. The brooding sheer cliffs on Mull seemed as if they had just risen out of the sea. Mull, I thought, is like the cross on top of a capital letter T.

18th December 1996
Midnight
Another biopsy.

It doesn't get any easier. It's like every day we have to climb a mountain, poor you. You are so brave, you poor sod. Panos had to take the biopsy out of your sternum because you had put on weight (I'm feeding you up on double cream so you will have some reserves for the next chemo).

Panos, as he's sorting out his bits and pieces, says there is a risk taking marrow out of the sternum; the needle could go through the bone and into the heart! He looks at both of us and we all laugh, Panos' shoulders shaking with hilarity. I trust Panos, he was hard work at first, but then he was the one giving us the bad news and, he being Greek, I wanted to shoot the messenger. You are now sleeping off the drugs and I'm sitting back in that chair, the blue leather chair in your old hospital room. I feel I've never left it. I've been real maudlin all morning, I went for a walk after I took the kids to school and walked through the graveyard. The Victorians, the clever buggers, built the railways and graveyards on the outskirts of London. This is where we live. I hate this grave-yard because I cannot help but think about death. I think about you. We re-examine all your full blood count results and add them to the pile. We neatly hoard the slips so we can compare them from week to week.

10th January 1997
Midnight
You had a meeting with the producer of a French film. You really want to do it BUT they may not be able to get insur-ance for you. That would be awful, you are on tenterhooks. We might go to a showing of Hamlet *four-and-a-half hours long. It better be good. You tell me you felt weird when you filmed this at Blenheim Palace early last spring, you felt odd. Panos tells us you were probably showing the first symptoms of acute myeloid leukaemia. It was snowing…you couldn't get warm.*

20th January 1997
Midnight
I shouldn't write at this time of night because it's when I'm most prone to negative thoughts. I go to bed before you,

now you are stronger. You enjoy your half hour on your own downstairs. When you first came home, it was very different. So I find myself alone in this bedroom we share, and it takes little imagination on my part to recall all those weeks when I wrote in this midnight notebook with panic in my pen. But still the panic lurks.

What happens when you are not in bed with me, what happens even at this moment in time when you are downstairs being normal, is that I become abnormal, my imagination hyperventilates. In the morning I'll take the kids to school and pick them up and cook the tea, but every time I kiss you goodnight and leave you sitting on the daybed in our living room I sense something horribly bad might happen. I pinch myself. I had to learn how to conjure you up, like some mad witch-doctoress, when you were in hospital, and I can still feel the leather chair underneath my thighs in that room in PW4 in UCLH…I've had too much to drink, you Mr Sober and me Mrs On-The-Cusp Lush.

It's been a shit week, one way and another. Last Monday you met with the French producer and director of the film Bosnia. *They had seen you in* Secrets *and* Lies *and want you to play the lead BUT…insurance…illness…It's a carrot dangled in front of a ravenous donkey. The chance of getting insurance appears to be remote. Poor you, you were so unhappy, you want to work. It's made me afraid…phone calls to agents/ directors/producers. On Tuesday you felt it best to turn the job down and you were so disappointed that I bullied you into buying a Rolls-Royce, which now stands in our driveway. You perked up. It's clapped out and old, but you insist it's a classic. 'When or if I get better,' you had said on so many occasions, 'we'll get two things, a Rolls-Royce and a boat.' One down…*

BUT IT'S YOUR 40th BIRTHDAY SOON, we've sent out invitations to everyone we like.

I rejoined Tim in the wheelhouse. 'Is Tilda OK?' he asked me.

'She's fine,' I replied.

'You missed the whirlpools. I timed it perfectly getting through the sound,' Tim informed me. 'All we have to do now is get out into the Atlantic Ocean. It'll be choppy when I turn hard to starboard into the Firth of Lorn, but nothing we can't handle. I'm going to keep well away from Mull, as that's where the rollers will hit back from, but that Welsh bloke in Craobh says we'll get some protection once we go inside the Island of Insh.'

'Right then, I'll leave you to it, my darling, and go below and keep my eye on Til, she's getting a bit too adventurous,' I commented, before heading for the steps to the saloon.

I perched in the saloon for about fifteen minutes feeling *The Princess Matilda* shuddering as she took on the force of the Atlantic, and I watched what was happening ahead on the web cam. Tilda carried on colouring; our granddaughter and her namesake were handling the ocean well. Eventually, the sea became calmer and small yachts and speedboats began to fill the screen. Tim had correctly predicted the Atlantic swell would soon give way to gentler waves. Dougal, the cab driver from Craobh, had told us that Oban was Gaelic for 'little bay' and it was obvious this horseshoe-shaped cove was a sheltered haven. He had also informed us that Queen Victoria and her consort had dropped anchor on the royal yacht, and they thought it one of the finest spots they had ever seen. The fishing town of old Oban may have changed since the royal visit in 1847, but the Isle of Kerrera, to our near left-hand side as we travelled up the Firth of Lorn, had not.

The surface of the Firth shimmered in the sunlight, an azure greasy slick leading us towards Oban. I recognized the royal-blue *Hebridean Princess*, the Queen's temporary royal yacht. The ship was moored on the north quay where we had had our lunch a couple of weeks previously.

'Do you want to come up in to the wheelhouse, Til?' I asked our own princess.

She put down her felt tip and stood.

'Best if you hold my hand,' I told her and we both staggered a little as a jet ski had stirred up the bay. We laughed and joined Tim.

'Jenny just phoned,' Tim said, indicating my mobile that I had left on one of the director's chairs. 'She says she's on her way back from the hotel in Fort William, so might stop off and get a ferry over to Kerrera.'

'Aunty Jenny can share my cabin,' Tilda said thoughtfully, before adding, 'and my binoculars.'

Tilda and I each had our own wheelhouse door to look out of, but, before we could focus our binoculars, Tim announced that we were picking up speed.

'It must be the pull of the tide as we go up the Sound of Kerrera,' he said, as he checked his various electronic gadgets.

'It's a long island,' I commented. I put down my binoculars, as I didn't need a sharp focus.

'About six miles long and acts like a breakwater,' my husband replied. 'Protects Oban except in strong so'westerly or nor'westerly winds.'

'Why's it called Oban Marina when we're going to be mooring on Kerrera?' I asked him.

Tim shook his head. 'I don't know, darlin', but it looks a pretty place. What do you think, Tilda?'

'I can't see any goats,' Tilda complained, as she twisted the focus on her mini binoculars.

'We'll walk up the hill to that monument on top of that mound,' I said, pointing towards a lush green flat-topped hill on the island, 'and I bet we smell the billy goats before we see them.'

'You! Walk all the way up there?' Tim teased me, throwing down the gauntlet. 'Don't make me laugh.'

'Well, I would've climbed Kilimanjaro in '96, if you remember. I was as fit as a fiddle, but you spoilt it by getting leukaemia.'

'I was just showing off,' he laughed. 'Now I think it's time you sorted out the ropes, 'cos my autopilot says we've arrived at our destination.'

'Is this it? It doesn't look like a marina, more of an anchorage,' I said, as I surveyed the small picturesque island harbour.

Kerrera has a foot ferry that leaves on the hour to cross the bay to Oban. Tilda and I left Tim hosing the salt off *The Princess Matilda* and filling Matt in with tales of our recent adventures. The last time Tim and I had seen him was in the Crinan Basin. Tilda rudely ignored Matt as if he had a contagious disease. The small ferry was next door but one to where we were moored. It only takes ten minutes to cross the bay, but Tilda and I didn't get off, as Jenny was waiting for us at the ferry-stop that was just around the corner from the *Hebridean Princess*.

My sister waited patiently for the passengers to alight before she embarked. 'I seem to be the only person getting on without any bags,' she commented, as we watched shoals of fellow passengers boarding.

The ferryman was very patient as he held the boat on the slipway and helped everyone to load their luggage, booze, babies and dogs. Tesco shopping bags were deposited on the deck as well as picnic baskets, cool bags, suitcases, rucksacks and bikes, along with school children and satchels. Scottish schools have different holidays to their English counterparts. Once everyone had found a seat, the ferryman and his deckhand began to load bags of building sand, fence posts, gates and brown paper parcels of every shape and size.

'On the hour, every hour, ten past from Oban,' Jenny said,

handing her great-niece a magazine. 'And I shall get the last ferry back this evening, so I won't be sharing your cabin this evening, Matilda, because I have a great deal of work to do – because next week, you and I and your mummy will be getting a large ferry to Coll, a ferry like that big black and white one over there,' she said, pointing towards the now familiar CalMac with its distinctive red lion on the black-tipped funnel.

Our eldest daughter Pascale and her boyfriend Cyrus were going to be driving up to Scotland, and planned to join us on *The Princess Matilda* a few days hence before catching the ferry over to Coll with Jenny.

'If you think how much stuff is taken over to Kerrera by this little ferry, can you imagine what CalMacs take to the Western Isles?' Jenny said, as we prepared to disembark a few minutes later. 'Our friends that run the hotel on Coll go to Glasgow twice a month with a trailer to pick up supplies. It's a twelve-hour round trip.'

'And there's me thinking it's going to be a palaver getting the shopping in from Tesco before we leave,' I replied, as the ferrymen offered his arm for balance so I could climb off his boat.

'It will be my pleasure,' he assured me, 'to help you off with your messages.'

For years, Jenny had told us that this is what the Scots call 'getting in the shopping', but this was the first time I had heard it being used.

Tim and Matt were waiting for us. I had explained to Tilda that Matt might have his camera. 'But I don't want anyone to film me,' she had complained.

'That's fine, Til, we'll get them to blur out your face so no one will know it's you.' But she had her own solution: she used the *Disney Princess* magazine that Jenny had given her to cover her face.

Her shyness with Matt didn't last long and she was chatting away ten to the dozen over dinner; the 'restaurant' was a temporary marquee by the marina gantry. Tim had booked us a table while I had collected Jenny.

'Just as well you did, Timmy,' Jenny said, as we were shown to our table.

The Waypoint Bar & Grill is only open during the summer and is a popular seafood restaurant and has a great selection of vegetarian options too. Much better than Loch Fyne, Jenny and I agreed.

'Why is *The Princess Matilda* still encrusted with salt from Cuan Sound?' I asked Tim, as I dipped the marquee baked bread into an olive oil and sea salt dip. Tim laughed and explained that he had been told off by a delightful girl from the marina office, because the island had no mains water and relied on a well.

'The amount of rain we get up here, I'm sure it doesn't run dry,' Jenny laughed. 'How long do you think you will be on Kerrera, Tim?'

'A few days. I listened to the Met Office forecast and there are gale-force warnings, so we'll stay where we are; there's worse places to be weathered in,' Tim replied.

'Well, let's go and make the most of the fine weather we have at the moment,' I suggested.

Tilda had her scooter outside the marquee. We took it in turns to ride it down a concrete slope behind the marina office, to see who could go furthest without using a foot to propel ourselves forwards. Tim tried to cheat by giving an extra kick, so he was disqualified.

We walked Jenny and Matt to the ferry, and Tim, Tilda and I bade them farewell. We were rewarded with unconstrained waving from our departing shipmates and the ferryman.

The horseshoe seafront of Oban was lit up like Blackpool during the illuminations, but on Kerrera the western hills were washed out by the late-setting sun. Blackness swiftly followed. Tim put Tilda to bed, with her *Pirates of the Caribbean* hot-water bottle and read her *Billy Goat Gruff*, but she was fast asleep before he could do his '*I'm a troll fol-de-rol and I'll eat you up for supper*' voice. She usually fights sleep to hear his troll rendition.

Tim and I knew the weather was badly misbehaving when we were woken by rain and a screeching banshee wind. We could hear the angry roar of the Atlantic in the distance, but even in our safe haven we had slopping waves bashing under us on the incoming tide. *The Princess Matilda* was swaying from side to side like a cradle being rocked by Mary Poppins on too much caffeine. It was Tim's turn to make the tea, and he did so quietly, as Tilda was still fast asleep. I refused to get out of my warm bed.

'It must be the hypnotic motion of the boat,' he whispered.

'That or the sea air,' I replied.

Tim handed me the laptop, with my tea, so I could check the weather, but we didn't need to be told a gale was gathering strength. We could hear and feel it and, as we suspected, the Met Office map of the inshore waters of the British Isles were enveloped in an angry, 'stay where you are' traffic-light red.

It was the hailstorm peppering our steel boat with lumps of ice that dragged Tilda out of her bunk. I insisted she put on her dressing gown for warmth and we all went into the wheelhouse where the noise of the hail was nearly deafening. Oban across the bay looked dreary and depressed so we were content to stay aboard *The Princess Matilda* and play dominoes. Tilda and Tim, when they became bored of my winning, tried to build a domino castle, but the rocking of the boat demolished all their attempts. At least we only had one child aboard to keep amused; when we had our narrowboats, Rafe and Sadie would bicker and Pascale sulk, and then we would all get cabin fever on rainy days.

I was about to prepare some lunch, when the rain stopped, so we quickly locked up and ran to catch the ferry. It was about to depart, but even I can run twenty feet without losing breath. The little ferry was busy and it was difficult to find a dry seat, but someone kindly cleared a space for Tilda over the engine. 'It's nice and warm sitting here,' she commented, as the ferry left the pontoon.

A forceful gust of wind caught us all by surprise and blew the well of rainwater from our sagging tarpaulin rain cover into the open-sided boat. Everyone except Tilda got a drenching, which is just as well as she wasn't dressed for Scottish weather.

'The first thing we do is get Tilda some wellies, a mac and a fleece,' Tim said, tipping the rain out of the hood of his mac.

The sun came out for a few minutes as we crossed the bay and the ferry had to do a small detour as a cruise liner was lying at anchor in our way.

'People pay through the nose to experience what we're doing,' Tim commented, as some of the ferry passengers took photographs of the ship. The passengers aboard the cruise ship took photographs of us as they queued to be ferried to Oban by the liner's tenders.

'They can't pay for good weather, though,' I replied, snapping away on our camera too.

Oban was again teeming with tourists, and we joined them as they promenaded, umbrellas at the ready, along the seafront. Eventually, we found a shop that sold children's clothes that were not completely tartan. So now the three of us wore wet-weather gear and this took some time to get out of so we could enjoy our lunch. By the time we had finished our meal, we were peeling off jumpers and fleeces too.

'Four seasons in one day, from ice to sunburn,' I said. 'And time for an ice cream before we get the ferry.'

There was an Italian ice-cream parlour by the slipway to the ferry and we sat with our legs dangling over the sea wall watching the CalMacs and fishing boats crisscrossing the bay.

The rain stayed off for the remainder of the day after our ferry ride back to Kerrera, so we decided we would follow a boggy footpath around one of the hills behind the marina, up to the monument we had seen when we had arrived. The boggy, squelching, wellington-boot-sucking footpath gave way to a rugged sheep path, and Tilda and I stopped to pick flowers. 'Just take one or two,' I said to her. There were plenty to choose from. We heard someone shout and we looked up and saw a family with children zigzagging down a steep path.

'Can we go that way,' Tilda asked us, 'and find the goats?'

The hill flattened out to a small plateau, but still we had a way to climb, so we stopped to catch our breath. The three of us, Tilda included, lay on Tim's plastic mac that he had put on the soft springy grass. Above us, swift-moving, skeletal fingers of clouds were being blown across the blue of the sky. Tilda sat up, bored of clouds and listening to birds trilling out their tunes. Tim tried to pull me to my feet. 'Come on, let's climb to the very top.'

I resisted his entreaties; the craggy path above us was now, to my eyes, a vertical cliff, and it was lichen-encrusted and decorated with moss that oozed water from the morning's rain.

'Come on, Chum,' Tilda begged me. 'Let's get to the top.'

'I think it will be too steep for you, Matilda,' I answered, but she had already began to climb like a sure-footed alpine goat, followed quickly by Tim, the Billy Goat Gruff, in case he needed to catch her should she fall. But not once did she look back; she was completely fearless.

Eventually, I hauled myself skywards, grabbing on to tufts of turf on my hands and knees. Tim occasionally had to yank me up the steepest parts of the hill. At one point, I had to push myself into bracken to let a striding, bearded Viking with a screaming two-year-old on his back go by. All he was missing was a horned helmet and a set of earplugs. The child had a piercing cry. My granddaughter and Tim had already caught their breath by the time I joined them at the top, and whatever breath I had in reserve was blown away by the vista. Before us were mountains and islands skirted by swathes of shimmering turquoise sea.

'No wonder they call Oban the gateway to the Western Isles,' I said, taking hold of Tilda's hand. I was still convinced she might drop over the side.

'She's fine, darlin', it's only a hill,' Tim admonished me. 'And you would never have got to the top of Kilimanjaro...' But before I could say anything in my defence, he put his arm around my shoulder and with his other hand he pointed north. 'That's Lower Loch Linnhe. I reckon we'll be going up there on Sunday.'

I sat down next to Tilda on a lump of granite in front of the iron-grilled fence to the monument. Someone had told us it was a memorial to one of the founders of what was to become the CalMac ferries. We could see three of them heading out into the Atlantic.

'Breathtaking, completely breathtaking, I feel we're on top of the world,' I said. 'I think Matt should come up here with his camera, get shots of the loch and islands. It could be the Mediterranean.'

'What about Matt having to climb all the way up here carrying all his gear?' Tim asked me.

'Oh, he's young, he'll cope, and that bloke did it with a yelling nipper on his back,' I replied. We all watched and heard the striding bearded man and his baby running down the zigzag path. 'And think about the poor sods who built this monument, having to heave all the granite up here. I'm going to go back down on my bum.'

Tilda and I took the ferry across to Oban the following day, leaving Tim to plan our next passage up Loch Linnhe. Having seen the numerous islands and watercourses north of Oban, I didn't envy him. Til and I walked to Tesco's as I needed to replenish my store cupboard. Jenny was going to come with us to Corpach. 'I've driven that road to Fort William so many times,' she had told me, 'it will be great to do it by boat.'

Tilda also had a shopping list that included some of her mother's favourite food and some new DVDs. 'And Cy is going to bring his fishing rod, so Mummy says we need to buy some lemons.'

'Well I might treat myself to some gin,' I laughed, winking at Til. 'I'm not sure how many fish Cy will catch.'

We got a cab to take us back to the slipway to get the ferry. There was an elderly lady wearing a rain hat tied over her neat blue rinse. She was primly sitting with her ankles crossed on top of an old-fashioned suitcase. She watched the cabbie unloading my shopping.

'Are you having a party on the island?' she asked me.

'No, we've got a boat moored there and I like to get in emergency rations, in case we become marooned,' I laughed.

'Och, there's nothing worse than running out of tea when you've rain blasting in on the teeth of a wintery gale and the ferry's nay running,' she remarked, as she shielded her rheumy eyes from the sun. 'And I just missed that boat,' she continued, pointing towards the bobbing ferry crossing the bay. She must have noticed Tilda pulling on my arm and added, 'I'll keep an eye on your messages if you want to take the wee lassie for a wander; we've got an hour to kill and I'm happy enough sitting here in the sunshine.'

'If you're sure, that's very kind, thank you,' I gratefully replied, before asking my granddaughter if she would like to take a walk along the seafront. Tilda shook her head and pointed across the road.

'You want to look in The Clearing Shop?' I asked her, wondering what would interest her in a boring discount shoe store that wouldn't have been out of place in Essex.

'No, behind there,' she answered. 'I want to go in that big grey building with the red chimney.'

The lady sitting on the suitcase laughed. 'I believe they now do guided tours around the Oban Scotch distillery. My father used to supply them with barley, but that was an awful long time ago.'

Tilda had questioned Tim and I numerous times about the distillery over the few days we had been moored on Kerrera. Her binoculars had been put to good use. She became bored looking for goats, and the tall chimney bellowing out the potent clouds of steam across the bay had intrigued her. We crossed the road, hand in hand, dodging lorries, coaches and camper vans. Tilda waved a shy goodbye to our messages' watcher when we safely reached the pavement of the A85. As we walked into the tranquil Georgian courtyard behind the 1960s-fronted shoe shop, I asked her, 'Are you sure, Matilda?'

She nodded her head and we entered the black arched door of the distillery. Unfortunately, we only got as far as the shop. A security man questioned Tilda about her age.

'Five,' was her reply.

'I nay can let ye in, lassie, the fumes from the vats may kill ye. Ye can come in when ye're twelve.'

'Never mind,' I said, seeing the look of disappointment on her face, 'Aunty Jenny's coming tomorrow and the day after that your mummy and Cy will be joining us too. But how about we get your granddad to teach you to fly a kite tonight?'

The last time Tim and I had flown our kite was in Weymouth, New Year's Eve 2008. It was raining too much to do our traditional New Year kite-fly in Penarth 2009, so the kite had been in the drawer under the table ever since. But every time Tilda went into the drawer where we keep all our board games, spare batteries and tea lights, she would drag out the kite and look at us with pleading eyes.

Kerrera is a lovely island but you have to be careful flying a kite, as we discovered a couple of hours later. We chose one of the few spots that had overhead electricity cables. A few attempts were made to get off the beaten path away from the lines, but this resulted in us getting stuck in muddy and mushy peaty bogs. Tim wouldn't give up and eventually managed to get the kite flying without the danger of death from the cables, but by this time Tilda had become bored, and then the kite became snagged in a tree. Then there was lots of shouting as Tim threw branches trying to free the kite, and Tilda found this far more fun. Eventually, he and Tilda just tugged and tugged until the kite came free, but the string was unwindable, full of knots and kinks.

'New kite-string goes on the shopping list,' I said to Tim, as Tilda and I walked back to *The Princess Matilda*, but my granddaughter's cheeks were rosy and I could see that she had had a thoroughly nice day. This is what memories are made of.

Chapter Thirty-One
HEADING FOR THE UPLANDS

Kerrera to Corpach Sea Lock: 28 nautical miles

Jenny caught the ferry to Kerrera with a good hour to spare before our planned departure. Someone from the Highland Hotel in Fort William had dropped her off in Oban so she could pick her car up from the hotel later. Fort William is near to the sea lock that is the start of the Caledonian Canal. Jenny was an authority on the canal not only because she is a keen walker and mountain climber, but also because she works in the Highland tourist industry.

'The Great Glen's coast-to-coast canal is made up of thirty-eight miles of natural lochs, joined together by twenty-two miles of canal cuttings and twenty-nine locks all dug by hand,' she had told me as I helped her off the ferry. 'It was surveyed in the early 1800s by James Watt, John Rennie and lastly by Thomas Telford. This feat of engineering would cut through mud, quagmire, rock and granite and take over two decades to complete, the summit level is Loch Oich, 160 feet above sea level.'

'Wow,' I replied. 'We'd best have a cup of tea first.'

'You might like a slice of my homemade bread to go with it,' she laughed, handing me a loaf wrapped in a tea towel.

'You've got a perfect day for it,' she later said to Tim, as she drank her tea. 'What's our ETA in Fort William? I want to wave to the staff at the hotel; they're all so excited about seeing *The Princess Matilda* on Upper Loch Linnhe.'

'About five, I think, we should have a fast passage as we'll travel up with the tide, and I need to go through Corran Narrows at slack water,' he replied. 'But to tell you the truth, Jen, I didn't for a minute think we'd ever get to Scotland, never mind this far north, and tomorrow we go through the Caledonian Canal and eventually come out on the east coast, but we'll get a seven-day licence and take our time.'

'And once you get out into the Moray Firth you'll begin the home run back to where you came from?' she quizzed him.

'Not this year, maybe we'll stay in Inverness or Aberdeen for the winter,' he answered thoughtfully.

'I reckon Newcastle,' I butted in, 'with some fine weather we could get there in a week, couldn't we, Tim?' I had my AA map on my lap, as I relaxed on the back deck enjoying the sunshine.

'I think that might be pushing it a bit, darlin',' he laughed. 'But wherever we end up this year will be a bonus. That's why we're loving doing this so much,' he said, turning to Jen. 'Last year was such a rush, after being stuck on the Helford River we had to make a dash to find a winter mooring, and I was starting a job, but this year I've turned work down. Moreover, we have more options this year too. It was Hobson's choice last summer in North Cornwall. It was only because Patch, the coxswain of Penlee lifeboat, put a good word in for us that we were able to stay overnight in St Ives before we went into Padstow.'

'Same ocean though,' I said, 'but, once we go through that sea lock in Corpach, I won't be sad to leave the wild Atlantic West Coast behind.'

'Nor me, when you think how far those mountainous waves have travelled before they crash over here,' Tim replied.

'All the way from America?' I quizzed him.

He nodded, then added, 'But you do realize that Newcastle is on the North Sea?'

'No, it's not, it's on the foggy Tyne and *"the fog on the Tyne is all mine, all mine"*,' I sang.

Matt had caught the same ferry over as Jenny, as he was going to be filming us over the next couple of days. He had mentioned to my sister that he had been staying in a rather basic B&B in Oban. 'Well, tonight, Matthew, you will sleep at the Highland Hotel in Fort William and will be treated like a VIP. I'll let them know to expect you, but just mind you keep your door bolted at night – the average age of our clientele is seventy-two and we have a couple of cougars in at the moment.'

We left Kerrera at noon. The next two hours passed swiftly, Tim was able to put *The Princess Matilda* on autopilot once we had a clear run. Loch Linnhe is a long, tranquil waterway, yet it may have been my imagination but it became moodier the further north we travelled. Cascading waterfalls scarred the purple mountains.

'I never have time to admire the views when I drive,' Jenny said on more than one occasion. 'The scenery is stunning.'

'And there's no one else here,' Tim also said on more than one occasion. 'It's like a dreamscape or photographs from a brochure.'

Tilda spent most of the time in the saloon watching a DVD, but every twenty minutes or so she would join us all in the wheelhouse. We had set ourselves a competition as to who would spot Ben Nevis first.

'It's the highest mountain in Great Britain,' Jenny had told her, 'and I've climbed it.'

'Here comes the tricky part,' Tim said, as he turned off the autopilot and steered *The Princess Matilda* himself. 'What was I saying about there being no one here? Isn't it always the way, whenever we've something difficult to do, there's always a ferry intent on stopping us?'

The loch had suddenly narrowed and white candyfloss clouds were rolling over the tops of the mountains, draining out the colour as shadows replaced the emerald green of the mauve undulating hillsides. To the left of us, just above a thin skirt of beige shingle, was a large whitewashed house with a lighthouse.

'That lighthouse looks out of place here,' I commented, noting how sharply it contrasted with the black–green hills behind it. The loch was also changing colour and texture, gently rippling as the ferry crossed a hundred yards ahead of us.

'That's the Corran Ferry,' Jenny said. 'It's run by the council and links the A82 Fort William Road to the A861 on the other side of the loch.'

Tim had slowed down the boat to allow the ferry to cross the narrow sound. 'But I'm still doing seven-and-a-half knots with the tide and once I put my foot down we'll do ten.'

No one spoke for the next few minutes, all eyes glued on the ferry that was discharging cars now at Corran.

'Right then, let's roll,' Tim said, upping the revs, and we fair blasted our way through the sound.

The high mountains closed in on us from both sides of the loch, until we thought they might block out the sun all together, but, just as I was about to put on a coat, the loch widened out once again. Jenny appeared out of the saloon with Tilda, and they were whispering like conspirators.

'Look, Chum,' my granddaughter said proudly, pointing out of the right-hand wheelhouse door. 'That really big mountain is Ben Nevis. Can I have my prize now?'

23rd February 1997
Midnight
I've been so busy the last few weeks organizing your fortieth birthday party and writing my thesis. You have not had

a blood test for two weeks, which has made us exceedingly anxious. We try to keep everything on an even keel, try to keep our underlying sense of foreboding under control. I woke the other night sweating, trapped in a chaotic confused dream, unable to escape and I woke you up – everything in our bedroom was unfamiliar – then I remembered, between the confusion, what had happened and I cried. I think I need therapy. How can I curb my fear? My imagination? My anger? My anger and fear has always been about your illness, but my ANGER now is directed elsewhere.

We had been in Cambridge. I was researching in Churchill College Library and you had driven to check out the B&B we'd booked, but you didn't like the look of it. Then you said that Pascale had called you on your mobile, excited. She said Secrets and Lies *had been nominated for five Oscars. You asked her to tell you who: Brenda Blethyn, Best Actress in a Leading Role; Marianne Jean-Baptiste, Best Actress in a Supporting Role; Mike Leigh, Best Director; Simon Channing Williams, Best Picture; Mike Leigh, Best Screenplay. And when you hung up, I have only just found out, you cried for half an hour, but you kept this from me for a couple of days.*

You picked me up from the library and I was excited because I had made a breakthrough with my research about Dame Edith Lyttelton but I could tell there was something wrong. You told me about the five Oscar nominations. As always you try and keep a brave face and tell me how pleased you are for them all. But you are a nicer person than I am, because all I feel is anger that your performance has been overlooked. You couldn't do the press junkets, the publicity tours, the chat shows, the radio shows, because you were fucking fighting for your life. You tried to stem my negativity by saying, 'Well, you can't recover from leukaemia and win an Oscar, can you?' How many times have I told the kids, 'Life's not fair'? And it is unfair, it is. Everyone else in Secrets and Lies *has an Oscar nomination and all you have to look forward to is another bloody bone marrow biopsy.*

10th March 1997
Midnight
Rafe's 14th birthday. We all had dinner at the Chinese, and Michael Mayhew brought the photos from your birthday. You go in for another bone marrow biopsy tomorrow, you are also going to have your stem cells harvested and put on ice – for a rainy day. We plan to go to the bone marrow restaurant for lunch.

11th March 1997
We are waiting for Panos; he as always will be doing the biopsy this morning, and then you will come back to UCLH tonight so they can harvest your cells in the morning. I've just looked through your birthday photos again. You were 40 on 27th February. The party took a great deal of planning, Jen helped a lot. I'm just starting to enjoy it now...we spent half the night saying 'Hallo', and the other half saying 'Goodbye'. Most of the nurses from the ward came; it was funny seeing the real nurses dancing with actor doctors off Casualty. *They formed a line to dance with Big Clive Mantle, and there was Panos and Dr Goldstone the real McCoy. You turned 40. Spring is here, the sun always shines on Rafe's birthday. I spent all afternoon sorting out the lawn. The bulbs (THE BULBS) are up. I planted them a lifetime ago. <u>We need to plan for the future.</u> Back to my thesis...*

Jenny was thrilled to be passing the Highland Hotel, but unfortunately she couldn't get a signal to text the staff to let them know we were sailing by. The Victorian hotel stands on an elevated spot high above Fort William and looks out onto the Sunart Hills and Loch Linnhe.

'The hotel was used by the navy during the war,' Jenny told us. 'The admiralty built a floating dock near where we are travelling now, to train crews for the D-Day landings. And I better warn you that the RAF is pretty much in evidence. You will hear them before you see them,' she said ominously.

Corpach Sea Lock is much larger than the sea locks on the Crinan Canal, and there were several lockkeepers there to help us as we locked through into the basin. Team Matilda were all rather hungry, so Jenny called someone from the hotel to pick us up once we were moored.

'There's an excellent Indian restaurant on the jetty at Fort William,' she said.

It was still light when Tim, Tilda and I returned to *The Princess Matilda* after our five-course feast of Indian Highland cuisine. We left Jenny to drive back to Loch Long and Matt to the cougars at the Highland Hotel. *The Princess Matilda* was moored at the bottom of a couple of neat and tidy gardens belonging to pebble-dashed bungalows. Occasionally, we could hear the crunch of car tyres on the gravel of the road by the towpath. As I waited for the kettle to come to the boil to fill up Tilda's hot-water bottle, I looked out of my kitchen window. The peak of Ben Nevis had been hidden by a bouffant hairdo of cloud, but now, as the last of the sun went down in the east, the whole of the mighty summit was visible. The bright lights of Fort William twinkled a kaleidoscope of reflected colours on Loch Linnhe. The only noise, besides the sound of our humming fridge and the occasional car crunching over the gravel towpath, was the running of water. A few yards ahead of us was the first of the Caledonian Canal's twenty-nine locks. A deluge of fresh water was cascading over the lock gates.

Tilda woke us up; we always left her cabin door and ours open. She was humming to herself and Tim called out to her, 'Are you OK, Til? Do you want to get into bed with Chum and me?'

We heard the pitter-patter of her feet as she came through the saloon and galley, before slipping into my side of the bed. She was freezing cold, so I climbed over her to put on the central heating. I heard Tim groan as her feet came in contact with his back. It was a drizzly grey day, proper Highland weather.

'Ben Nevis is covered in mist,' I said to Tim, as I filled the kettle to make the tea.

'Jenny says it's mostly covered in mist,' he replied.

'Let's get you dressed, Til,' I said to her, as I lifted her out of the bed. 'And after breakfast we'll take a walk over the lock and see if we can get down on to the beach of Loch Linnhe.'

After our stroll, I left Tim chatting to one of the lockkeepers, while Tilda and I walked to the village shop. Toni, the petite lady lockkeeper, had warned me that on the canal the shops were few and far between. We had to cross a railway line and I looked both ways before we crossed it. When Sadie was eleven, she and I almost died when a silent intercity train appeared out of nowhere. We were literally seconds away from being smashed to smithereens. I threw my weight and pinned her to the crossing gate, or I was sure the vacuum created by the rushing train would have sucked her into oblivion.

Corpach is a small village with the canal and railway line on one side and the A830 on the other. It also has a Co-op, so I stocked up on some more long-life milk and toilet roll, things you don't want to run out of. Tilda pulled a frozen macaroni cheese out of the freezer, so that along with a cabbage was added to the heaped basket. The lady at the till asked me where I was from. I picked up the cabbage and explained that we had a boat that had once been moored near to a field where the cabbage had come from.

'Kent,' she laughed, appreciating my pathetic joke after she had inspected the label.

'Don't you have cabbages in the Highlands?' I asked her as I packed away the rest of the messages in a bag-for-life bag.

'Aye we do, but they send them down to Lincolnshire,' she replied.

'And the Lincolnshire cabbages are sent to Kent,' I said handing her a £5 note.

We both shook our heads at the stupidity of it. She looked at her watch before giving me change. 'If you hurry, the steam train will be at the station soon; the wee one would love to see it, I'm sure,' she said, handing Tilda a sweet out of her overalls pocket.

As it turned out, we had no choice but to see the train, as the barriers were down across the railway line. There had been several men with notebooks and large tripod-mounted cameras hanging about when we went into the Co-op, now their numbers were swollen tenfold. We heard the steam locomotive before we saw it, clickerty-clacking down the track. The locomotive huffed and chuffed, puffing grey clouds of smoke and belching steam. In the 1930s my dad used to operate a traction engine when he worked at a fair; he always said the steam was the blood of an engine, because it drives the pistons that drive the rods that turn the clackerty-clack-clack wheels.

'It's like the train in *Harry Potter*,' Tilda squealed with excitement, as the stately black locomotive chuffed and puffed slowly by.

'Aye, lassie, it is,' said a bearded chap with a notebook to our right. 'I believe this is the very train they use as the Hogwarts Express. Do you like *Harry Potter*?' he asked her.

'I'm only allowed to watch the first one; my mummy says the ones with my granddad in are too scary,' she said in a solemn voice.

He winked at me and rubbed his nose as if to say, 'we'll humour her'.

The locomotive had now gone by and the barrier was raised. I was expecting Tim to be standing on the other side of the track to help me with the shopping. It took a few moments for the steam to clear and I felt like Jenny Agutter in *The Railway Children* when her returning father gets off the train at the end of the film. The foggy steam evaporates and she runs into her father's arms. Tim spotted me and did a silly mime, coughing and spluttering as he walked over to help me with my bags. The bearded man did a pantomime double take as he recognized Peter Pettigrew.

'All right, mate?' Tim smiled, as he took Tilda's other hand.

Chapter Thirty-Two
LOCHS AND GLENS

'Ron the lockkeeper said they'd let us up the first three locks whenever we're ready, but wants to know if we intend to do Neptune's Staircase straight after,' Tim said, as we put the shopping on the boat.

'Let's do it,' I replied. 'I'll just get Tilda sorted out with a DVD; we don't want her getting in the way while we're going through locks.'

Tilda was more than happy watching Hello Kitty for the twentieth time.

I heard Matt's voice just as I finished putting the long-life milk away. I looked out of the window and it had begun to rain.

'Matt,' I called to him, 'you are going to need more than your TK Maxx to keep you dry today.' I found him a pair of waterproof overtrousers that he struggled into, then wrestled his camera in its waterproof condom. The lock was ready for us to enter by the time we were all sorted. Tim had helped zip up my bright yellow mac so I would be weatherproof on our bow.

'Are you sure I don't look fat in this?' I asked him as he used two hands to tug up the zip. I was wearing a thermal and a fleece and suspected I looked like an Easter egg.

'You look fine. Now hurry up get down the front and get ready to throw your rope up to the lockkeeper.'

After doing three of the connecting locks, I became rather good at it, but I had rain going down my arms every time I raised them. Toni, the lady lockkeeper, suggested I might like to change my clothes before the next flight. 'You've got about ten minutes,' she warned me. 'My colleagues are getting the bridges and staircase ready for you.'

I discarded my canary yellow and exchanged it for an old dusky olive-green Driza-Bone before making my way back along the gunwale. Halfway along, I stooped down to look through the window to see if Tilda was OK; she saw me and waved. I returned to my wet pitch just in time to see two swing bridges opening for us to go through. The railway and the A830 both cross the canal, and straight ahead was the longest staircase lock in the British Isles.

Over the years, on our narrowboat travels, Tim and I have experienced quite a few staircase locks. As the name suggests, the water level goes up or down in steps, depending which way you are travelling. When ascending a staircase, a vessel enters a deep cavernous empty lock. Opening the sluices of the lock above is like pulling the plug out of a bath, but the water isn't wasted as it raises the water level in the bath/lock below. When the two water levels are equal, the lock gates above open, allowing a boat to float into the connecting lock, then the doors behind are firmly shut and the process begins all over again.

There is a bit of a difference between narrowboating locks; narrow is the clue. The ones we were about to use, on the Callie Canal as it is known locally, were built for ships, so the locks are 180 feet long and 40 feet wide; on many narrow canals, the dimensions are 70 feet by 6 feet 10. But, whatever the size of the locks, they serve the same purpose: getting from A to B. Neptune's Staircase lifts the canal 64 feet up (or down) a hill. It is lined with a quarter-of-a-mile of continuous masonry, and each of the locks was dug by hand. By the time *The Princess Matilda* had entered the third of the eight connecting locks, I had become bored of the bricks, and I was thoroughly soaked once again. Rain was dripping of my nose and, as if this wasn't bad enough, I was enveloped in clouds of midges.

The locks took a while to fill, so Tim, from the shelter of the wheelhouse, and me, from the open foredeck, were able to chat to the lockkeepers; although I only did so with the knowledge that I might drown in rain every time I opened my mouth more than an inch.

'Bet you're glad these locks are all mechanized now?' I spluttered to Toni. I felt the lady lockkeeper and I had become good friends.

'I am indeed. Back in the day, as I've been told, it would've taken a great deal of sweat and half a day to do what we do now with a press of a button. Och, it's a shame you're doing it in the rain. We had Griff Rhys Jones and *Three Men in a Boat* come up last week – they had fair weather.' Toni whispered this, in case she was speaking out of turn.

'So we believe, Toni, you're not the first to tell us this,' I gossiped, also lowering my voice in case anyone was eavesdropping, not that anyone else was as stupid as us to be standing out in the rain. Well, apart from Matt, who was on the lock gate above us filming, and he couldn't hear a word we were saying over the noise of water gushing from the sluices filling up the lock. 'We also heard,' I said, looking from left to right just in case, 'I heard from the horse's mouth, well a friend of a friend, that they arrived by seaplane on Loch Linnhe so I think they cheated a bit.'

'We all watch your programme too,' Toni said, pulling a hanky out of a zipped oilskin pocket to blow her nose. 'But I thought you'd have more cameramen with you and support, like *Three Men in a Boat*.'

'We don't have their budget, and anyway it's what Tim and I do, it's not just for a TV programme.' I was continually flapping my hands, trying to swat the midges away. 'Tell me,'

I said, 'how do I stop them? They're driving me mad.' Then I began to splutter and spit, not so much because I had imbibed the torrential rain; I was convinced I had swallowed midges.

'Sorry,' Toni replied, trying hard to suppress throaty laughter. 'They are particularly bad today and your boat is acting like a midge magnet.'

It took us an hour and a half to get to the top of the staircase of locks with the quarter-of-a-mile of continuous masonry. The midges, never mind the hard graft, must have sorely tried the navvies that built the canal. We moored above the staircase, and Toni slipped on a pair of rubber gloves so she could fit a contraption to a valve on our gunwale that sucked out the less than salubrious contents of our holding tank into the main sewage system. Usually, we jettison it several miles out at sea; Tim and I like to swim on beaches too.

'It's been lovely meeting you,' Toni said, after depositing her gloves in a bin. 'If you've had enough of the rain, I suggest you moor on the Banavie jetty just upstream. But keep your windows shut and don't turn on the lights unless you draw the curtains. That's the only way to keep out those pesky midges.'

'It was lovely meeting you too, Toni, and thank you!'

Matt was waiting for us on the jetty, looking like a drowned rat. He had planned to film us as we went by. Tilda was still watching Hello Kitty, but Tim asked her to put it on mute. She knew all the lines anyway, and so did he, because he had listened to it all the way up Neptune's Staircase.

Tim helped me peel off my not-so-waterproof trousers.

'Time for a beer. Do you want one, Matt?' Tim asked him, multitasking as I passed him a towel to pass to Matt so he could dry his hair.

'That will be great, thanks, Tim,' Matt replied.

Once free of my un-waterproofs, I rummaged in the wardrobe in our cabin, trying to find me and Matt something dry and clean to wear. It was difficult, as I needed to do a wash and the laundry bag was overflowing. For some strange reason, our young cameraman rejected my choices: a pair of khaki moleskins or a pair of shocking-pink leggings.

'Now tell us, Matt,' Tim asked, as he snapped off the cap of a bottle of Beck's, 'did you get anyone knocking on your door last night?'

Matt got a cab back to the Highland Hotel, assuring us he was quite safe from the old ladies. 'All they wanted to know is if I was going to the ceilidh tonight and if so could I do the "Dashing White Sergeant" or the "Gay Gordons".'

'Just keep out of the way when they "Strip the Willow",' Tim laughed as he waved Matt goodbye. 'See you tomorrow, mate.'

Rain hammering on the roof woke us all up the next day and we resigned ourselves to another wet day.

'It's only water,' we kept saying to each other, as we stared out of the windows.

Tilda, however, was fidgety, not just because the weather was keeping her boat bound, but also because her mother was due to arrive that morning. Pascale and Cy had spent the night in Loch Long with Jenny, and they brought the sun with them, as the rain stopped the moment they parked their car.

'Mummy, Mummy!' Tilda shouted with excitement as they came aboard.

'I love it when we have crew,' I said to them both as we welcomed them.

'So we do all the locks, while you drink gin,' my eldest daughter cheekily said.

'The locks are all manned,' Tim laughed, as he gave them both a hug. 'But your mother got a fair old drenching yesterday when we came up Neptune's Staircase—'

'And I watched Hello Kitty,' Tilda interjected.

'I can see that, Til,' Cy said, raising an eyebrow at the TV, 'you've still got it on pause.'

I sorted them out lifejackets, which they both made a fuss about wearing, until Tilda told them they had to wear one, it was the rules.

'And so does Matt,' I said, as Tim introduced him to the new crew. 'This is going to be Matt's last day with us for a while,' I explained.

'I have to go back to London tomorrow – I have a holiday booked, but I'm looking forward to today's trip,' he said, with a beaming but shy smile.

I was crushing some garlic in the galley preparing a marinade for the evening's dinner. Suddenly, as I looked out of the galley window, I had a sense of déjà vu; we were travelling through a dark canal cutting. Everyone else was chatting away in the wheelhouse, but I found myself thinking about a time when Tim was recovering from his illness and we bought a rust bucket of a canal boat that we loved. We spent a few years pottering up and down the canals in England; even the kids enjoyed it before they got fed up of being crammed in a narrowboat when it was pouring with rain.

Tim joined me in the saloon leaving Cy to steer; we were only travelling at four miles an hour.

'I feel wistful,' he said quietly, putting his arms around my waist. 'Our kids have all grown up; this canal cutting reminds me...'

'Me too,' I said, wiping away a tear. 'It went in a blink of an eye. I'm sure they were all Tilda's age last week.'

'Come on,' he said, slapping my bum, 'snap out of it, we have a new generation onboard. Matilda loves *The Princess Matilda*, and we don't have to worry about tides, gale-force warnings, tidal rips, overfalls or sunken wrecks.' He took my hand. 'Let's go join them.'

But I could see he had tears in his eyes too.

The narrow manmade canal cutting stopped at Gairlochy, and by means of four locks we came out into our first freshwater loch.

'It looks more like a fjord to me,' I said to Tim. Loch Lochy has steep, forested hillsides that were perfectly reflected in the still waters. Cy already had his rod out on the back deck, while Tilda and her mother sat on the gas locker on the bow.

'I'm going to put a chair on the roof and really enjoy this,' I said, before grabbing one of our director's fold-ups.

'So you should, my darlin',' Tim replied, 'the loch's over ten miles long so I'm going on autopilot. Will you keep an eye out?' he said to Cy. 'I showed you how to override, didn't I?'

'Aye, aye, ye did, capin',' Cy acknowledged, saluting before winding in his fishing rod, then casting it out of the wheelhouse door.

Tim walked along the gunwale, stopping to chat with Matt, before taking up the seat on the gas locker that had been vacated.

Tilda and Pas had joined me on the roof and we chatted and tried to identify the violet-trimmed mountains from my AA map that I had secreted within the fold-up chair. We rolled the Gaelic words experimentally around our tongues; *Sròn A'Choire, Meall Coire nan Saobhaidh*. Tilda, we suspected, had the best pronunciation. Whatever these words meant, they evoked a sense of timelessness, of a landscape that had not changed for millennia. Loch Lochy and the two other freshwater lochs of Loch Oich and Ness run through the valley of the Great Glen, a geological fault that was formed over 400 million years ago. It was the genius mind of Thomas Telford that engineered the manmade cuttings to link the lochs of the Caledonian Canal together.

I wondered if there was a Gaelic word for the wispy tendrils of mist hovering in patches, like Guinness-smeared moustaches, halfway down the mountainsides. Telford may have seen these patches too. Perhaps, like me, for a second he believed these transparent spectres to be the ghosts of the dead, but I quickly realized they hovered below the bruised heather and crags, where the mighty mountains gave way to a thick, emerald belt of forestry. The trees were the mist magnets.

Tilda had been tapping me on the shoulder trying to get my attention as I'd been daydreaming. She loved to point out the waterfalls that fell gushing and foaming, as if in competition to see which would fall first into the loch. It had become cold and Pas kept Tilda on her lap for warmth. Cy had been excused his autopilot watch duties and cast his fishing rod off the port side of the prow. In the distance, the loch disappeared into a deep V-shaped gorge. It seemed, to my eyes, to be impossible to go any further than this.

It took another hour before we reached the gorge, we had come to the head of the loch; 200 years ago, this is where we would have stayed. But Thomas Telford engineered a canal cutting through the rock that was in the way, and with two locks he raised the canal through a narrow dark cutting into the next loch. Matt abandoned ship as he too had been studying my map.

'I should get a good shot of you going into Loch Oich,' he had said, as he broke into a run. *The Princess Matilda* was only doing four miles an hour, so Matt had a head start.

The A82 abuts part of the east side of Loch Lochy and crosses Loch Oich at Laggan.

Tim had radioed ahead so the bridge was open for us to go through, and we waved to Matt as we sailed by.

One of the lockkeepers had suggested we moor at the Great Glen Water Park, just through the bridge. The park wasn't on any of our maps or charts, but we saw a number of 'Scandinavian'-type log cabins in the woods and a couple of timber-effect buildings with a water-sport shop and half a dozen empty pontoons. Tim timidly pulled alongside a hammerhead, half expecting someone to rush out of a log cabin and say, 'Clear off, pal!' But no one did.

No sooner had we moored and all exclaimed how lucky we were to have such a tranquil mooring, than half a dozen teenagers arrived in swimming suits. They were bubbling with laughter and high spirits and their laughter was infectious, and we laughed too as they screamed as they threw themselves into the freezing loch. Then they all climbed out and did it again. Tilda thought they were marvellous and kept looking up as she fished with her net from the end of our pontoon, Pas and Cy keeping a close eye.

For a few minutes we had heard a roar of an engine and couldn't work out where it was coming from, but the roar was getting louder. The noise was coming from two huge fishing boats heading pell-mell down the still waters of the loch; they must have been doing twenty knots.

'They're in a bit of a hurry,' I said to Tim, as I hung my washing out on the back deck. The next moment I was almost thrown overboard by their wake.

'I think they want to get through the swing bridge before it closes for the night,' Tim said, as he steadied me.

Through the tangle of laundered socks and Tilda's T-shirts, I noticed Matt had reappeared.

'Are you staying for dinner, Matt?' I asked him. Chicken marinated in garlic and lemon was simmering in the oven.

'I'd love to, but I have to get back to the Highland Hotel – Jenny very thoughtfully booked me in for another night – then I'm off back to London first thing,' Matt replied.

'At least have a beer with us?' Tim asked him.

'I won't say no to that, thanks, Tim.'

We all watched as the two navy-blue and white trawlers passed by us again, but this time at a more leisurely pace. One of the Glaswegian skippers shouted down to us from the bridge, 'Is it OK to moor here, pal?'

Tim walked to the end of the pontoon and shouted back, 'I think you might be a bit too big for the wooden pontoons.'

'Aye, pal, I think ye're reet.'

Instead, he moored against the concrete pilings by a slipway near one of the lodges and the other fishing boat rafted alongside. 'You'd think they'd be worried about running aground?' I remarked to Tim.

'No, the loch's about 200 feet deep, but it's weird to see fishing boats like that 100 feet above sea level,' he replied.

'It is,' I answered, 'but we've forgotten the fishing industry was one of the main reasons behind linking the east and west coasts of Scotland. The canal can be done in fourteen hours.'

'Well, I'm glad we're taking our time,' Tim said thoughtfully. 'It's such a relief not to be scared to death, and that's how I feel every time we go out to sea.'

'Then why are we doing it?' I asked him for the umpteenth time.

'Because I'm alive. It's as if I want to cock my finger up at fate.'

'And I've got some cock for your dinner,' I said, laughing, as I checked how the chicken was doing in the oven.

I am not sure if it was the fishing boats that sent the teenagers running back to their holiday homes or the chill of the late-August afternoon. The sun was behind us, drying my washing on the back deck, and Cy had his fishing rod out again now. I suggested through the galley window that he might have more luck if he used the dinghy. Tim was in the bathroom, so I dragged *New Si* around the side of the boat and to my husband's amazement – he was watching me out of the bathroom window – I climbed in on my own and waited for Cy to join me. We took it in turns rowing into the centre of the narrow loch. I lay back while Cy cast out his line. 'We might have a three kilo Atlantic salmon for tea,' he said, as if he sincerely believed it would happen.

'Or we can go to a fishmonger tomorrow when we get to Fort Augustus?' I suggested.

Matt called to us and waved. 'My cab's here, bye!'

Pascale had lit a fire and the candles while Cy was fishing, and Tilda had laid the table. There was no salmon, just my chicken for everyone but me, with roast potatoes, leeks, carrots and the Kentish cabbage. After Tilda was put to bed and the washing up stowed away, we converted our dining table, without too much cursing, into a double bed for Pas and Cy. But none of us wanted to go to sleep; it had been a perfect day, and we were loath to let it go. So we crept up into the wheelhouse where a full blousy moon greeted us. The luminous harvest moon had risen high above the forest, casting a silver shimmering ribbon of light – as if it was seeking out the deepest darkest secrets that were hidden beneath the tranquil waters of the ancient Highland loch.

11th March 1997
Midnight
This evening we returned to UCLH so you could have the stem cell harvest in the morning. Panos knocked on the door with that other doctor, Andy 'somebody', another specialist. You and I were having a hug, laughing and joking, but immediately we knew something was wrong. Panos was very serious and he and Andy sat down and Panos looked at the floor at

his feet before looking up at us as we both sat on the single bed. Then he quietly said, 'Timothy, your blast cells are back…I am so sorry…but the results from the bone marrow aspiration I took this morning indicate that you have relapsed.'

In a split second our world stopped turning. No one spoke, we did not move, and then I heard an echo and I realized it was you that was speaking. It took me a few seconds before I understood what you were saying. 'What are my chances, Panos?' But it was in slow motion that Panos looked towards Andy, who shrugged and said, 'Not good, we'll go for a bone marrow transplant, but with that fungal chest infection…' I don't remember anything else, all I could think about was that you will probably die as soon as they give you chemotherapy again, you will die, the fungus will grow and spread. I can't even recall which of us drove home. They had told us to go back to the hospital in the morning when your treatment will begin. All of the way home we just cried and cried and cried and cried. At least the younger kids were in bed. I quietly told Pascale in the kitchen, and she went into the living room to you before disappearing into her bedroom. I don't know what you said to her, or she to you, and we got horribly drunk and laughed and took photos of each other and discussed what would happen if you died. We both think you will die, and you are worried that I won't be able to live without you and of course I could not, and then we talked about how I'd bring you home if the transplant is unsuccessful…Our idyll is shattered. Quite dispassionately we discussed what 'I would do'…we should get the will changed…you were so close to death last time… our conversation, for want of a better word, was profound… we talked about life and death and 'what if?' scenarios… But we didn't talk about when you get better. WHY NOT?!

Over and over I chant as I scrawl, if I write and say it enough times it will happen. Don't you dare blub!

Don't you dare blub!
Don't you dare blub!
Don't you dare blub!
Get on with it!
Get on with it!
GET ON WITH IT! GET ON WITH IT!
This is what I say to myself over and over but my tears stain the page. I must not cry anymore...no more negatives...I'm so tired and drunk...You said that you had asked Panos if it was OK for you to have a couple of glasses of wine and he replied, 'I'd have two bottles if I were you!' So you did. Shock, oh God what a shock. I can almost taste it. You have relapsed. We talked about life and death and 'what if?' but we did not talk about when you get better.
WHY NOT?!
WHY NOT!?

Coming into the busy tourist hub of Fort Augustus, the mid-point of the Caledonian Canal, was a bit of a shock after a bucolic day's sailing. The day had begun with Cy and Pascale diving into Loch Oich for a swim before we had breakfast. Our picnic lunch was collected from a swing bridge near Cullochy. The bridge keeper was on his lunch break, so we moored and awaited his return before spotting a sign that said tea room. Pascale and I strolled up there to see what they had to offer. A well-built late-middle-aged man took our order and informed us that it was his day off and he was going to get out his train. And that is exactly what he did; after he gave us our picnic lunch, he used a mini JCB and lifted a steam train out of his shed. By the time *The Princess Matilda* sailed by the teashop we could see clouds of smoke puff puffing behind the garden fence.

*

A staircase of five locks takes the canal downhill in to Loch Ness, cutting right through the heart of Fort Augustus. The top lock offers one of the best views of the loch. There was also a bottleneck of boats waiting their turn to go down, and we came in to the top lock last. *The Princess Matilda* was immediately surrounded by gongoozlers; hundreds of them. My sister Jen had warned me it was a popular stop-off for coach parties doing the Highland Experience in a day. The lockkeepers were rather more regimented than they had been when we had gone up Neptune's Staircase, but this was because going down has more problems.

Pas, Cy, Tilda and I stepped off the boat onto the lock side. Pas had the bow rope and Cy the stern. 'One of you take the bow line and one of you the stern. Skipper, turn off your engine and stay where you are!' the lockkeeper instructed us, but I had already briefed Team Matilda.

'OK, me and Pas and Til will stand at the front of the boat and keep her tight to the side of the lock when the water goes out, then when the lock gates open we'll pull her into the next one. You do the back end, Cy.'

'Aye aye, capin'.' Cy saluted me.

'But I want to stay with Cy,' Tilda pouted.

'OK,' I replied 'but stay right away from the edge of the lock because it's very dangerous and if you were to fall in you could get crushed and die!'

Pascale had been Matilda's age the first time Tim and I took a holiday together. We hired a narrowboat. I recalled so vividly giving her these exact instructions; I have an old photograph somewhere of her wearing her nightie and dressing gown underneath her lifejacket. It was past her bedtime but I promised she could stay up and 'help' me as we went down a staircase lock somewhere in Shropshire.

There must have been half a dozen other boats in the Fort Augustus locks with us, which was a bit of a mystery as we had hardly come across any other craft. The small boat in front of us was crewed by a team of tiny Japanese ladies who all wore cotton gloves and huge white beekeeper-like helmets with muslin that covered their faces and gathered tightly under their chins. It took me a while to work out they had hired them along with the boat to keep the midges from biting them. Since we had left Banavie jetty above Neptune's Staircase, we had had no more problems with the pesky blighters.

It was a sunny afternoon and we enjoyed travelling down the staircase; it was a slow procedure that allowed us to take it in turns to nip into the lock-side shops. I came back with a couple of large, deep-fried macaroni cheese pasties that we shared.

'Bloody 'ell,' Tim said, after taking a bite. 'How many bleedin' calories and heart attacks in that?'

By the time we reached the bottom lock, an hour had flown by. The lockkeeper instructed all boat crews to re-board their craft. 'We'll drop down your ropes when you're done. And, *Princess Matilda*, if you plan to stay overnight, you're too large for the visitor pontoons, so carry on by them and tie up at the pier.'

'There is no pier,' Tim said twenty minutes later, after we had come out of the lock and into a narrow channel that heads out into Loch Ness. On one side of the channel, there was a sign for boat excursions and there were mooring pontoons on the other.

'She said opposite the abbey,' I said, pointing towards a gothic-looking structure.

'So, this wall is the pier then?' Tim queried, before putting the boat into reverse.

The top of the wall was level with the roof of *The Princess Matilda*.

'Cy mate,' he called. 'Can you jump off the roof?'

I followed him up there and passed him a rope from the boat to the bank. There was a couple of cleats to tie on to, but I suggested to Tim he might like to use a mooring pin too. He disappeared into the engine room and came out with a hammer the size of his leg and a huge rusting mooring pin. He heaved them onto the wall and climbed up there too.

'We need the gangplank now for your mother to get off,' Tim announced.

'We've not used that for a couple of years,' I said, as I watched my husband lift the gangplank from the roof to make a bridge to the bank.

'Gweek Quay, last summer,' Tim commented, as he reached out to take Tilda's hand for her to walk the plank, 'on the Helford River, where we left her to have some work done while I was working in Manchester.'

With Tilda safely across, I put out my hand and Tim firmly gripped it as if I might fall down the gap. 'We should have had the boat painted while we were there,' I said as I crossed.

'Yes we should, the salt's turning her into a bucket of rust, and if we don't watch out the steel will corrode and disintegrate.' Tim pulled me to him. 'Then what will happen?' he said to his granddaughter, who was bending down picking buttercups off sparse clumps of grass.

'Will *The Princess Matilda* boat sink?' she replied, before holding the flower up towards him. 'Bend down, do you like butter, Granddad?'

Chapter Thirty-Three
MONSTERS
AND MIDGES

Team Matilda left us the following day as they were meeting Jenny in Oban to get the ferry over to the Isle of Coll for the August Bank Holiday weekend. Tim and I felt quite bereft when they left. Tilda had a bag full of golf balls that she and I had found that morning while paddling on the shore of the River Ness, just the other side of the pier.

'Aunty Jenny will love these,' she assured me as she dived beneath the surface of the freezing water for another white ball.

After our little family left in their cab, which would take them along the coast, back the way we had come by *The Princess Matilda* from Oban, Tim and I stood on the back deck and watched a boatful of tourists getting ready for an 'Exhilarating Ride on a Power Boat'. This is what the sign had said. As soon as the RIB (rigid inflatable boat) had gently but noisily motored by us, we noticed four red-throated divers doing what they do best, diving not flying. They were youngsters and copycats, so when one went under they all followed suit, emerging yards and yards away from where they had started. The same cannot be said of the RIB, because now they had cleared the pier the powerboat roared away.

'Cor, look at that go,' Tim said. But I was more concerned for the little chicks as they were now bouncing on a tidal wave from the wake from the powerful engine.

'That RIB must be doing forty knots,' my husband continued, 'it'll be at Urquhart in half an hour.'

'How long will it take us to get there?' I asked him.

'About three hours,' he replied.

Tim did his usual engine checks before we left.

'Damn it,' he said, as he climbed out of the engine room. 'I forgot to do the greaser last night. It's been dripping for twelve hours. Put the bilge pump on, darlin'.'

The 'greaser' that Tim was referring to is a tube that is stuffed with grease that stops drips from the propeller from leaking into the engine room. When we were stupid on our first rust bucket canal boat, we almost sank because the drips kept dripping until water almost covered the engine.

The Princess Matilda left the pier after we had had a stroll around the tourist-packed town of Fort Augustus. It was a beautiful day; the infamous loch was a sheet of plate glass except when the powerboats went by, and the visibility infinite. We had our own air show coming down the loch, phantom bombers on training exercises from RAF Lossiemouth flying barely 200 feet above us. The noise of the aircraft reached us seconds before they flew over. Tim and I waved. We didn't see anyone wave back.

After Loch Lochy and Oich, Loch Ness was a disappointment, with densely-packed forestry commission plantations that sat like dark shoulders along the banks of the loch.

'There's not much to see,' I observed. 'And I doubt we'll see the monster...'

'I think the monster was a ploy to get the tourists in,' Tim interrupted me, 'but it's deeper than the North Sea, so who knows what lurks beneath our feet?'

'Urquhart Castle,' I replied, going off subject, 'is that it? I bet there are a few ghosts and monsters prowling around there.' I was peering through my binoculars at one of Scotland's most iconic ruined castles.

'We should be in Drumnadrochit Harbour in about half an hour then,' Tim said. 'The bay is tucked behind the castle and I've been warned to keep to the buoyed channel as we go in. We don't want to end up being towed in by the RNLI.'

'TBI?' I said. 'What are you on about?'

'You need to get your ears syringed,' Tim replied, tutting.

12th March 1997

You have been readmitted to PPW4, Dr Goldstone wants you to go straight into transplant. You are going to have two days of chemo then spend four days at the Cromwell Hospital so you can have TBI (Total Body Irradiation) and then be given your brother Richard's marrow on Good Friday... Easter uprising...resurrection...death and rebirth...Richard's in for tests. I got up at seven, so I could prepare myself for telling the kids. We told Pas the night before. I phoned Jen and I cried and then I had a wash and got the kids up. How do you tell your kids their dad might die? I told them you were going to live...I took them to school and had a word with a teacher. I was worried about Rafe, it was his birthday two days ago, no wonder he's so upset. Sadie was fine, carried on eating her breakfast. When we're together we try to put on a brave face. You have just gone up to the operating theatre to have another Hickman line fitted.

Midnight

I almost disintegrated with grief when you were taken to theatre. The surgeon couldn't put the line back in your chest because the veins wouldn't take it...it was put in your groin. Richard came into the room after having his tests done (for when he gives his marrow, thank God it's a match) and I tried to be calm, but then one of the cleaners came into the room without knocking and I went mad and started to shout

'Can't you knock?' Richard tried to put his arms around me and I wept, 'I can't live without him, he's asked me to, but I won't be able to.' Then Jane, the chemo nurse, came in, and I said, 'I don't want him to die in this room...'

13th March 1997

We're at the Middlesex Nuclear Medicine Department, you are to be injected with radioactive something or other, so they can test your renal function in preparation for the transplant. The nurse tries to find a vein in your hand for a catheter and you ask the doctor, 'Why don't you use the Hickman line?' and the doctor says, 'Oh it would make it radioactive.' I'm asked to leave, which I do gladly. I sit outside in the waiting room. Tap tap on my laptop, trying to hang on to my sanity, but I look around me and wonder, are the people waiting here radioactive?

While you were having your biopsy done on Tuesday I opened this file on my laptop and started to read it from the beginning. How did we manage? How did you cope? How did I cope with the hellishness of the situation? Watching you as a 'healthy' man being reduced to a bag of bones, hardly able to walk to the bathroom. I remember how you had cried in July, the only time I saw you cry the whole time you were in hospital, as you held on to the side of the sink to stop yourself from collapsing. 'Look at me, I can't even take a piss,' and I couldn't hold my tears back anymore either, and we both wept, me trying to hold you up...the lowest point. I went to Sadie's leaving assembly that day and envied all those women as they indulged themselves in tears of nostalgia, I could not afford to weep...and I thought the same thing last night after I'd consumed a bottle of your birthday champagne and I looked at my reflection in our bathroom mirror at home. All day I've been telling you, 'You are going to get *better, live in the moment, don't think about the future!' I cannot take my own advice.*

How quickly one forgets the torment, we've just spent eight months forgetting all about it (except we never really forgot). We both kept saying it was like it had happened to someone else. As we came back into the hospital on Tuesday night for the stem cell harvest, you said, 'Well, at least I'm only going to be in here for two nights, it's not as if I'm coming in for a bone marrow transplant!' and this was what we were laughing about, our relief at our escape, as Panos and Andy came into the room. Panos had looked at the marrow at 8pm, poor Panos, he was visibly moved by his task. He has a great deal of dignity that man.

You were readmitted to PPW4 at 12.30 yesterday afternoon, and when Panos came in you asked him, 'Are you sure you've not got my marrow mixed up with someone else's?' Panos said, 'If that were true it would give me a great deal of satisfaction to tell you so.'

As we were leaving the ward to go over to the CT Scan department, you saw Cathy by the lift. You told her you were worried because Panos had looked serious. Was there anything that you had not been told? And Cathy replied, 'Panos is very upset; we're all very upset to have you back in here, Tim.' You have been greeted with hugs and very sincere commiserations...believe me when I say this feeling of goodness and love helps the pain. One day at a time...

Apparently Goldstone has suggested it would be better for you to be treated on PPW2 when you are transplanted because they have an air-filtered room down there. The fungus is still there in your lung, and we all know that, as soon as your immunity is flattened by the chemotherapy and the TBI, the fungus will grow and spread into your – heart? Brain? The nurses want to keep you on PPW4. We'll see. They were all dancing at your birthday a few days ago.

We can go home for the weekend to make the most of our
time as a family before they proceed with your treatment/
death sentence next week...

There were three people waiting to greet us as we pulled into
the strangest harbour we have ever used. Behind us were the
craggy ruins of the medieval Urquhart fortress, sitting on a
high headland, and before us was a car park, except it had small
boats in it. It even had a machine to buy a boat parking ticket.

'Hello, I'm Martin,' a small dark-haired man said, as he
reached out to take a line from Tim. I had already stepped off
with the bowline.

'And I'm Viv,' a vivacious, curly-haired woman said, as she
helped me pull the boat in tight to the side.

'And that's our son Lewis,' they both chorused, pointing
to an embarrassed teenager who looked as if he wanted to be
anywhere else in the whole world rather than in a car park off
Loch Ness.

'You've picked a great weekend to come and visit!' Martin
exclaimed.

I had been communicating with Martin for a few weeks
over various social media sites and understood he was a volunteer with the local lifeboat. We had passed the tiny lifeboat
station as we came into Drumnadrochit. 'We're the newest
RNLI station,' he had proudly declared. The first message I
had received from him was when we were moored in Douglas,
the home of the first lifeboat station. 'Don't hold your breath,'
I had messaged back, 'but, if we ever make it to Loch Ness,
we'll say hello.'

'Hello, Martin,' I said shaking his hand, 'this is my husband
Timothy.'

'Oh we know who Mr Spall is,' Martin laughed, 'and we'd
all be delighted if you joined us this evening for a drink and

a look around our station. I know it might not be as grand as some you have seen...'

'We'll leave you to it,' Viv said, taking Martin firmly by the hand.

Lewis had been left behind and seemed to be rooted to the spot.

'I love *Harry Potter*,' he whispered, and then quickly covered his mouth as if the words had slid out.

I had a few unread text messages, one from Paul Crompton who was on a family holiday: 'Thinking about sending cameraman to film on Loch Ness & hiring a RIB, get some sail by shots of P M in front of castle.'

I phoned him. 'I thought Matt was on holiday?'

'Yes he is and so's Phil, so is it OK if Roger does it?'

'Yes, of course,' I replied.

Roger had always done the long panoramic shots in Cornwall and Wales.

'But I just found out it will cost £300 to hire a RIB for a couple of hours,' Paul added, speaking in hushed tones. 'Look, I better go, my wife's glaring at me.'

'Hang on Paul, I'll find a RIB; we can spend the money on better stuff.'

Next, I phoned Freddy, our shipmate from the Crinan Canal, and asked him if he knew anyone with a RIB. 'My brother Jeremy,' he said instantly, 'I'll give him a call.'

After a few moments, Fred called back: 'Jeremy would love to, and all he wants is the petrol money to fill up the RIB – those enormous outboards are a bit juicy on the gas.'

Jeremy Moore arrived on Sunday morning, before Roger the cameraman. Like his brother Fred, Jeremy has a droll sense of humour. The first thing he said as he entered the harbour on his RIB was, 'What are those silly buggers doing?'

Earlier in the day, Tim and I watched a little yacht leaving the harbour; we thought they must have some insider knowledge because they took a shortcut through the buoyed channel. However, they didn't get very far as they ran aground. It was a small yacht and there were five hefty youths onboard. I had shouted to them, 'HAVE YOU RUN AGROUND?'

They were testing the level of the water with a boat hook, and they shouted back, 'YES!'

I replied, 'STAY WERE YOU ARE!'

'I don't know why you just said that,' Tim commented, 'they ain't going anywhere.'

'I know, but while you were having a shower they were taking the piss out of our boat, the smug little twats. I thought I might rub their noses in it. Anyway, I just phoned Martin from the Drumnadrochit Lifeboat Station.'

No sooner had I said this than Martin arrived in his car and assessed the situation. He saw the occupants were in no danger and yelled, 'DO YOU HAVE A RADIO?'

They yelled back, 'YES!'

'I'LL CALL YOU WHEN I GET TO THE LIFEBOAT STATION!' Martin shouted in reply.

Tim turned on our radio and I put on the kettle, and returned with a brew in time to hear Martin's voice crackling out of the VHF radio: '*Yacht run aground! Yacht run aground! Yacht run aground! What is your call sign?*'

'*Mudlark.*'

Jeremy by this time had tied against us, complaining as he boarded that we were a midge magnet. We explained to him what was going on with *Mudlark*. He took stock of the situation and said, 'Why don't they climb out and push it off the mud?'

Meanwhile, Martin had called the trip boat, *Deepscan*, which operates out of the harbour, and asked if the skipper could pull *Mudlark* off.

'This is much better than watching the TV,' I laughed.

'Don't laugh, Shane,' Tim admonished me. 'If you recall, we've run aground a couple of times.'

'Aye, so have we all,' Jeremy piped up, 'but not in one of the deepest lochs in the world, and they should've had more sense. They're sea cadets and could've used the buoyed bloody channel.'

By the time Roger arrived, it had begun to rain, but, after a few false starts, Jeremy and our cameraman buzzed out onto the loch on the RIB, using the buoyed channel out of the harbour. We followed them just as the sun came out, so I put the chair on the roof and did a bit of acting until a downpour sent me scurrying for cover.

'So that's show business?' Jeremy said an hour later, as he towelled his hair dry. 'But I've had a great day, one of the best Sundays off for a long time!'

Midnight
I can't write about the weekend – too too painful…

God, I can't remember the date, it's Tuesday/Wednesday (18th/19th March), and you were WERE due to go back in hospital tomorrow, BUT…yesterday, Monday, you had another bone marrow biopsy because the cytogenetics on the last marrow are normal. Panos tells us not to build our hopes up, and is going to do another one… He's just phoned and says he's just looked at the slides and it's borderline. What does borderline mean? He told us but I can't remember anything, except the transplant has been postponed. Let it be a miracle, God, please let it be.

What a day, what a week, living from minute to minute, and if our hopes have been raised to be dashed how shall we bear it? Tomorrow Panos is going to take another biopsy and some bone...a trafine? He says it will take several days or more to get a result, but it will show one way or another if you have relapsed or gone back into remission. This is all very unusual. So much happening. Jimmy Nail just phoned, he said, 'The roller-coaster goes on.' It's all too profound.

Meanwhile, when all this was taking place – LIFE and DEATH phone calls with Panos – Kelly, Jimmy's PA, phones to say The Daily Express *have been sniffing...they'd just phoned your mom at home. Poor Sylvia sitting, waiting for the phone to ring, wondering what's going to happen with her son, and some journalist calls her. She was very upset. The solicitor's been on to them to leave us alone, we're going through hell enough without the papers getting involved. I'm so exhausted. Please let there be good news with the cyto-genetics...Panos won't let us off the hook, he doesn't want to build our hopes up. I daren't think. You and I, we are extraordinary. I'm too tired to write anymore...*

It was the midges that drove us out of Drumnadrochit. After Jeremy left us, I stopped up any sneaky holes with toilet paper because the insects sneaked through any gaps. They infested our ropes and I am sure they would swarm down the chimney if I had not lit the fire.

'But, darlin', it's too warm now,' Tim complained.

'Don't you dare open a window!' I snapped

The following afternoon, I was attacked by the midges we'd imported; they came out in clouds from our ropes as we locked through Dochgarroch, a drop of a few inches as the Caledonian cutting took us off the River Ness, which comes out of the loch. We could not see the river that runs parallel with the cut, the trees were too high.

'I'd like to climb onto the roof,' I said to Tim, 'to take a look, but I feel like Katharine Hepburn in *The African Queen* flapping away the mosquitoes.'

'Why don't you take a leaf out of her book then?' he asked me.

I disappeared in to our cabin and came back with a fine silk scarf that I draped over my hat.

'We have a swing bridge and four more locks before we reach the city of Inverness,' Tim said casually, as if this was something we did every day of the week.

'That means we are now about to come out on the east coast!' I said, hugging him with all of my might.

'We've all but done coast to coast, darlin',' he laughed, swinging me off my feet.

Chapter Thirty-Four
ON THE HOME STRAIGHT

Clachnaharry Sea Lock to Banff: 72 nautical miles

Tim and I wore sun hats – me without the silk scarf this time – as we came out of the sea lock from the Caledonian Canal. It must have been 22°C and the Beauly Firth at high water was a mirror; not a breath of wind fluttered our ensign. A lady lock-keeper called Val had operated the lock above the sea lock. She used to be a stage manager and lighting designer at the Lyric Hammersmith and shook Tim's hand. 'I never got to work with you in the theatre, but I suppose I am now.'

She told us she had come north a few years ago with her partner, but said she still gets twitchy about 7pm.

The Princess Matilda didn't go very far, barely a mile to tuck into Inverness Marina, which was a stone's throw from the huge Kessock suspension bridge. It was a wonderful sight, with cars and lorries roaring over, plus the odd tractor. But it wasn't just the thundering traffic that had our attention, as we spotted a head breaking through the satin of the Beauly Firth.

'It's a seal,' Tim had said, but I disagreed.

'It didn't dive like a seal.' I consider myself to be a bit of a seal expert.

David, the marina manager, who helped us tie up on our hammerhead berth, said he suspected we had seen an otter. He used to be a fisherman and had more experience than Tim and I about the wildlife around the east coast.

'Why did you stop fishing?' Tim asked him, as we walked along the pontoon to the marina office.

'I'll show you a photo when we get inside and you can make your own mind up.'

The photograph he was referring to was a beached fishing boat being battered with mountainous waves.

'Aye, that was mine,' he laughed, 'and I'm still living it down, but that's not the real reason I quit fishing,' he continued, as he took down our details. 'I got sick and tired of the fish quotas so I sold ma boat. I'm happy enough in ma new career, but I miss Whitehills. It's where ma family are from and we fished out o' there for three generations.'

'Bloody hell,' said Tim, still studying the photograph. 'Is this what we have in store?'

'Och no,' David replied, 'it's only stupid fishermen that go out in seas like that.'

I changed the subject quickly. 'Why's there so many lifeboats in the marina, David?' We had counted three so far.

'They use them as spares; if a lifeboat is needed in an extreme emergency on the west coast, they can steam through the canal, and if one's needed out on the oil fields or the Hebrides there's always a spare, just in case they have to rescue some daft bugger like me.' He pointed to the photograph again.

'Anyway,' he continued, 'ye're more than welcome to stay here for the winter. But then it's only the end of August. No doubt ye'll want to push on, it's up to ye.'

'Thanks, David,' Tim replied, 'that's given us some food for thought.'

'Aye, but enjoy the evening,' David said, as he gave us a card to get in and out of the marina gate. 'If ye're lucky, ye may see dolphins and more otters, they often come and have a nosey where ye're moored.'

The wind had picked up by the time we had walked down the pontoon to our hammerhead. We were moored opposite the breakwater entrance to the marina. Tim and I sat out on the back deck, nursing a glass of chilled wine.

'I think mulled wine might be a better option,' I said, stamping my feet.

Tim disappeared below and returned with his UGGs.

'Put these on,' he said, breathing deeply. My husband has huge lungs, well he used to…

'It's wonderful to smell the ocean again,' he said. 'Those clouds don't bode well, but we ain't going nowhere until we're ready, and we could stay in this marina for the winter. What do you think, darlin'?' he asked me.

'If we see an otter or a dolphin that's what we'll do, but I'm going to find myself some gloves,' I replied.

Tim went into Inverness the following morning; I stayed onboard as we were expecting Matt and Paul to join us. They arrived an hour before Tim came back.

'We're running out of budget,' Paul told me. 'We've enough for one more day's filming and I don't know how we'll finish it.'

'How about coming under that bridge?' I said, pointing towards the huge span of the suspension bridge crossing the Moray Firth. 'Tim plans to leave here at a quarter past two.'

I left them in the wheelhouse and went below. They were looking at my AA map when I came back.

'We've worked out how we're going to do it. Matt's got the car and hopefully he'll see you going through Chanonry Point as well,' Paul informed me.

'Are you wearing enough clothes?' I asked Matt.

He laughed and assured me he was.

'We'll see you when we get to Lossiemouth, Matt, then?' Paul queried.

Matt nodded, obviously wanting to go so he could find his locations.

'Hey, Matt,' I said, giving him a cling-filmed sandwich, 'put this in your pocket, you'll be starving in an hour.'

'What's Tim doing in Inverness?' Paul asked me, as we watched Matt striding up the pontoon.

'A voiceover,' I replied. 'It's a lovely city. Have you had a chance to look around?'

Paul shook his head. 'No, we came straight from the airport, but it looks pretty amazing from the air. When I spoke to Tim last night, he mentioned you'd moored the night on the canal before coming in here. What was that like?'

'Felt like a canal,' I answered thoughtfully. 'But we could walk into Inverness, unlike here.'

'I must admit we had a problem finding you; it's like an industrial estate outside the marina gates. Is that the reason you're not spending the winter here?' he quizzed me.

'No, it's only the first of September and we didn't see the otter again,' I replied.

We did see some dolphins, however, an hour into our journey out into the Moray Firth. Paul was even more excited than Tim and I.

'I hope Matt saw them too,' Paul said, after we had all finished hooping and hollering as we watched the bottlenose dolphins spinning and diving. We were going round Chanonry Point that lies on the end of a spit of land off the ominously named Black Isle, a peninsula, and opposite Fort George on the mainland. The sea had suddenly become agitated as we passed through the narrow sound and the rush of the tide funnelled through. The waves were short, nippy and choppy as if being pinched with spiteful fingers.

'*This must be why the dolphins love it, the fish are forced through with the tide,*' my husband said, as if he was doing a voiceover for a wildlife programme.

Tim pushed down on the accelerator and we could see just how fast the tide was running as it rushed either side of the Riff Bank West Buoy. The hulk of the buoy was coated in pearl-white slicked guano. This was from the spread-winged black cormorants, who were drying their feathers before diving back into the sea, competing with the dolphins in their fish-feasting frenzy. I turned to look behind us as we left the swirling confused sea of the sound, my eyes drawn skywards towards the dark summit of Ben Nevis. Now, for the first time, we were seeing the eastern slopes. It made me want to cry for the good times we had had, with friends and family onboard. I felt I was nine again, when the day trip to the seaside on the coaches from the working men's club was over; I would sob myself to sleep, knowing it would be another twelve months before it came around again. But I knew Tim and I would never go back – it had been a once in a lifetime experience.

'Life is like a carpet rolling up behind you as you walk into the future,' my favourite teacher, Mr Pilsbury, used to tell me. 'You can only walk it once; this is why you must make the most of every day.'

'Look to starboard, darlin',' Tim said, grabbing my attention away from the past; he could sense a melancholia creeping over me. 'Take a look at those golden beaches. Where's your map book?'

As he always does, Tim snapped me back into the moment and I picked up my road atlas. 'That must be Nairn, it's just off the A96, and over there,' I said, pointing to our left, 'is Cromarty on the A832. And if I'm not mistaken…' I paused for a few seconds before continuing, 'those are diving juvenile gannets. Look at them, they're like bullets; there must be something very tasty down below!'

Ben Nevis remained visible for another four hours.

*

The Princess Matilda arrived in Lossiemouth, just off the A491, at eight; Matt was waiting for us. Ian the harbour master helped us moor. 'Just watch out for those steps,' he warned us, 'they get a wee bit slippy when the tide's out.'

Tim walked Matt and Paul back to their hire car, as I had volunteered to do the greaser in the engine room. This is something that needs doing every day. As I climbed up the ladder to get out, I heard Tim's voice: 'Quick, quick, I need a carrier bag, someone's giving us three lobsters, hurry up!' Before adding as an afterthought, 'He's got a septic finger!'

I wiped my hands on some kitchen roll. 'Who's got a septic finger?' I asked him.

'The fisherman. Quick, get a bag for the lobster,' he said frantically.

I suspected the Tim Spall loose cannon was about to begin firing again. I blocked his path so he couldn't go below.

'These lobsters – are they alive?' I quizzed him.

'Yes, yes, quick, get the pans out.'

'Oh, for goodness sake, what size pans? How big are they? Can't we put them in a bucket?'

But Tim had pushed by me and searched for a carrier bag from under the sink before rushing back the way he had come. I washed my hands and poured myself a large G&T; I sensed I would need it. Sure enough, Tim returned with the now full carrier bag that he placed gently on the floor by the fridge. One of the lobsters tried to make a run for it.

'Oh my God,' I shouted, swallowing down hysteria. 'Put them in the freezer. I'm sure I've read it's the most humane way to prepare lobster...'

I took a step back into our cabin, in case I needed to shut the door should the lobster attack me. Fortunately, Tim managed to contain the errant crustacean. I knew I needed to take control, so quickly I opened the fridge, then the flap to the freezer compartment. He rammed the bag in – the little flap was still ajar, but he slammed the fridge door anyway. We both made a grab for my gin, but he got there first. Luckily, I hadn't put the Gordon's or the bottle of tonic back in the fridge.

'We can manage without ice,' I said, as I searched for my *Wild Food Year Book*. I found it among my secret stash of road maps.

'We've done the right thing,' I said, taking a glug of gin. 'The RSPCA say freeze them for two hours then plunge them into boiling water, but we'll do it after we've been to the Indian.'

Matt had done a reccie and said there was one near the harbour and we had arranged to meet them there in 'half an hour'. Just as we were locking up, the fisherman with the septic finger turned up; he had it trussed in a dirty-looking bandage that he wore like a trophy. I couldn't understand a word he was saying, but Tim assured me he had said, 'Cook them for eight minutes.'

This is what we did two hours later, on our return from the curry house. I brought the pans to the boil and Tim did the plunging. We stood in silence like a couple of murderers as Tim counted down: 'Eight, seven, six, five, four, three, two…' I filled up a bowl with cold water and used barbeque tongs before shoving the boiled corpses outside the galley window to finish chilling. It was perishing out there.

'I'll have a jam sandwich for my lunch tomorrow. I'm sure Matt and Paul will enjoy eating those with you in the morning.'

The next day, I took a walk around the town, while Matt and Paul chatted to Tim. Paul likes to do audio recordings to tie up any loose ends for the TV series.

I had done my recording first.

'So, Shane,' Paul had quizzed me, 'just a few questions about when we were in Aberystwyth and you took me to see where you lived with your first husband, Alec. You never finished telling me what happened.'

I had a mike on, but this question completely threw me. He sensed I was having difficulty speaking. 'Sorry, sorry, Shane, sorry…'

My throat had constricted, but somehow I managed to form three quivering words. 'He…died…overdosed.' I felt like the breath had been crushed out of me.

19th March 1997
Biopsy and trephine

You are really knocked out for this one. Panos has already explained that besides the 'routine bone marrow biopsy' he was also going to take a splinter of bone that would be sent to a laboratory in Cardiff to see if it would produce leukaemic cells. 'How long will that take?' I ask him, as you arch your back in pain like a medieval saint being tortured. 'Tim won't remember any of this, Shane,' Panos assures me. 'But the trephine test can take up to two weeks before we get the results, and I'm sorry to say that your husband can't be given the all clear until these are through.'

I watch him inserting the huge needle into the marrow, I'm not squeamish any more. I sit holding your hand, talking to you, I don't know if you hear me, but I can tell the trephine is giving you grief. Panos tells me again that you won't remember any of it, and says he will look at the slides of the bone marrow biopsy at once and call your mobile this evening with the first test results. As usual before he leaves us, he tries so very gently to rouse you from the stupor. 'It's OK, Panos, I'll do it.' An agency nurse comes in to do your vital signs; I already had you almost upright, with three pillows behind your head. I drove home; we didn't have lunch in the bone marrow restaurant. Panos called about 6pm, and told us the cells from the bone marrow aspiration are normal: 4 per cent, but we must wait for the cytogenetics and the results of the trephine. This hugely relieves you, and I cannot burst your bubble. Panos says we must wait, until we get the results from Cardiff we must wait...

The front page of the Express *today has another 'Exclusive' 'Transplant Ordeal for Spall in Fresh Cancer Setback'. They had promised Keith Schilling that they wouldn't publish any more stories about your health. It's hard enough dealing with it all from day to day, without the whole world knowing about it. The distress it causes is horrendous, it's so fucking intrusive. I hope this doesn't mean another media frenzy like there was last time. I've told the kids not to answer the phones.*

20th March 1997
The Standard *picked it up last night 'Timothy Spall Hit by Cancer Setback'. Today it's the* Mirror *'Bone Op for Star Spall' and the* Sun *'TV actor Spall in Op Drama'. Drama, they haven't a clue what the word means, except that now, instead of spending fucking quality time, for want of a better word, with you, I have to spend the rest of the day on the phone speaking to the solicitors who are trying to get an injunction. You got this in the post today, a bit of light relief from Stephen Fry.*

Dear Tim
I hear this bastard luke has come back to give you another tickle. Tim, at the risk of sounding maudlin and soppy, can I just let you know how much you're in my thoughts and how deeply, deeply loved you are by all those who know you and millions who don't. There's no point asking the gods why they do this kind of thing, but at least it gives me a chance to tell you how important you are. If you carried on in your

normal rude health all this time, instead of giving us all the fright of our lives, then perhaps we would never have bothered to let you know just what a solid stand-up diamond geezer you really are. So maybe we should look on this arse of an episode as a kind of gigantic fishing expedition on your part, trawling for compliments like the consummate old queen you always were...haul up your slacks, tighten your pants and gird your loins for this new assault...I'm thinking of you and doing the atheistic equivalent of praying for you... Meanwhile spit in the face of fate, scrunch its testicles and all strength and power to you, old darling.

    Much, much love

    Stephen

27th March 1997

Midnight

Four weeks since your birthday party. We got the Rolls-Royce back today because on Wednesday I discovered the hubcaps and silver trim around the headlights and the Spirit of Ecstasy had been stolen. So what does that matter when you are waiting for the results of the trephine test? It was NORMAL! And Secrets *and* Lies *didn't get any Oscars and what does that matter when you are waiting for the results of a TREPHINE? 'Yes Timothy Spall won the Trephine Award for Normality!' So what difference does a few stolen hubcaps make to our lives? We see Goldstone at 8.00am because it's Good Friday and we are going away for a few days before you have that horrible fungus cut out of your lung. We are going to look at a narrowboat; apparently she's called* Cassien. *I'm fucked, relieved, done in, knackered. I'm a Christian (I think): I prayed with the vicar last Thursday, went on my knees. Me who swore at God...*

Tim was in the wheelhouse chatting to Matt; we always do the audios separately.

'You OK, darlin'?' he said, sensing something was wrong.

'Everything fine, my love,' I assured him. 'Paul's ready for you. I'm going to go for a walk, take a look at the fishing museum.'

I spent a few minutes chatting to Matt before I left.

'We're going to miss you both,' I said. 'We've had some good times, hey, Matt? Looking back now, even that stinking voyage to Fishguard wasn't that bad.'

Matt laughed. 'It was pretty bad at the time, but I've really enjoyed it and only wish we could do some more filming, but the money's run out on this series. Are you still planning on leaving this afternoon?' he asked me.

'It feels pretty fresh outside the harbour, but if we go Tim says we'll leave about two.'

'We'll be long gone by then,' Matt remarked sadly. 'I'd love to wave you goodbye.'

'Oh shut up, Matt,' I said, giving him a hug, 'you'll have me crying in a minute. I'm going.'

The fishing museum was closed, which was a shame, so I carried on around the corner towards the 'new basin' – it was built in 1857. I noticed several older gentlemen disappearing into a little concrete hut; intrigued I approached one of the chaps and asked him what was going on.

'It's where old men go to talk about the size of the fish they almost caught and how they got away,' he laughed.

As we stood there chatting, people, young and old, called out his name: 'Morning, Jimmy, a lovely day.' The older men went into the hut and the younger ones headed away from the harbour. Jimmy said that he used to be a fisherman and told me the harbour, in his youth, used to be full of fishing boats and the hut was where the crews passed the time of day. Old habits die hard; the old fishermen still congregate, chat and play cards.

In the nineteenth century, herring, whiting, mackerel, cod, haddock, crab and lobster, depending on the season, were the mainstay of the Lossiemouth fishing fleet. The town was prosperous, the harbour had warehouses, ice stores, banks and churches. It was a busy place. Herring was the most profitable catch, as it could be salted into barrels and exported as far away as Russia. Lobster and crab were kept alive, and the other fish packed in ice, and put on the train down to Liverpool; the lobster and crab for the Cunard Liners sailing to America, the rest travelled down south to Billingsgate in London.

The herring was processed on-site in the harbour. Gutting was done by women, they were known as quines, and they had backbreaking and stinking work. The quines travelled around the east coast following the fishing fleets into the harbours of Buckie, Findochty, Portknockie, Cullen, Portsoy, Whitehills, Banff and Macduff, and then into England as far south as Lowestoft.

We didn't see a single commercial fishing boat in Lossiemouth. Jimmy said the fish market was due for demolition: 'Ta make room for waterside lifestyle apartments,' he sneered, as he lit another roll-up.

'How far is it to Buckie, Jimmy?' I asked him.

'Eleven nautical miles and ye won't find any lifestyle apartments there,' he replied, as he pulled tobacco off his top lip, 'it's an ugly old place.'

Tim and I left Lossiemouth on a fresh breeze with waves breaking over miles of the deserted beaches that skirt Spey Bay.

'I love this sea,' Tim said, putting his arms around my shoulders, 'six months ago we wouldn't have put our nose out of the harbour, but we know *The Princess Matilda* can take it.'

We both watched with awe as the long rolling waves broke over the bow, showering the wheelhouse in froth.

'How far do you think we'll get this year?' I asked him as I braced my knees, ready to ride over the next wave.

'Who knows, darlin'?' Tim replied. 'The world is our oyster. And talking about fish, Paul and Matt demolished that lobster.'

'I know, I saw the remains in the bin.'

'It was bloody delicious,' Tim responded, licking his lips.

'I had a chat with an old fisherman in Lossiemouth; he reckons Whitehills would be a good winter home.'

'We'll see, but one port at a time, and today that's Buckie,' Tim replied.

'My fisherman said it was a dump, let's go to Whitehills.'

But Tim would not be swayed.

We were to discover that Buckie is the largest harbour on the south side of the Moray Firth and still has a fishing fleet. After we moored against a high wall, we also discovered it still had a flourishing shipbuilding and repair facility. There was a phone number above one of the sheds.

Tim called it. 'Hello, we've just arrived and wondered if you could give us a quote for a paint job?...*The Princess Matilda*. We're right opposite your yard...OK, see you in twenty, bye.'

I was making a cup of tea and noticed two men climbing down the ladder. Tim invited them onboard.

'I'm Colin Taylor, the general manager of Buckie Shipyard, and this is James Grala-Wojrezyk, our shipyard manager,' he said by way of an introduction. James nodded and said hello in a broad Scots accent. Colin we suspected was a Geordie. James we could see was a working man; he was wearing overalls and declined a cup of tea. He was a wiry man, the sort that is never still. He ran his dirty thumbnail along the seal on the window by the TV. 'It lets in water.' It wasn't a question more a statement of fact. 'Aye, we could fix that,' he said, taking out a notepad and pencil.

Within half an hour it was arranged that they would have us lifted out of the water and put in the boatyard for de-fouling then painting. We all shook hands and agreed that Tim and I would take *The Princess Matilda* by the slipway so she could be craned out at high tide.

'Looks like this is going to be our winter home, then?' Tim said after they left.

'How the fuck are you going to get me up that ladder to see in Hogmanay?' I asked him. We always try to see in the New Year afloat.

'In a sack,' he laughed. 'And we need new line for the kite, but you'd better get online and work out how we get home while they do the work.'

The Princess Matilda stayed in Buckie Shipyard for several weeks, getting what Tim called 'a Buckie-wood makeover'. She looked brand spanking new when Colin Taylor and his team were finished with her. The new paintwork almost reflected the smiles on our faces, but it wasn't an option for us to winter *The Princess Matilda* in Buckie. I had had enough of clambering up filthy ladders, and Jimmy the old fisherman from Lossiemouth had been correct about the harbour. It was not the most picturesque part of Scotland. So we spent our first Scottish Hogmanay in the handsome county town of Banff. Jim Henderson the harbour master had said he could give us a pontoon mooring for the winter. Banff was only a few nautical miles away from Buckie, but it was one hell of a roller-coaster ride to get there.

We left Buckie Harbour an hour later than we should have and ploughed over waves the size of terraced houses. This was hardly surprising as it was mid-November, but what amazed me most was Tim's calm. The shaking nervous wreck that he had been when we came out of the Cardiff Barrage that spring had disappeared. It was as if he had put all of his fears and anxieties to bed as he skippered our craft around the Moray Firth on an angry unforgiving sea.

We had a welcoming committee of salty sea dogs and fishermen to watch as we came into the old historic harbour of Banff. The briny bush telegraph had signalled that we were on our way. Banff is an old port, with parts that date back to 1625; two centuries later, Thomas Telford extended it with the building of the northern breakwater and lighthouse. This was where the ex-fisherman Jim Henderson and Colin Taylor, et al, were waiting for us.

It was low tide and surf waves were swelling across the approach to the entrance of the outer harbour. Whether it was just by sheer luck or Tim's fine skippering, we managed to get into the port without getting any of Colin's paintwork scratched. In fact, the paintwork could have been more abused than scratched, because if Tim had lost his nerve by putting *Matilda* into reverse gear to abort our entry, the rolling swell would have lifted us up like a rubber duck and smashed us into the opposite historic wall. Instead, the skipper increased the revs for more speed. For a split second I thought it would be all over, that our luck had finally run out, but by going faster we outran the surf wave before it ricocheted with twice the force.

The Princess Matilda and her crew had been centimetres from destruction. Jim Henderson said it was Tim's fine seamanship that saved our bacon, and we're told the old fishermen still talk about our entrance – most of them saying it took a brave man or a fool to do it at low tide when the surf breaks. At high water, unless there is a northerly gale blowing, the sea usually trickles in. The only casualty to *The Princess Matilda* that day was a stress crack in the marble worktop in the galley. Jim said it probably happened when we fell off the top of a fifteen-foot wave and did a belly flop as we landed, which would have sent vibrations running all the way through the hold.

Chapter Thirty-Five
THE PRINCESS MATILDA HEADS HOME

Banff to England: 169 nautical miles

Tim and I left Banff the following spring and in the course of just six days we crossed over the border into England. We had the weather and the tides on our side. I kept remarking to the skipper, 'We're picking up speed, we're heading downhill!' But perhaps most important was the fact that heebie-jeebie Timmy had disappeared; nothing like the bag of anxiety he had been when we left Penarth the previous year.

Banff Harbour had been a perfect winter home, a short walk along the shoreline to the nearest pub. We had even managed to fly our kite on New Year's Eve, although the might of the wind had us running back to the warmth of our log fire. Some of our neighbours came first footing on New Year's Day. Fortunately, we had a bottle of single malt, so we made many new friends, some who saw us off in their own boats when we left. A photograph of *The Princess Matilda*, covered in snow, appeared in the local newspaper, and Tim and I did a radio interview the day we left. A third series of our programme had now been commissioned, so Paul Crompton was with us.

We put into Amble south of Berwick-upon-Tweed on 26th April 2011, so I removed the Scottish ensign and replaced it once again with the Union flag. Our next milestone was going into the Tyne, where we left *The Princess Matilda* for a couple of weeks in a tiny marina called St Peter's Basin, just seven-and-a-half miles upstream from the estuary and less than a mile away from Newcastle's 'Toon quay'. My best friend Miriam was with us the day we left the Tyne, taking an excursion under the famous bridges: the Millennium, the Tyne, the swing and the High Level bridge. The last of these was a rail bridge that had been opened by Queen Victoria in 1849. Then we headed back downstream to the North Sea and Hartlepool. Bad weather kept us there for a few days before we set out again, heading south. Tim and I had a yearning to get back to the Medway and Thames estuary, from where we had started. I ticked off the ports in my road atlas: Whitby, Scarborough, Bridlington and Hull. But then summer storms threatened to keep us from pressing south; common sense and a meeting with another RNLI lifeboat crew gave us pause for thought.

The deep water of the Humber estuary is the historic boundary between East Riding of Yorkshire and Lincoln-shire. This boundary was of utmost importance to us, because we were now a couple of hops away from the start of our homeport estuary, the Thames. All that stood in our way was the Humber, the Wash and the nobbled rump end of England that is made of the counties of Norfolk and Suffolk. For Tim and me, North-folk is where the 'north ends' and Sarf-folk is where the south begins. But first we had to wait for fair weather before coming out of the mighty Humber to cross the square-mouthed bay of the Wash and put in at the Norfolk town of Wells-next-the-Sea.

Humber Lifeboat Station sits on a remote windswept peninsula called Spurn Point. The North Sea slaps in on one side of the narrow spit and the River Humber tumbles out of the other. I had been given the phone number of David Steen-voorden, the coxswain of the lifeboat station; he was a friend of Patch Harvey, the coxswain at Penlee Lifeboat Station who we had become pals with when we had moored in Newlyn in 2009. David, 'call me Spanish', generously offered us the use of an RNLI swing mooring close to the mouth of the Humber estuary. 'You'll be safe and sound there,' he assured us in his rich lumbering Lincolnshire accent, 'you can't miss it, the lifeboat lies afloat off the end of the Humber Pilots Jetty. The buoy you want is just upstream.'

I had a feeling he would be looking through a pair of binoculars as we attempted to get attached to this swing buoy.

I now quite enjoyed getting swing buoys, but it had been a while; the last one was by Piel Island the previous summer. However, this brute on the Humber had no float for me to grab with my boat hook. Tim approached the buoy slowly to see what the tide was doing. Fortunately the sea was flat calm, but the ebb tide was rushing out and was swirling angrily around the huge yellow lump of metal that was stopping its progress.

I knew I would be unable to secure us, so after bickering for a few minutes Tim and I swapped places, Tim on the bow and me on the helm. I used the bow thruster to bring *Matilda* close enough for Tim to lie flat on the gunwale; he got our rope through the iron hoop and in moments we were secured to the buoy. If he had fallen in, the ebb tide would have swept him out to sea. I hoped that Spanish, the lifeboat man, had been keeping an eye.

No sooner had Tim tied up than my phone rang. I had been right, we had been observed. 'Spanish here, why don't you come over and meet the crew? I'll nip over in the boarding boat and pick you up.'

'Speak to the skipper,' I said, somewhat ungraciously, almost throwing the phone at Tim. I was peeved he had got the mooring buoy, but I was hoping he would decline, because I knew that I would need to climb a ladder up to the top of Pilots Jetty. Tim gladly accepted the invitation, so I sat in our cabin and sulked.

We had Phil Shotton the Geordie cameraman onboard, so this was the third year that he had filmed with us. He was easy to be around and we had become really good friends.

'What's up, Shane?' he asked me as he leant against the stove in the galley, rolling a cigarette to smoke on the back deck.

'Fucking ladders, Phil,' was my reply.

Spanish and one of his crew turned up twenty minutes later, and held on to the side of *The Princess Matilda*, their small craft bouncing up and down on the low tide swell.

Spanish was the older of the two; he was wearing an RNLI hard hat that emphasized a strong square-jawed face. He reached out a calloused hand to help me step down from the wheelhouse into the lifeboat's boarding boat. 'No need to lock up,' he said to Tim, who had a set of keys in his hand. 'Now't goes on around here without me knowing about it, hey, Steve?' he said, turning towards his companion who was simi-larly clad in well-worn wet-weather gear. Phil quickly joined us, after stubbing out a half-smoked roll-up and popping it in his pocket. I had once accused him of being a dirty chucker after he threw a fag end in the sea. He had been vigilant with his butts ever since.

Once we were all safely aboard the boarding boat, Spanish casually swayed with the tide. He reminded me of one of those men that spin the Waltzers at the fairground. The crew of *The Princess Matilda* all quickly grasped on to a grab bar as we rolled from side to side. Steve and Spanish could have been standing at a bus stop. They were best mates, this was obvious, but Steve was a few years younger than his boss to whom he appeared to defer. It wasn't hard to see why; Spanish had been around the block a few times and had taken some hard knocks, but it was clear that he loved his job. Tim later said that he had a face that was always on the edge of a smile, but it was his 'blue Spanish eyes' that caught my attention. My dad had eyes like these – as a nipper, I could never lie to my father unless I was looking at my feet.

Steve was at the helm and he put the little boat into forward gear and did a slow circle around *The Princess Matilda*. He briefly pulled back on the revs as we came by the buoy; he and the gaffer were diplomatically checking we were firmly tied on to it.

'Do we pass muster, guvnor?' Tim said anxiously. He then pointed to a tear on the knee of his white linen trousers. 'I did this kneeling to get a rope in that hole…'

'You did well, skipper,' Spanish said; he was a man used to taking charge and missed nothing. 'When you arrived,' he continued, 'there was a five-knot tide pushing against you; we've the winds and tides from hell here on the Humber, it makes you humble. Even Steve and I sometimes have problems tying the lifeboat up to these buoys!' Tim was delighted with this endorsement.

'You live in a beautiful part of the world,' Phil remarked. The retreating tide had left a pristine beach on the spit, with the remains of what looked like an old wooden sea break. Phil was mentally framing a shot, but, like the true gentleman he is, he asked them, 'Would you mind if I filmed you both with the sun setting behind *The Princess Matilda*, like?'

Both Spanish and Steve nodded.

'But I don't have any consent forms on me,' Phil said quickly, as he grabbed his camera out of its case, before they changed their minds.

'No need,' Spanish replied, as he and Steve both turned towards the camera and looked straight in to the lens. 'David Steenvoorden, superintendent coxswain of Humber Lifeboat Station and…' 'Steve Purvis, crew, Humber Lifeboat Station,' then in unison, 'hereby give our consent.'

'Will that do?' Spanish said with a huge grin creasing up his face.

'I think you've done that before,' Tim said, laughing, 'a couple of pros!'

Spanish nodded. 'We often get local news teams down here; we've got one of the busiest shipping lanes in Europe, so there's always something going on. Some days there's over a hundred shipping movements coming in or out of the Humber and some of our shouts can be sixty miles offshore; that's why we're the only full-time lifeboat crew in the country, and we are unique because we live on the job with our wives and kids.'

Tim sheepishly explained to them that, when we had been complete idiots, we had once thought about bringing our narrowboat from the River Trent onto the Humber estuary. Spanish chuckled and replied, 'Aye, and we'd have lassoed you as you shot out into the North Sea – that would've made the news!'

While this conversation was going on, I was looking towards the jetty, trying to work out how far I would have to climb. Steve slowed down by the ladder, and I swallowed hard as I looked high above me – this ladder was even longer than the one in Fishguard Harbour – but Steve steered around it towards a landing platform at the base of the jetty. A series of concrete steps with handrails led up to the top. I took David's hand as he helped me disembark, and my relief was palpable. Phil and Tim followed close behind; the coxswain jumped back into the boarding boat and Steve steered back to the ladder. In seconds they had it attached to a crane that lifted it out of the water and onto the jetty. The two of them scrabbled up the ladder like a couple of monkeys. Neither were spring chickens, but they were fit.

A few minutes later, we were sitting at crowded picnic tables in the middle of a semi-circle of half-a-dozen identical houses.

*

'Why do they call me Spanish?' the coxswain said, as he poured us a drink. 'I used to fish in Spain, thus the nickname. This is my wife Karen,' he said, presenting us to a handsome middle-aged women who had just appeared out of one of the houses, 'whose maiden name is Spall. Maybe you are related, Timothy?' We shook her hand. Then he introduced us to the rest of the crew, their wives, children and even grandchildren. The kids played on their bikes and the grown-ups chatted and told us a little about their lives.

'We all live here together, each crewmember has their own house. It's our own little village,' Karen explained. 'In eight minutes the men can be on the lifeboat. If one bell sounds in the house, the crew walks down the jetty, but if it's two bells they have to get on their bikes because this means it's life threatening. It's a way of life for the wives, we're used to it, but the younger ones feel the isolation more than me. Sometimes during storms or tidal surges, the road gets washed out and we can't get the kids to school, or get to the shops or doctor's appointments, but me and Spanish love it!'

Her husband gently patted her hand. 'Aye we do, I've got the best job in the world, but I couldn't do it without you.'

It was now completely dark and had become chilly, but none of the families seemed bothered about going indoors. Tim was worried they were just being polite so we stood up to take our leave and looked around to see where Spanish had gone.

'He'll be getting changed,' Karen said. 'Come on, I'll walk you to the jetty.'

Steve and Spanish had only been missing for a few minutes but were already rigged out in their protective gear, as were some more of the crew that operated the crane that lowered the boarding boat.

'It's all good practice,' Spanish said, as he led the way down the jetty.

I chatted to Karen as we slowly followed the men.

'Do you worry when they go out on a shout?' I asked her.

'I wouldn't be human if I didn't,' she replied. 'Especially when there's a force 10 blowing, but the sea's in his blood. I fretted more when he was a fisherman. He was rescued himself, not once but twice by a lifeboat, but at least now he's going out on an all-weather, self-righting boat, not an old rust bucket of a trawler!'

Just then a child ran behind us, she was about nine with bare arms and feet. Karen shook her head and put her arms around the girl. 'You know you're not supposed to be on the jetty,' she chided her, at the same time as rubbing her to get her warm. 'Now run home before anyone sees you!'

We both watched as the child went back the way she had come. Suddenly, I understood exactly what Spanish meant when he said he couldn't do his job without Karen. Humber Lifeboat Station was as much her responsibility as her husband's. She didn't go out on the shouts, but I would bet my life she was always available to give advice and support to the crew's families.

The boarding boat was now being lowered, and Spanish and Steve scrambled down the ladder ready to ferry us back to *The Princess Matilda*.

'It's been an honour to meet you, Karen,' I said, as I gave her a hug. She waved us goodbye and watched as the boarding boat took us back to the buoy.

Tim and I were lulled into the arms of Morpheus by the soporific slipslop slap of the tide trickling under the bow. The skipper was out for the count, but I was woken about 1.30, with the weight of Tim on top of me. I think this is what stopped me being rolled out of bed. It dawned on me that we had been hit by an enormous wave. Then seconds later the wave must have bounced off the beach and sent us flying back the other way;

Tim rolled off me. The ropes holding us to the great heavy buoy grunted and groaned but held us tight. I promptly fell back to sleep, thankfully in my bed and not on the floor. I woke to bright sunshine at 7.30 and reached for my laptop to check the weather forecast; it showed near-perfect conditions for us to leave. I wanted more than anything to get back to the non-tidal Thames. Tim was sick of hearing me say, 'No tides, or overfalls, no jelly fish, no gale-force winds to blow us onto rocks, no sand-banks to run aground on, no oil tankers or fast ferries, no wind farms, no getting lost!' We were so tantalizingly close to home.

We had a few visitors while I made breakfast (pork sausages for Tim and veggie ones for me and Phil). Our first callers were the crew of a Humber pilot boat. They said *The Princess Matilda* intrigued them and were fans of my husband, so I put the kettle on. Half an hour after they left, another pilot boat dropped by for a chat, then – from the other side of the mouth of the Humber – the Cleethorpes Lifeboat Station's inshore RIB pulled alongside. They all said the same thing: the sea was pretty beastly out on the estuary. The original pilot boat came back about an hour later and said there was a three-metre swell coming from the south-east, so they advised us to stay where we were. This was good enough for us, so I prepared dinner.

By teatime, we had a high-tide swell swinging us back and forth, as if a manic baby-sitter on Red Bull was rocking us. It was a bouncy hour in my galley, but I am pretty good at cooking when the sky disappears and the sea takes its place. I even managed to make cauliflower cheese. After dinner, Phil washed up at slack tide; he was first up the following day. He likes to film the sun rising and had his camera out of his cabin window when a boat came alongside and gave him four lobsters. 'I wasn't wearing any kecks,' he told Tim sheepishly.

Tim had also got up early but I stayed in bed; I was feeling under the weather.

'I think we might go today,' Tim announced, as he handed me a cup of slopping tea. '3 to 4 so'easterly decreasing 2 to 3 later.'

'You must be kidding, I think I'm going to be sick!' was my reply. My view through the skylight showed fluffy cotton-wool clouds rushing across the blue of the sky. On our mast was a free giveaway royal wedding flag, with a picture of Kate Middleton and Prince William that was flapping so quickly it was hard to tell which was which. This made me feel a little more nauseous; I was suffering from the effects of the Humber swell. I staggered out of bed and waddled into the galley, hoping to find something to settle my stomach. I knew there was a low-fat yogurt lurking somewhere in the fridge, instead I found the lobsters in a black bin liner. I almost threw up but screamed instead, the bag was moving.

'No, they are dead!' Phil assured me. 'The gadgie on the pilot boat said they were definitely dead.'

'I want them out of my fridge now,' I said, stamping my foot.

Tim and Phil both shrugged their shoulders and shuffled their feet.

'So I have to do it?' I shrilled, filling pans of water to bring to the boil.

Tim carefully removed the bin liner out of the fridge and put it on the marble work surface. We all stared at it for a few seconds, but I bolted into the bedroom when one of them tried to make a run for it.

'Put them in the freezer!' I shouted.

The Humber lifeboat boarding boat pulled alongside about eleven, with Steve and Spanish aboard.

'Looks a good day to go. I expect you're planning to leave about one before the last of the ebb?' Spanish said casually, as if he didn't notice the white horses galloping our way. He must have seen the look of apprehension on Tim's face. 'Oh, it will all calm down soon! We'll pop by in an hour and look at the charts with you if you want,' he said, with a grin that spread across his face. They sped back over to the lifeboat, so Tim went back to his charts and me to the stove; the water for the lobster was once more coming to the boil.

With my eyes shut, I had pulled the bag out of the freezer. Tim took the bag out of my trembling hand and reached inside and pulled one out. 'Yep, fully anaesthetized,' he said, before dangling it over my head.

'Stop it, Timmy,' I screamed at him. 'Just put them in the pots NOW!'

Spanish and Steve came back about 12.30, and as predicted the swell had now died away. Tim had his charts and passage plan on the table, and Spanish sat and studied them. 'You are a far better skipper than you give yourself credit for, Tim. I wish I could see the same amount of planning going into a passage as you do!'

Tim's face lit up. 'Thanks, Spanish,' he replied, 'that's the best review I've ever had.'

We had about twenty minutes to go before we slipped the buoy, so we all chatted over coffee, Tim to Spanish and me to Steve. I think Steve and I had a great deal in common; we spend most of our time with larger-than-life, rumbustious men. Steve quietly told me a little bit about himself. He was a veteran of the Falklands War and had served aboard the *Stena Seaspray*, a support craft that repaired the navy taskforce ships.

'You must have seen some grim things out there?' I questioned him.

He shrugged his shoulders and quickly changed the subject. 'Tell me about your worst experience on *The Princess Matilda*.'

Without thinking, I immediately replied, 'Coming around Rattray Head—'

'It was biblical,' Tim said, interrupting, 'we left Banff on a perfect spring day, no wind, flat calm sea, blue sky, then I came in too close coming round the headland. I should have gone out four miles, but stupidly took a shortcut. One minute it was dead calm and the next we were being tossed like a ragdoll in the mouth of a rabid dog, then we were hit by a hailstorm that battered us with lumps of ice the size of snooker balls. It sounded like someone was firing peas at us from a bazooka!'

I looked at my watch. 'We'd better go now, Tim, if we want to make the most of this tide.' The lifeboat men both stood and I gave them two cooked lobsters for their lunch.

'Do you have any advice for us?' I asked them, as they prepared to untie the boarding boat from *The Princess Matilda*.

'If you need help, call the coastguard, sooner rather than later,' Spanish said, looking us both in the eyes. 'Then the lifeboat can get to you before things get really bad. Rather a bruised ego than broken hearts.'

I thought about the Penlee RNLI crew of the *Solomon Brown*, who in 1981 lost their lives because the captain of a ship had asked for their assistance too late.

Tim and I meet so many interesting people, especially in his line of work, but it is characters like Spanish, Steve and all the other lifeboat crews who are our heroes. Selfless is a word that springs to mind, plus true grit and valour, because they go the extra mile when others throw in the towel.

The Humber coxswain and his mate waved us off at quarter past one as we headed out on a flat calm sea, even the sun came out and there were a couple of nosey seals watching us go. We heard Spanish yell from the boarding boat, 'KEEP YOUR FEET DRY!' I wasn't sure if this was a warning, but shortly afterwards Tim began to wrestle with the steering wheel as brown frothing breaking waves hit us all 54 feet along our side. He had to turn *Matilda* to meet them so we could climb over the rollers, which was far more comfortable than being smashed from side to side. Unfortunately, this meant we were going in completely the wrong direction, heading back up north to Bridlington, not south towards Skegness. We all held on to the grab bars as the nose of the boat went into the spume of sludgy, silty foam that sprayed all over the bow. It seemed like an age before the sea changed colour and the swell died down. Once again we were heading due south. Spanish was right; the Humber is a humbling river, and it had disdainfully spat us out.

Chapter Thirty-Six
A WASH

Spurn Point to Wells-next-the-Sea: 45 nautical miles

It took us over eight hours to get from East Yorkshire to North Norfolk, but the last third of our journey was crossing the wide-open wilderness of the Wash. On my road atlas, the square-shaped Wash looks friendly and benign; it doesn't give any indication just how lonely crossing this bay can be. The estuaries of four rivers, the rivers Witham, Welland, Nene and Great Ouse pour into this bay. In the southwest corner is King's Lynn, on the Great Ouse, and to the north is Boston, on the Witham, and in between are the flat fenlands of Lincolnshire, East Anglia and Cambridgeshire.

Years ago, when we explored the inland waterways on our first narrowboat, *Cassien*, we often discussed leaving the Grand Union Canal to join the River Nene in Northampton and get down to the Wash. On the canal guides, it sounded such an idyllic journey to the sea; through meandering rivers, manmade drainage ditches and sluices, but boaters more experienced than us would shake their heads and tell us stories of the tricky tides of the Wash.

Maybe this was one of the reasons we saw no other boats as we did our crossing on *The Princess Matilda*; indeed, for many hours we could not see anything of the low-lying land, just the grey, gloomy, grim sea. I kept looking through my binoculars, yet it was seven in the evening before I saw what I thought were Norfolk street lights. And then a mist came down and once again we were alone.

It is so comforting to be able to see the land on our journeys and my heart sank when Tim mentioned we still had another nine miles to go; and to add another layer of anxiety he added, 'I don't understand it, we've a seven-knot tide behind us, but we don't seem to be making any headway. I think it's all those rivers debouching into the North Sea, that's slowing us down.'

It seemed like hours before Robert, the harbour master of Wells-next-the-Sea, came out in his launch to guide us into our next port of call. He had warned Tim before we left the Humber that the dogleg channel into Wells (no-longer-that-close-to-the Sea) was continuingly changing because of shifting sands; we were more than glad to have an escort, especially now it was twilight. I had turned on all of the lights within the boat, as well as the navigation lights, an hour before, even I knew there was a wind farm with supply boats somewhere off the Norfolk coast. Phil and I hung on to grab bars as the sea on our approach was spitefully choppy. 'We're crossing the bar,' Tim said quietly, almost to himself not us. He was hanging on to the steering wheel, concentration etched across his face, as he followed the harbour master's launch along the confusing buoyed channel, one minute heading south, the next north.

I was too knackered to ask him what he meant about the bar, as I was preparing the ropes on the back deck.

'*Turn around by the warehouse,*' Robert's voice crackled over the VHF radio a few minutes later. He was now along-side us and pointed to where we should go. The channel had opened out to a wide lagoon, with fishing boats moored against the harbour wall under the old warehouse. '*We're just passing your berth on that starboard pontoon,*' he said, pointing to our right-hand side, '*but you won't be able to moor with the tide flooding!*' He and two others were waiting for us after Tim had followed his instructions, spinning the steering wheel and using the force of the tide to push the arse of

Matilda about. He kept the engine in a gentle forward gear as we drew alongside the pontoon. This gave the harbour crew enough time to take and secure our ropes. We thanked them and fell into bed, not even the funfair on the town quay kept us awake.

I was woken by a belly-bubbling gurgle; it wasn't Tim, because I turned over hugging him instead of turning away, luxuriating in the womb-like sloshing that was inches from where we lay. Our bed is below the waterline and tucked behind the bow. Usually the tide glugs and slip-slip-slops, but I sensed something different. This rising tide had more urgency and our bed and the whole of the boat began to writhe, pulling against the mooring ropes, vibrating. I threw on a dressing gown and tripped over Tim's pink crocs as I made my way through the untidy saloon to the wheelhouse. I thought it was the end of the world; that while we had slept the four horsemen of the Apocalypse had come upon us.

There was a small space between the side of the boat and the pontoon, and unconstrained energy was rushing through the gap, the sheer force of the water was humbling. We had not had time to take much notice of our new temporary home, but now I could see just how narrow the channel behind us was, and the tide was being funnelled, and we were in the way. Across from our mooring, I noticed there was a small beach, but in seconds it was enveloped with an angry frothing sea. *The Princess Matilda* groaned and bucked on her mooring ropes, as the tide seemed determined to rip us away. I was hypnotized by this surging water and in my slippers I inched my way along the gunwale, so I could sit on the gas locker and watch the miracle of the fast-rising tide.

'No wonder Robert told us to turn around last night, we'd have never stopped else!' I said to Tim, as I woke him up to give him a daybreak cup of tea. 'You know I never use this word, but this is an awesome tide.'

Tim grunted, farted and went back to sleep.

We had to leave *The Princess Matilda* in Wells-next-the Sea for a couple of weeks because of family birthdays and Tim's work commitments. Robert said he would keep his eye on the boat, but, because it was such a small port, he might need to raft boats against us. Our new neighbour on our return was to be a Dutch barge called *Angell Hardy 11*.

I knew a little about this vessel because the skipper had been communicating with me on social media sites. He had seen our series on TV and asked our advice about making a passage from the River Trent to Wells. He said he had done it once before, but had come out onto the Wash at Boston. This time he planned to do it the long way round, coming out on the Humber then on to Wells via Grimsby. Our suggestion was to come out on the Wash, and I relayed what Spanish had to say about the Humber having 'the wind and tides from hell'.

By all accounts, *Angell Hardy 11* had a pleasant trip down the Humber to Grimsby, making a liar of Spanish and us, but then the weather changed. We were still chatting online, and I advised the skipper and his wife to wait for a couple of days, as the Met Office forecast said it was going to be blowing a force 5 to 6, with a moderate to rough sea. A slight to moderate sea is enough to keep Tim and me in port.

Angell Hardy, with four people aboard, was rescued by the Wells lifeboat off the North Norfolk coast. It was found helplessly wallowing with a broken engine in a heavy swell. According to the RNLI website:

> *Conditions were extremely difficult...as the waves were breaking over the casualty vessel's foredeck. Care had to be taken to minimize the water flooding into the accommodation*

which wasn't watertight. On reaching…Wells the lifeboat also had difficulty in negotiating the bar in the seas, which were beam-on to the two boats. Also they were rapidly losing water as the tide was ebbing fast. Despite the lifeboat crew's best efforts, the barge had taken on a lot of water…

We arrived back in Wells a few days after they had been rescued. Robert had rafted *The Princess Matilda* to the outside of them, so we had to cross their deck to get to ours. 'Permission to come over?' Tim said to a tall, bearded man who was adjusting fenders on *Angell Hardy*. He turned and saw us and held out his hand. 'I'm a right prat,' he grimaced.

That evening, Tim and I sat on our deck and silently surveyed a full-blown blousy harvest moon rising over the tide-swollen Norfolk wetlands. The great buttery globe of the setting sun had rippled streaks of bleeding crimson until it disappeared over the horizon. There was no wind or tide, just chatter drifting over the dusky satin of the water.

It had been a while since we had been in such proximity to other craft. Our last mooring had been on the bouncing Spurn buoy and before that an uneven mudbank in the drying part of Bridlington Harbour. We sensed a change in the air, or rather the conversations. People were sitting out on decks rather than lifestyle apartment patios, but the talk was the same: politics, wine, careers, the cost of living and school fees. I whispered to Tim, 'We're definitely getting closer to London!'

The moon cast an inviting slither of a pathway across the port of Wells-next-the-Sea. If I had had webbed feet, I swear I could have followed the silvery trail to a secret place. My kids grew up with me telling them nothing ever stays the same, except the sun rises, the tide will turn and your dad will knock over a glass of red wine. Tim was now on his hands and knees cleaning up the Chianti by the light of the moon.

Chapter Thirty-Seven
RELAXED FISH

**Wells-next-the-Sea to Southwold via Lowestoft:
67 nautical miles**

We were heading to the port of Lowestoft, the most easterly point of the British mainland, with a spiteful wind blowing down from Siberia. The tide was with us for a few hours, speeding us on our way, which was just as well as we had fifty-five miles to cover that day; then it turned and so did I.

'We're going backwards,' I grumpily complained.

'No, we're not,' Tim replied. 'We're doing three-and-a-half knots, but we'll pick up a bit more speed once we cross this estuary,' he said, pointing to his sea chart. 'That's the River Yare that's spewing out from Great Yarmouth.'

'I can see the bloody estuary, it's been in the same position now for half an hour, and why can't we go up it and put in at Great Yarmouth?' I asked him for the tenth time, but his answer was the same.

'I've plotted our course to Lowestoft, and then we'll only be about eighty nautical miles from the Thames Estuary!'

'We could walk there quicker,' I responded irritably.

'Not even you can walk on water, Shane,' my husband replied, as he thrust down on the throttle to give us more power. *The Princess Matilda* did her best but the five-knot tide kept us firmly in our place. It took us two hours to cover two miles. We left Wells before breakfast and arrived in Lowestoft at dinnertime.

*

Matt our young cameraman was there waiting for us, shivering on the pontoon. As usual he was wearing inappropriate clothes; his shorts and T-shirt weren't made for the bracing Suffolk breeze. I put the kettle on to make him a cup of tea but Tim thrust a chilled beer in his hand instead.

'Have you had a chance to look around, Matt?' Tim asked him.

'You're not moored in the prettiest part of town,' Matt replied, as he swigged out of the bottle. 'I think the docks have seen better days—'

'The fishing industry is almost dead in this country,' I said, interrupting him. Then I added, 'Think of those young fish-gutting girls from the Hebrides, who used to follow the herring fleets all the way from Lossiemouth down the east coast to here. I used to think Lowestoft was such a long way from Scotland, but here we are!'

We heard an old diesel engine spluttering towards us and we all peered out of the saloon windows. There was a small fishing boat heading our way.

'Oi recognoize thes bloody boot, boi!' the ruddy-faced Norfolk fisherman drawled as he came alongside us. Tim went into the wheelhouse to take a rope from him and spent the next ten minutes answering the fisherman's questions about how *Matilda* handled in a rough sea. Well, I think that is what he was asking; I only managed to understand half a dozen words as he busied himself gutting fish.

'Yer oft amara?' he asked us, as he slid fillets of Dover sole into a tatty Tesco's bag.

'We're going to Southwold Harbour,' I quickly responded, hoping I had answered his query correctly. I had studied my road map and knew the harbour was on a river. The fisherman stopped what he was doing and, with a sharp intake of breath, he balefully shook his head and said something that I guessed meant, 'the tide rushes up the River Blythe and if you are not exceedingly careful you may be dragged under the bridge and be decapitated'.

'Now these Dover sole,' he drawled, as he handed Tim the bloodied carrier bag, 'put them in the fridge for a couple of days, then freeze them. Don't eat them fresh, they won't taste as good, the flesh needs to relax.'

'Thanks for the fish and the advice about Southwold,' Tim ventured, while rooting in his pocket for cash with one hand and rubbing fish scales down his trousers with the other.

'Oi'll tec north-in-boi!' The fisherman winked as he undid his rope. Then I think he said, 'Tim, your work has given me and my wife a lot of pleasure and we've been watching your *Somewhere at Sea* programme on the TV. We both like a laugh, but you have my admiration for sticking at it. What will you do when you've finished the circumnavigation?'

Tim and I didn't have an answer to that.

We had one goal in mind when we left Banff in the spring, and that was to get back to where we had started our proper circumnavigation in 2007. It felt as if we had been running a maritime marathon, albeit a slow one, but at long last the end was in sight. Our finishing line was the River Medway, where Tim had taught himself how to navigate and about the tidal pull of the sea. We both longed to walk along the seawall and look at the lights in Upnor Castle from Chatham dockyard.

We had spent eighteen months in Chatham Maritime Marina after our first disastrous expedition out of the Thames, when we had been rescued by a pilot vessel and Sheerness lifeboat. We were determined our return would be different, because now we were a couple of salty seadogs. We would spend a couple of days in Chatham, glorifying in our achievement. Then in triumph we planned to sail up the Thames, through the Thames Barrier, and go back into Limehouse

Basin. Maybe the next day, if the weather was fine, we planned to go back upstream to Brentford where our sea odyssey had really begun. But first we had to go to Southwold, for this is where my sister Jenny and old friend Frances Barber were to join us for our final passages.

It is only twelve miles from Lowestoft to Southwold Harbour. The dead calm sea glistened in the sunlight as the gulls flew alongside us, as if guiding us home. The Dover sole fisherman was right about the might of the tide that could drag the unwary up the River Blyth, but this couple of old seadogs had learnt a few tricks along the way. We did our approach at slack high water, when no tide ran. The harbour master was waiting for us and helped us tie up on one of the wooden stagings. 'Very handy for the pub,' he said, indicating the conveniently sited Harbour Inn above the moorings. Halfway up the building was a sign that said 'FLOOD LEVEL 1953' and below the sign my sister sat, looking at her watch.

The floods of 1953, coincidentally the year that I was born, devastated the east coast of Britain and the Low Countries of Europe. On the night of 31st January, a high spring tide coincided with gale-force winds out in the North Sea. The result was a storm tide that surged down the east coast of Britain and the Netherlands. In places, the sea level was eighteen feet higher than usual, killing hundreds of people. The worst-affected areas were the flat counties of Lincolnshire, Norfolk, Suffolk and Essex. In the Netherlands, where towns and farms lie below sea level, the death toll was in the thousands.

'The might of the ocean,' my sister remarked, as we made our way around the museum in Southwold, looking at photographs of the destruction left in the wake of the surging tide.

I nodded, then took her arm and led her towards the exit. 'Come on, let's get back to that pub we left Tim in before he finishes off the bottle. He's got to get us to Harwich Harbour tomorrow, making the most of the weather, and then Frankie's going to join us!'

'Hurrah!' said my sister. She loves Frances Barber as much as Tim and all of our children do.

Frances took a train to Ipswich, arriving just as the Dover sole had become 'relaxed' enough to eat, and joined us in Shotley Point Marina near Harwich; she was laden with Chablis, champagne and several hats.

Chapter Thirty-Eight
WHAT THE SHUCK

Shotley to Brightlingsea: 34 nautical miles

If Tim is a loose cannon, Frankie is his ammunition; her throaty smokers' laughter can be heard ricocheting in Rotterdam. One of the first things Tim said to her was a slip of the tongue: 'Welcome to Shitley.' Frankie thought this was hilarious.

We showed her around the boat – she had often been on our narrowboats, but this was her first time aboard *The Princess Matilda*. She was also a fan of our TV series and had not missed a single episode. The second episode of the second series of *Somewhere at Sea* was airing at the time of her visit, and Matt was still with us filming for our third series. I had forgotten to mention he might be around. She didn't seem to mind Matt trailing behind her as she took the guided tour. Meanwhile, Jenny and I were getting shipshape, putting away breakables ready for our next trip down the coast. Frank was given a lifejacket and she stood chatting to Tim in the wheelhouse as he finished his own preparations.

'I'd better call the lockkeeper, let them know we want to lock out of the marina,' he said, as he tuned the VHF radio to Channel 80, 'and for God's sake don't let me call it Shitley Marina!' In his usual efficient and serious skippering voice, he began his radio transmission: 'Shitley Marina, Shitley Marina, Shitley Marina, this is *The Princess Matilda* over.'

Frankie's laughter could be heard in Newcastle.

*

We only went a few miles that day as we were spoilt for choice; this was a first for us, mostly our sea passages had been dictated by the next suitable destination. While moored in Shotley, Tim and I had had several arguments about our next ports of call; there were so many places we could go. Large swathes of the coast of Great Britain are too wild to have ports; high cliffs and saltmarshes don't offer a safe harbour. Our first trip of 2011 was from Banff to Peterhead, which was thirty-eight nautical miles, and the next, from Peterhead to Stonehaven, was the same distance. Now we were under the bulbous buttocks of Norfolk and Suffolk, we had lots more options.

Shotley is on the River Stour, opposite two of the busiest ports in Europe, Harwich and Felixstowe. Frankly, the cranes unloading the huge container ships scared me as much as the ships themselves. The size of Harrods, they are not attractive-looking vessels and they don't stop if you get in their way, nor do the fast ferries that leave Harwich for the Netherlands. Tim knows all the rules about giving way to these ships, but it is stress-inducing to have thousands of tons of metal crossing your path.

As a compromise, we had decided we should put in at Titchmarsh on the Walton Backwaters, which is only seven nautical miles from Harwich but feels like another country. This is where Arthur Ransome, the author of the children's classic *Swallows and Amazons*, sailed his small sailing yacht the *Nancy Blackett*.

The south-east coast of England is ribboned with pretty inlets, backwaters, rivers and creeks. I wanted to get back on the Medway and Thames as quickly as possible, something inside me said our luck might run out. But Tim wanted to explore all of the backwaters of Essex. In hindsight, we should have done just that.

Jenny left us in Titchmarsh, as she had problems at one of her hotels, but Frankie stayed onboard, regaling us with stories as she demolished more Dover sole. After dinner, Tim put his sea chart on the table and showed her exactly where we were and where we were heading.

'Some people say the Thames Estuary begins as far north as Felixstowe, but I think it starts at Clacton,' he said, as he traced the chart with his finger. 'But tomorrow, we're going to do twenty-seven nautical miles and go to Brightlingsea, then it's just a few hours from Brightlingsea to the Medway.'

Alas, Brightlingsea on the Medway would be where our odyssey began to unravel. But still, the day began well enough, the sun was shining and we were moored in the middle of the creek on a floating pontoon. Tim called for a water taxi on the VHF radio, so Frankie and I could get in some supplies; we also had a changeover of cameramen. Phil, our Geordie mate, was going to do our penultimate passage over the Thames Estuary and up the Medway to Chatham.

'We'll leave about two,' Tim shouted over the rumble of the water taxi's engine as he waved us goodbye, 'and Rennie's train gets in at one, so bring him back with you!' Rennie Silva is Tim's oldest and dearest friend; they had been to RADA together.

'I think Tim's glad to have a bit of peace and quiet. He says crossing the Thames Estuary is complex,' Frankie commented, as the water taxi crossed the creek to the landing stage below the town.

'According to our pilot book, it's one of the trickiest estuaries in the country, with sandbanks, tides and loads of shipping. He's got it all on his paper chart, but now he'll be putting his course into the chart plotter,' I replied. 'It drives him mad, it's quite an old model, so I always keep out of his way!'

We quickly forgot about Tim's problems as we got out of the water taxi, because there on the jetty was a fisherman selling fresh oysters.

'I adore oysters!' Frankie exclaimed. 'Can we get some?' she pleaded.

We both stood looking at the pile of closed shells sitting on chips of ice, then at the fisherman.

'How do we open them?' I asked him. 'Do we need a special knife...'

'To shuck them,' Frankie joined in. 'It is called shucking, isn't it?' she continued, licking her lips. 'I love slurping oysters.'

The fisherman coughed and tried to regain his composure; listening to Frances say shuck and slurp is more than most red-blooded men can stand.

'I recommend you lay them on a hot skillet for a few seconds and then they open straight away,' he responded, looking at his feet.

'We'll take a dozen,' Frankie said, rooting around in her handbag, 'and we'll pick them up when we come back from the shops!'

'We'd better get a couple of bags of ice to put in the cooler bag, to keep them fresh,' I groaned as I dragged her away.

I left Frankie to pick up the oysters and meet Rennie off his train, and I went back to *The Princess Matilda* with most of the shopping. Tim, as I knew he would be, was still fighting with the chart plotter, so I went below to do some ironing. I had done a load of washing that morning as I needed clean linen and towels for Rennie to use. The sheets had already blown dry in a gentle breeze on the washing line on our back deck. I went up and down the steps to the wheelhouse half-a-dozen times, replacing the un-ironed with the newly ironed so they could air in the sun. Tim would smile at me and I would pat him on the back.

'You all right, love?' I asked him more than once.

'Not really, I can't get all the waypoints in, and if we go today I have to catch this tide to take us across the estuary—'

'But, once we're on the Medway, we'll be home and dry,' I said, interrupting him as I unpegged a couple of his shirts.

'Yes,' he answered me, as he kept putting in his waypoints; tap tapping on the keypad, like some ancient mariner sending out an SOS.

'So you don't have to worry about the navigation from Sheerness to Chatham, we've done it so many times!' I added.

Chapter Thirty-Nine
DÉJÀ VU

Brightlingsea to Chatham Maritime Marina:
40 nautical miles

Our trusty vessel fairly flew across the Thames Estuary at a speed of eight knots, which for us is fast. The sea was so flat that Frankie cooked a shepherd's pie, as a second course to follow the oysters, to eat when we arrived in Chatham. Occasionally she came out of the galley to have a cigarette break on the back deck with Phil, who was happy to have a fellow smoker onboard. Rennie, in a deckchair, gossiped with his old friend Timothy about fellow students from their time at RADA, while I kept looking at my road atlas.

'Just look how far we've come,' I kept saying to no one in particular. 'Just look how far we've been!' Then I stood and saw a familiar sight; Frankie had seen it too.

'What's those things sticking out of the sea?' she asked us.

'That's the wreck of the SS *Richard Montgomery*,' Tim and I said at the same time.

'This is where we lost our steering the first time we ever came out of the Thames, in 2005,' I continued, before Tim took over telling the tale.

'It's a wreck from the Second World War; she broke her back on a sandbank. It's a 3,000-ton time bomb that would take away the Isle of Sheppey if it was to blow—'

'And when we lost our steering, Tim saw the masts and thought about throwing a rope around one of them, 'cos we didn't know what it was,' I added, before Tim continued.

'But I saw a boat heading our way and did this,' he said, waving his arms to demonstrate.

'It was the pilot from Sheerness,' I said, interrupting him once more, 'and they gave us a tow, then the crew from Sheerness RNLI helped us, and a young lad called Little Ray went in the water and mended the rudder and escorted us up the river.'

'You could say this is where it all began,' Tim said thoughtfully.

The sun was low in the sky as we made our entrance into the Medway and I pointed to the small harbour that the Sheerness pilot boat had towed us to. Tim slowed down as we went by; we both half expected to see someone, Little Ray maybe. We wanted to wave and shout, 'HELLO, WE'RE BACK!'

'I cannot believe we are back, Shane, I cannot believe we are back,' Tim said over and over again.

'I cannot believe the Medway is such a wide busy river. It feels like it's a big lake,' Rennie piped up, as he peered through the binoculars. 'What's that industrial sprawl with the big tower on the right?'

Tim and I were standing arm in arm, both quite dazed that at long last we were back to where we had started our circumnavigation in 2007. 'That's the power station on the Isle of Grain,' Tim eventually replied, 'and this is where I have to find all the buoys the hard way,' he added. 'The autopilot stops here; I didn't have time to put in all of the waypoints.'

'It's such a wide space,' Frankie commented, as she took everything in, 'it's hard to see where you are heading for.'

'I don't recognize anything,' Tim replied. 'It's been six years…'

Frankie picked up Tim's iPad and looked at the interactive map. She studied it for a few minutes, looked around her and said, 'I know where we are, it says we are here!'

With that, she disappeared below to check on the pie, before reappearing at the bottom of the steps to the saloon with a huge smile across her face as she proudly showed us the golden baked fruit of her labour.

'It smells delicious,' Rennie enthused, 'and I can't wait to try those oysters!'

But Tim was too busy concentrating to make a comment, as two container ships were overtaking us, one either side, as they made their way towards Thamesport (upstream on the Medway and not, as the name suggests, the Thames).

'Ooooh, it's busy,' Rennie continued, as *The Princess Matilda* bounced over the wake of the container ships, 'and just look at that sky,' he added.

We all looked behind us and saw the sun dipped in the west, bleeding reds and purples across the estuary. The tall black chimney of the Grain Power Station was silhouetted against the Turneresque sky.

I looked at my watch. 'What time is it?' Tim asked me.

'7.45,' was my reply.

'You'd better put on the navigation lights, darlin',' he said quietly.

While I put on the streaming and green and red navigation lights, by the coat rack at the bottom of the steps, I had a chat with Frankie. She was busy tidying up the galley after her uncharacteristic culinary outburst. All the lights in the saloon and galley were on.

'It became dark so quickly,' she said, as she dried her hands. 'I'll need to warm the pie and put the runner beans on to cook. What time will we get to where we're going?' she asked me, as I lifted the lid of a saucepan.

Once again, I looked at my watch and tried to remember how long it would take to get upstream to Chatham. Tim and

I had done this passage many times when we moored on the Medway, but my brain had turned to mush. I shrugged my shoulders and replied, 'I reckon we should be there in about forty minutes. What shall we do with the oysters?'

Frankie shivered and disappeared into her cabin, pulling on a hat and fleece, before following me back up the steps to the wheelhouse. As it turned out, shucking live oysters would be the least of our problems.

'It's like the Magic Kingdom up here,' Rennie enthused as we joined him on the back deck.

Ahead of us was an illuminated power station with hundreds of spotlights, making night into day. The busy docks of a container port were also lit up. The lights were doubly dazzling as they reflected off the black satin of a tide-swollen river. I was confused and struggled to make sense of what I was seeing.

'Why are we heading back downstream?' I asked Tim, who was pressing buttons on his chart plotter.

'We're not!' he replied irritably.

'Yes we are, that's Grain Power Station. Look at the chimney with the red lights going up it – it has to be Grain and we passed that ages ago.'

'Are you sure?' he asked me with even more irritation in his voice.

'Yes, yes, I am sure, you have to turn around.'

We spent the next hour going around in circles, dodging container ships going to Thamesport and tankers taking fuel to the oil refinery upstream from the power station. Tim and I, when we weren't bickering, looked desperately for a flashing buoy to get a fix on our position. The illumination from the oil refinery merged into the dazzlement of the container port that blurred into the illumination of the power station. The flashing buoy was impossible to find. Rennie and Frances went below, as Tim and I continued our heated squabbling in the darkness of the wheelhouse. The loud volatile bickering was interrupted by Frankie, whose head appeared beneath the hatch. 'Darling,' she said to me, 'how do I find BBC4 on your TV? It's almost 8.30, your programme is about to start.'

Somewhat exasperated, I may have raised my voice: 'Frankie, this is real life, we are living the fucking programme.' Phil was standing behind me recording it all.

For another hour, I pleaded, cajoled, threatened and swore at Tim to call the coastguard. We were lost, hopelessly lost. The tide was going out. It was pitch black except for the blinding confusement of lights from the industrial banks of the wide river. Large container ships were heading both ways, but we were not sure if they were heading out to sea or heading upstream. Eventually, Tim gave in and called Thames Coastguard for assistance.

'I swore I would never do this,' he said under his breath, as he tuned the radio to Channel 16.

Sheerness inshore lifeboat launched at 9.30pm.

While waiting for our knights in high-visibility lifejackets to come to our rescue, we almost rammed a large tug that was tied up to a mooring buoy. Tim pulled alongside and shouted to someone on the deck, 'CAN WE TIE ALONGSIDE PLEASE? WE'RE WAITING FOR THE LIFEBOAT.'

I was already on the bow, and a deckhand leaned down, took my rope and secured *The Princess Matilda* against the craft. I turned and saw Tim doing the same on the stern. The chap at my end asked me if I would like to take a look around their vessel. Tim and our passengers were in conversation with a few deckhands at the back. It seemed bad manners to say no and I was given a guided tour. It was an odd experience; all was calm on their ship and ours had just turned into an episode of *Dad's Army*.

This is where the lifeboat found us, tied alongside the tug. A young, petite helmswoman came onboard and helped Tim navigate back the way we had come. It was too late to get upstream to Chatham as the tide was against us, so she suggested we spend the night in Queenborough on an all-tide landing pontoon on the river Swale. I thought back to how clever we thought we had been the afternoon we managed to get attached to a mooring buoy, the day before we left on our proper sea voyage. We had been so full of ourselves when we arrived in Ramsgate from the Medway and Swale in 2007, but now we were back where we had started, with our tails between our legs.

Once the lifeboat crew and the waiting coastguards in Queenborough had us securely tied up for the night, Tim invited them aboard. I put the kettle on to make them tea, while he continued to apologize. Nicki, the girl that had helped Tim navigate, kept reassuring him that he had done the right thing. 'There's a lot of mud out there!'

Our visitors' book was on the table and one of the lifeboat crew picked it up and flicked through the pages.

'I see you've lots of comments from lifeboat crews,' he remarked. 'I'm familiar with a few of them from Poole, where we all go to train. I know Spanish from Humber and Patch from Penlee, oh and Hosey the mechanic from Fishguard. He's a character,' he said with a laugh. Then he looked at Tim who was standing with his head hanging down over rounded shoulders.

'And if I'm not mistaken,' he continued, handing the book, open on page one, to Tim, 'this is where my crew signed your book.' Tim took it from him and I looked over his shoulder.

'What happened to Little Ray?' I asked him, but before I got a reply Tim looked closely at the speaker and said, 'Of course, you are the Sheerness coxswain. Sorry, I should have recognized you; you've saved our bacon twice…things really have come full circle.'

The oysters had gone off as the ice had melted, and Frankie's pie had gone stone cold, but we were safe. I made Tim eat his supper and insisted he go straight to bed. My loose cannon of a husband was in danger of falling overboard, as he wanted to go out in the darkness and check all the ropes. He was having a mini-breakdown, furious that, after circumnavigating the British Isles, we had fallen at the last fence. 'I feel such a twat,' he said, as I tucked him up. 'I feel such a twat!'

We left Queenborough the next morning, using the floodtide to take us upstream to Chatham. In the light of day, we knew the way, but we also saw how close we had come to running aground on the ebbing tide. At low water, the Medway has many islands with muddy causeways that are lost as the twice-daily sea sweeps in. Indeed, the smaller of these islands are completely covered during a high spring tide. Should you be unfortunate enough to run aground on one of these temporary hidden islands, you can be stuck there for a month waiting for the next spring tide to lift you off. The Medway is littered with the shells of wrecked boats. I truly believed we averted a disaster by calling for help when we did.

In the late seventies, Rennie had been a dresser in the West End, and now tried to cheer us up, regaling us with outrageous stories. Usually, Tim laughs like a drain, but even his best friend's tales of West End Wendys could not snap him out of his depression. We had a black cloud hovering over the boat and none of us, not even me, knew what to do to get it blown away. 'You made one mistake,' we all kept reassuring him. 'You navigated this boat to Weymouth with just a compass. You are allowed one mistake.' But the cloud refused to budge – unless

Phil and his camera was about, then Tim would try and lighten the mood.

I went below and sat on our bed, thinking about all the times I had been thrown across it in rough seas and how I had opened the porthole to drag in the trailing rope that could have fouled our propeller. Tim and I were a team; I married him for richer, for poorer, in sickness and in health, so I wasn't going to let one setback make him doubt his capabilities. Especially as now we were on our way home, back to our homeport. That morning, before we left Queenborough, he told me that he had had enough, that he couldn't go any further.

1st April 1997
Midnight
You should have had loads of platelets today to prepare for your thorax section tomorrow, and I packed the pyjamas, toilet bag and the laptop, but we've come back home because Panos phoned while we were having lunch and told us there were not enough platelets because of the Easter Bank Holiday. So you and I go to sleep thinking about tomorrow…BUT we went to Northampton on Good Friday, after Goldstone said, 'Yes, I think you are in remission, but let's think about having the section done.' We looked at boats. We are thinking of buying one. You say we should buy a narrowboat, our first holiday was on a narrowboat. As soon as you are fit after this operation, we shall go back to Northampton and buy that boat. You say you are not afraid of the operation, because you just think about the future. Our future a couple of weeks ago, we had no hope. You told me that you had had enough, that you couldn't go any further, that you couldn't bear to think how I would cope, if you were to die…but then you and I went to that church St Andrews in Holborn and a ray

of light streamed through the stainglass and touched your head. You said, 'That's when I knew it would all be OK!'

UCLH
3rd April 1997
It's 9pm, you should be down soon from the recovery room. The operation went very well apparently, although the anaesthetist had trouble putting you under as you wouldn't stop talking.

 How still it is in this hospital room, how empty. They took your bed up to recovery, and an ITC nurse will be with you all night. I may go home, I'm no good if I don't sleep. You'll be fine with the nurse. I wish they would bring you back down, I wonder what you will look like. The daffodils we bought today have all opened. I must be the only person in the hospital who has cheerfully kissed her husband 'Bye bye' before he is taken up to theatre for a major operation, but both you and I are so relieved that you are not having a transplant that we're almost nonchalant about the section. It's a piece of cake. On the wall is a map of the British Isles, that I stuck up with Blu-Tac. It was free with a canal boating magazine. We had looked at it most of the day before they took you away. Every single navigable river and canal is highlighted. Now as I tap away on my laptop, killing time, I keep looking at the canals that go through Scotland, the Crinan and Caledonian canals, I bet that would be a great trip...I wish they would bring you down. I keep listening and staring out of the window down the corridor.

Midnight
Just after I wrote that, I heard a throaty laugh coming down the corridor. It was Frankie Barber, she had nipped into the ward to see how you were doing. Good old Frank,

what a consistent and good heart she has. She swept me into
her arms and stayed with me until they brought you back to
the room, attached to pipes and drips and tubes, but clear
of that disgusting fungus that would have killed you if had
gone into transplant.

You live. We shall live and grow old together, you and I.

I thought back to our first trip up the Medway in 2005. Six years have passed in a blink of an eye. Seventeen years since we bought that old rust bucket of a canal boat in Northampton. Where has the time gone? I peered out of the porthole and saw something so familiar that I began to cry. I heard the echo of a young man's voice; his name was Little Ray, a volunteer from the RNLI who has since moved from Sheerness. 'That's the gasworks at Gillingham,' he had reassured us, 'you can't get lost now...'

Frankie was in the galley, she could see I had been crying. 'Darling, what's wrong? Are you all right?'

'I didn't know how far we had been until just now. We used to go to that pub over the river,' I said, pointing out of the window, 'and walk down that jetty...it's just all so emotional, we spent so much time here...it's all a bit weird. We are back. I didn't know it would affect me like this.'

I left her and joined Tim in the wheelhouse, tears silently rolling down his face too. All kinds of memories were flooding back.

'You're in tears,' he said, as I laid my arm around his shoulder, both of us looking ahead. Tim turned to face me, and smiled. 'We're back!' he said. 'We made it.'

We had travelled over 2,000 miles and visited over 90 ports and harbours and were now about to lock in to Chatham Maritime Marina. We were back, we had made it; with a little help from our friends and the RNLI.

AFTERWORD

March 2014 Hellevoetsluis, the Netherlands

In August 2011, we finally went back up the upper Thames –
'No tides, or overfalls, no jellyfish, no gale-force winds to blow
us onto rocks, no sandbanks to run aground on, no oil tankers
or fast ferries, no wind farms...' said Tim happily – without
getting lost. *The Princess Matilda* got as far as Abingdon in
Oxfordshire before the skipper and galley maid decided to turn
around and go back down the Thames Estuary. The rough
sea-passages, like childbirth, were all but forgotten: we wintered
in Ramsgate in 2011 before crossing twenty-two nautical miles
from Dover to Calais. It was then only a short hop up the coast
to get to Belgium. *The Princess Matilda* remained moored in
Ostend until August 2013. We didn't manage to get to see her
often, because during 2012/13 Tim was working on a film
about the artist J M W Turner with Mike Leigh. They say things
go full circle: this film, *Mr Turner*, will be shown at the Cannes
Film Festival, where *Secrets and Lies* won the 1996 Palme d'Or,
while Tim was having his first course of chemotherapy.

One of Turner's paintings is *Helvoetsluys* (1832). A scene
in the film *Mr Turner* takes place in the Royal Academy
during 'Varnishing Day' when the artists finish their work.
Helvoetsluys is a sea piece, with cool marine colours verging
on monochromatic. The painting had been placed by a huge
canvas, by Constable, *The Opening of Waterloo Bridge*, which
was comprised mainly of the colours crimson and gold. Seeing
this, Turner took out his paints and got some red on his brush

and put a big blob in the middle of his washed-out sea. He didn't say a word but walked into the next room, leaving the other artists aghast. Constable famously said, 'Turner has fired a gun here!' and was right put out. Later, Turner came back and turned the red blob into a red port buoy. It drew the eye away from Constable's lavish painting to Turner's. A clever trick from an old devil.

This is why *The Princess Matilda* is presently moored in Helvoetsluys/Hellevoetsluis. There are quite a few red blobs out there. In a couple of weeks, when the winter storms have died down, we plan to head north towards Russia. It may take us some time…

ACKNOWLEDGEMENTS

I would like to acknowledge the help and support given to me by my literary agent Laetitia Rutherford who believed I could write then suggested a better way to do it – 'paint pictures... show us, don't tell us.'

And for Liz Marvin my infinitely patient editor and the rest of the team at Ebury.

Also to Jake Lingwood at Ebury for taking a punt on an unpublished author who left school when she was 14: a baby-boomer – late bloomer.

Last but not least to the courageous volunteer crews, the mechanics and coxswains of the Royal National Lifeboat Institution and their families and fundraisers.